# DESI CRIME

**Aishwarya Singh** is half the voice behind *Desi Crime* and co-founder of Desi Studios. A political science and philosophy graduate with experience in nuclear weapons policy, she traded law school applications for a microphone and launched Desi Studios at twenty-three. Having lived in fourteen cities across four countries and four continents, Aishwarya now calls India home. In her free time, you can find her at the nearest gym or browsing through luxury real estate she cannot afford with the seriousness of a seasoned buyer. An ardent lover of wine, she'll be the first to admit she's largely faking any real understanding of it.

**Aryaan Misra** is the less funny half of *Desi Crime*, which might have something to do with his nerdy beginnings. He was all set to become a biologist after an experiment he designed for NASA in high school was carried out aboard the ISS, but it has been downhill since. He attempted a biology degree before dropping out to chase his dreams (money, fame and love) in New York. He found none of the above. The search for meaning continued as he hopped around the world, living nomadically in Africa and Europe, only to return home to start Desi Studios. Nowadays he squanders his rent in Mumbai by travelling half the year. He likes jumping rope, drinking coffee and publishing pseudo-intellectual video essays.

# DESI CRIME

**20 True Stories of Killers, Kidnappers and Other Sinister Criminals**

**AISHWARYA SINGH
ARYAAN MISRA**

PAN

First published 2025 by Pan
an imprint of Pan Macmillan Publishing India Private Limited
707 Kailash Building
26 K. G. Marg, New Delhi 110001
www.panmacmillan.co.in

Pan Macmillan, The Smithson, 6 Briset Street, Farringdon, London EC1M 5NR
Associated companies throughout the world
www.panmacmillan.com

ISBN 978-93-6113-325-1

Copyright © Aishwarya Singh and Aryaan Misra 2025

The moral rights of the authors have been asserted.

The views expressed in this book are the authors own and the facts reported by them have been verified by the publisher to the extent possible. The publisher hereby disclaims any liability to any party for loss, damages or disruptions caused by the same..

All rights reserved. No part of this publication may be reproduced, stored in or introduced into a retrieval system, or transmitted, in any form, or by any means (electronic, mechanical, photocopying, recording or otherwise) without the prior written permission of the publisher. Any person who does any unauthorized act in relation to this publication may be liable to criminal prosecution and civil claims for damages.

1 3 5 7 9 8 6 4 2

This book is sold subject to the condition that it shall not, by way of trade or otherwise, be lent, re-sold, hired out, or otherwise circulated without the publisher's prior consent in any form of binding or cover other than that in which it is published and without a similar condition including this condition being imposed on the subsequent purchaser.

Typeset in Garamond Premier Pro by R. Ajith Kumar, New Delhi
Printed and bound in India by Thomson Press India Ltd.

*To my parents*
*who filled our home with love, laughter and respect, making it the perfect playground for me to chase my dreams*

*To my English teachers*
*Seema Krishnan, Anju Soni, Neelu Yadav and Ghunghroo Misra – who fostered my love for this language*

# CONTENTS

Introduction   1

1. The Kolkata House of Horrors   5
2. Murder at Royal Park, Sri Lanka   18
3. The 100 Killings of Javed Iqbal   29
4. Gulshan Kumar vs. the Underworld   41
5. A Royal Wedding and a Vanishing: Vishal Mehrotra   56
6. A Case Study in Crime: Sajal Barui   74
7. The Gruesome Murder of Sister Abhaya   83
8. Occult Secrets and Mass Psychosis: The Burari Suicides   93
9. The Scam Call that Wasn't: The Aditya Ranka Kidnapping   102
10. Snuffing Out a Rising Star: The Murder of Qandeel Baloch   111
11. A Hasty Conclusion: The Confounding Case of Pravin Varughese   124

## CONTENTS

| | | |
|---|---|---|
| 12. | The Tandoor Murder | 138 |
| 13. | Not-So-Jolly Joseph | 149 |
| 14. | Missing Since 9/11: Sneha Philip | 163 |
| 15. | The Tale of Two Vishwanaths | 177 |
| 16. | Buried Alive: The Grisly Murder of Shakereh Khaleeli | 186 |
| 17. | The Sickly-sweet Smell of Murder: The Joshi–Abhyankar Massacres | 196 |
| 18. | A Deadly Viral Video: The Kohistan Killings | 207 |
| 19. | Gone Without a Trace: The Sudden Disappearance of the Chohan Family | 220 |
| 20. | To Be Hanged Until Death: The Case of Hetal Parekh | 235 |

*Acknowledgements*   247
*References*   251

# INTRODUCTION

## AISHWARYA

IN THE FRIGID MICHIGAN WINTER OF 2019, HUDDLED inside a dorm room at Alma College, a fledgling idea took shape.

'Why don't I ever see you listening to true crime podcasts from India?' Aryaan asked after weeks of being pestered to listen to a mind-blowing true crime podcast episode I had come across.

'Oh, I don't know. I don't think there are any,' I responded, marvelling at the oddity of the statement that had just left my mouth.

'Maybe we could start one …' Aryaan said casually, scrolling through my phone on a hunt for Indian true crime podcasts that led nowhere.

While it would be months before we could execute our idea, the underpinnings of *Desi Crime* were set that evening. We knew that India had no dearth of stories, yet we couldn't find a storytelling podcast that was doing them justice. The podcasting space was booming, but it was still dominated by hosts, accents, tales and viewpoints from the West. The subcontinent was merely a consumer and a spectator of this new and exciting format. The belief that stories of crime from the subcontinent offer a unique perspective – the way we view love, family, money, women, justice, sexuality, duty and more – became the foundation of *The Desi Crime Podcast*.

## ARYAAN

IT WASN'T ALWAYS *DESI CRIME*. OUR INITIAL HUNT FOR A worthy name took us from *Prime Time Crime* to *Indian Crime Podcast*. There was no podcast or a mic yet – just a vision to create something big. And to create anything, my brain needs a name. Whenever I begin a project – creative or otherwise – I always start with a name I love. I've already decided on my daughter's name (a palindrome of mine), after all.

Many titles came to us, but they never brought that sparkle to our eyes. Sometimes a title is the final piece in a convoluted jigsaw and sometimes it is the gold you strike while hopelessly scratching at the ground of ideas. *Desi Crime* was gold. The name allowed us to cover stories beyond India, including our neighbours – addressing their problems, our similarities. It would connect us to Brown youth across the world, creating a sense of camaraderie among scattered people. *Desi Crime* became more than a project for us when families of victims reached out to us, thanking us for shedding light on their case. It's devastating every time a victim's mother thanks us, some random twenty-year-olds, instead of the police. I feel like a charlatan every time a journalist calls us 'brave' for the work we do. We're just storytellers – brave are those men and women solving these cases on the ground. And I feel indebted every time someone tells us they caught a train to come see us. Why? It's still hard to make sense of this fortune of digital love we have received.

From the summer of 2020, when the first episode of *Desi Crime* aired, to the summer of 2025, as we put our finishing touches on this book, one thing has become abundantly clear: our love for creating and building our podcast was also driven by our love for writing. Behind each weekly episode are thousands of words, written with deep adoration and respect for the very real people whose experiences we are responsible for narrating. It is in these words that the living history of our nation – its citizenry and even its dark underbelly – come to life. Somewhere between carefully identifying the cases we wanted to cover, conducting research and then turning that research into stories worth reading, we've begun to feel a lot like writers in addition to podcasters.

This book you hold will allow you to experience each case the way we do first – written out, with our own view of the world filling in the scene, feeling shaken or affected by its dark turns. Our journey began with childlike enthusiasm over a seemingly fleeting, though ambitious, idea: about making lesser-known stories heard. As you turn the page, we hope you'll find it marked by the friendship that brought that idea to life and the memory of the victims whose tragedies push us to make the world a better place. Welcome to *Desi Crime*.

# 1

# THE KOLKATA HOUSE OF HORRORS

**ARYAAN**
So many true crime stories start with families gone awry. But this is not the case of a family that did not love each other – this is the case of a family that loved each other too much. Our viewers often ask: Do we get nightmares when researching for cases? And while most of the time, the answer is 'no', there are a few cases that stand out. They do give me nightmares. This is one of them. This is the tragic story of the De family.

ROBINSON STREET IN POSH, DOWNTOWN KOLKATA SITS at the crossroads of the city's two worlds. Crumbling colonial architecture makes space for the sweeping, if nondescript, facades of modernity. On the night of 10 June 2015, the city was moving at its usual pace. Officegoers returned to their homes after a long day at work; meanwhile, drivers of Kolkata's iconic yellow Ambassador taxis cruised the streets in search of the rare Wednesday night passenger to begin their own. Suddenly, the attention of both residents and visitors in the area caught on a cloud of smoke drifting out of a small second-floor window of one of the houses. Number 3, Robinson Street. Shaking off the inertia that often grips a large crowd witnessing a disturbing event, someone called 101. Soon, the fire trucks and the police arrived, pulling up and standing in front of the towering red-brick home. A knock on the front door received no response, even as the faint sounds of music and hymns could be heard from within. The possibility of a fire blazing unchecked became too urgent, and they decided to break down the door.

The horrors inside revealed themselves only gradually. First came the chanting; it grew louder, echoing eerily through the house. It wasn't coming from any living soul. Instead, five speakers, placed in different rooms of the house, played the same thing: a taped sermon by the controversial American TV evangelist, Joyce Meyer. Hundreds of books on spirituality were scattered on the floor, covered in a thick layer of dust. Countless handwritten notes had been tucked into corners, wedged into almirahs and hidden under pillowcases. The house did not appear to have been ransacked. Its chaos was lived-in and intentional.

#### ARYAAN
I know I've described a horrific scene for you, but what do you make of all of this?

#### AISHWARYA
I don't have enough information to draw any conclusions just yet, but this does sound like an unnervingly staged house. It reminds me of one of those haunted houses you see at carnivals, perhaps …

**ARYAAN**
If you think the hidden notes and chants are weird, it
gets even stranger.

Without pausing to observe and absorb the strange contents of the house, the cops rushed to the site of the fire: the bathroom. They were alarmed to find the source of the smoke. It was not a household fire as they had anticipated. Instead, they discovered a charred human corpse in the bathtub. Nearly unrecognizable, the body would be later identified as that of seventy-seven-year-old Aurobindo De. A container of gasoline and a box of matchsticks lay beside him, along with a note that read, 'Love you beta.'

Perhaps the man had set himself on fire; a highly unusual but not unprecedented case of suicide. But before they could investigate the bewildering scene any further, a sickening stench revolted them. It was emerging from behind one of the bedroom doors. As police officers, they were not unfamiliar with the odour. It was that of decomposing flesh. However, when they pushed the door open, they could not find any corpses inside. In fact, they couldn't see anything at first. The room was pitch black, with the curtains drawn and the windows papered over. It was only when the shades were removed that the macabre scene came into focus, and the most disturbing contents of the bedroom became all too apparent. Lying neatly in the bed was a fully dressed human skeleton surrounded by teddy bears. On either side, two smaller skeletons – non-human – were curled beside it. Likely the family's pets. There was a lunchbox filled with rotting food. The state of decomposition left little room for doubt. The person in the bed had been dead for a very long time. Long enough for their flesh to disintegrate, leaving only bones behind. This deepened the mystery and confused the police. If Aurobindo De had just died, then who had his final, loving note been meant for?

Their question was finally answered when the only living resident of the home, Partho De, Aurobindo's forty-four-year-old son, was discovered in a catatonic state in the living room. He was banging his head against the walls, his body caked in grime and the putrid stench clinging to him as heavily as it did to the dead bodies that surrounded him. Despite the delirium that had possessed him, Partho did not resist arrest. Speaking in a low, oddly gentle voice, Partho confirmed that the skeleton in the bedroom was his sister's. Her name was Debjani De. He admitted that he had been sleeping beside her remains since her death in December 2014. The smaller skeletons, he explained, were their pet labradors. They had been laid to rest beside her, to keep her company. The lunchbox found near her bed? He had used it to feed her daily. When asked if he had harmed Debjani, Partho scoffed dismissively – his actions had been motivated only by his love for her. It was love, he insisted, that had driven him to seal and darken the room to preserve her scent. It was love that had compelled him to sleep beside his sister's maggot-infested corpse, night after night, to feel close to her.

**AISHWARYA**
Alright, for argument's sake, I'll believe that Partho De didn't kill Debjani. That still leaves the question open: How did she die?

**ARYAAN**
In his frazzled state, Partho refused to answer that question. But he continued to claim his innocence, to the police and the media.

It quickly became clear to the police that this was no ordinary crime, and Partho De was no black-and-white villain. Instead of homicide or manslaughter, the man was booked under IPC sections 176 (omission to give notice, or information, to a public servant by a person legally bound to give) and 269 (negligently committing an act that is likely to spread infection of a disease dangerous to life). Both carried a maximum punishment of up to six months in jail. At the urging of medical professionals, Partho was committed to the Pavlov Hospital for the Mentally Ill. During his time at Pavlov, police access to Partho was restricted, and he was placed under close psychiatric supervision after being diagnosed with severe depressive tendencies. His initial days in the facility were tumultuous. A journalist from a Bengali daily, *Anandabazar Patrika*, who managed to visit Partho, described him as incoherent and agitated, his body reeking with infection, likely a result of prolonged exposure to Debjani's decomposing remains. Dr Sabyasachi Mitra, one of the attending psychiatrists, initially raised the possibility of necrophiliac tendencies – the compulsion to have sexual intercourse with corpses. At times, Partho would cry out for Jesus, and was soothed only by the assurance that Jesus and Mary would come to him, and touch him.

Once medication began to lift the fog of psychosis, Partho slowly warmed up to his doctors. He spoke at length about the still obscure events that had led him there. He described, in detail, how attentively he cared for his sister's body, changing the bedding she lay on daily, tucking her in at night and arranging elaborate meals to eat by her side. He spent as much as 600 rupees every day to buy pizza and pastries for his deceased sister. To a senior police officer, he confided something even more unsettling – he believed Debjani came alive every night to eat the food. 'I loved my sister and couldn't let her go. Besides, didi visits me at night, she talks and sings to me,' he said during the preliminary investigation. These details, while disturbing, offered rare insights into the psyche of the troubled man now in the doctor's care.

The autopsies of Aurobindo and Debjani's bodies revealed little additional information. They only confirmed that Aurobindo had died by suicide, and his daughter's skeletal remains showed no signs of physical trauma. Now, the police had to rely solely on the objects they found at 3 Robinson Street and testimonies from the De family's few acquaintances to further their investigation.

The handwritten notes found scattered throughout the house bizarrely appeared to be the primary mode of communication among its three residents. Investigators pored over them, trying to match the handwriting and piece together timelines. Some notes, dated and composed with relative clarity, were attributed to Debjani. Others, more erratic and disjointed, were believed to be Partho's. Yet the numerous jottings offered little by way of explanation. In one note, an unidentified person asked, '*Ei pothei ki jibon cholar chilo?* (Was this the path my life was meant to take?)' Some of the notes, penned by Aurobindo, spoke of practical matters such as his plans to divide his share of the family property between the siblings. This detail took on greater significance when his solicitor friend, Subir Majumdar, revealed that he frequently advised Aurobindo on issues of inheritance, but he never had an inkling that Debjani was already deceased. On 8 June, days before his suicide, Aurobindo asked Majumdar to serve as a trustee of his assets.

The cops must have felt defeated. They possessed an array of seemingly disparate pieces of the puzzle but struggled to put them together. That is, until they found the key.

When the police searched what the media had dubbed 'Kolkata's House of Horrors' in 2015, they unearthed more than just skeletal remains and handwritten notes. The house had an unbelievable 20,000 books on subjects related to spirituality. Among them, investigators found stacks of cursive writing workbooks that Partho used as journals. Many were abandoned; others, half-filled. For the first time, the police could chronicle Partho's life with a level of detail rarely possible for regular people. The tragedy at 3 Robinson Street had rendered Partho's life extraordinary, but to understand how it had come to that, one had to start at the beginning – the profoundly ordinary origins of the De family.

In 1968, Debjani De was born to a loving couple in Bangalore. A few years later, the birth of her younger brother completed their family. From the moment she became a mother, Aarti De became fiercely protective and vehemently sheltered her children from the outside world. Debjani and Partho grew up almost entirely in each other's company, playing indoor games like Scrabble. Unfortunately, the protective – perhaps excessively so – maternal instinct only hardened over time. Soon, Aarti's behaviour began to seriously inhibit the siblings as they grew older. Not only were they unable to connect with others their age, their personalities and relationships veered into territory that felt deeply unconventional.

Partho's journals paint a concerning portrait of an abusive mother who isolated her children but was unable to accept the closeness between them. Jealous and controlling, Aarti punished any attempts by Debjani to assert her independence. Meanwhile, she harassed Partho about his sexuality, fearing that a childhood spent cloistered with his sister had made her son 'effeminate'. In one of his diaries, Partho wrote,

> We went on vacation. My mother made us strip in the bathroom. My mother thinks I'm impotent. She wanted to see me develop a relationship. This is why she used to send a maidservant to my room to excite me.

Through all the emotional upheaval, Debjani remained Partho's constant companion. But when their parents decided to separate, they chose to split custody. Partho would live with Aarti, while his sister would live with Aurobindo. The separation was difficult for the siblings, whose lives had been closely intertwined. After finishing school, they both enrolled at the University of Calcutta's prestigious Rajabazar Science College to study BTech. Their professors would later recall in interviews that the siblings spent an unhealthy amount of time together. Among their peers, rumours floated about incest, though not too seriously.

After university, Debjani studied music at Trinity College London and returned to teach music at the prestigious Don Bosco School in the city. Colleagues described her as accomplished and cordial, though preoccupied with her family life. Meanwhile, Partho found it hard to adjust to the changing times. The young man had long relied on the twin anchors of an overbearing mother and a sister who was his only confidante and source of emotional support. Eventually, he joined the software giant, Tata Consultancy Services, and moved to the US. Little did he know that one of the two pillars of his life was about to come crashing down. At the turn of the century, Aarti De was diagnosed with breast cancer. By 2005, the matriarch of the family was dead and with her, the final strands of normalcy in the family.

Aurobindo De held unconventional ideas surrounding death. A believer of naturopathy, he did not pursue conventional methods of treatment when his wife was diagnosed with cancer. Moreover, for him, the death of one's physical body did not mark the end of one's spiritual existence. Debjani had inherited this belief, and when Aarti died, neither of them attended her funeral. Her body was cremated by a relative. Partho, still working in the US, was also unable to attend the final rites. The news of his mother's death was his breaking point. Despite their troubled relationship, she had been a cornerstone of Partho's chaotic life. He left his job and returned to 3 Robinson Street.

In the aftermath of her mother's demise, Debjani became completely consumed by her increasingly rigid spiritual ideas. It was a preoccupation that would cost her career. She was fascinated by TV evangelists like Joyce Meyer, whose voice had welcomed the police on that fateful night. The initial search had also yielded notes where Debjani claimed to have fasted rigorously to restore the family's spiritual balance.

> **ARYAAN**
> Now, to each their own - we're all spiritual in our way, and who am I to judge someone's beliefs? But Debjani followed not just one guru but twelve leaders from different religions, every single day.
>
> **AISHWARYA**
> I mean, we've seen that in the case of obsessive spirituality - like the Burari family suicides, there isn't one particular religion whose followers are more susceptible to this behaviour. It's more about their personality type and other factors, like isolation.

In time, verbal communication in the De family broke down completely. Their only source of income came from the tenants they rented a part of their house to. The trio isolated themselves in their apartment, and had the security guard bring them three meals a day. The house grew dark, dusty and desolate. And in August of 2014, this uneasy stasis plummeted into absolute turmoil.

Within a month of each other, the family dogs died in August and September 2014. Debjani's spiritual notions compelled her to believe that this was due to a curse, one that could only be exorcized by fasting. She stopped eating altogether, insisting that she would only consume food if God gave her a sign. That sign never came, and on 29 December 2014, Debjani struggled to take her last breath. She became the third corpse in that accursed room.

Incredibly, since the family only communicated through handwritten notes, Aurobindo did not realize that his daughter had died until three months later. Other sources say that given the layout of the space, Partho was able to conceal the fact from his father, who lived at the farthest end of the house. By then, the person he loved most in the world was gone, and with that unimaginable loss, Partho's grip on reality was completely shattered. Consumed by grief, he began hysterically safeguarding his sister's corpse, unable – or unwilling – to let her go.

**ARYAAN**
Partho may have done things no normal person would, but that's because his life had been absolutely out of the ordinary. He wasn't a psychopath or a killer. He was a broken person in need of help – serious medical help.

**AISHWARYA**
Do you think such an extreme case of mental illness and trauma can ever be addressed in its entirety? Is

there any hope at all for Partho to be reintegrated into society, maybe even live a normal life?

**ARYAAN**
Before I came across this case, my answer to that question might have been 'no'. It's difficult to imagine a situation where somebody with such profound mental health issues reintegrates into society. But this case was exceptional …

During his stay at the Pavlov hospital, Partho repeatedly expressed his wish to be closer to God and the church. After his release from psychiatric care, Father Rodney Borneo of the Archdiocese of Calcutta took him under his wing. The priest would later speak out against the media's treatment of Partho's story:

> The moment we met, it was so clear that this was not a person who needed interrogating, but someone who needed understanding … And I think from that point onwards, Partho was no longer someone who was a mystical figure surrounded in the fog of the "Horror House", but a very real person who could be a very real friend and who had a very real story to tell.

In time, Partho was able to find a strong and supportive community, despite the media circus that haunted him. He sold the sprawling house on 3 Robinson Street and moved to an apartment in Watgunge. There, he attempted to make amends with a society that had once labelled him a cannibal, murderer and necrophile.

On 20 February 2017, Partho posted a quote on his social media: 'It's better to light a candle than to curse darkness.' Tragically, the very next day, history repeated itself. Vegetable sellers were calling out their wares, yellow cabs circling the block for their next passengers, when a thick cloud of dark smoke billowed out of Partho's flat. The police were called once again. Inside, they found a scene disturbingly akin to the one from 2015. In the bathroom was a bottle of gasoline, matchsticks and the charred remains of Partho De.

## 2

# MURDER AT ROYAL PARK, SRI LANKA

**AISHWARYA**
This is a murder that took Sri Lanka by storm. Not just when it happened in 2005, but again in 2019 and 2024, years after the crime. Corruption, injustice, brute violence – this case lays bare the darkest shades of human impulse. This is the story of a young girl whose life was cruelly cut short despite her warnings that danger was close at hand. This is the story of Yvonne Jonsson.

On 30 June 2005 – a Friday night like any other – two sisters set out to enjoy a night out in Colombo, Sri Lanka's bustling capital city. It took some persuading to get their father to lend them his blue Jeep, but after they promised to return home together, he handed the keys over. 'You are going together and make sure you come back home together,' he told them. They left around 8:30 p.m. and headed to Bagatelle Road to pick up their younger sister's boyfriend. Their first destination was the popular pub White Horse. For the rest of the night, the group moved between three spots: starting at White Horse, then on to Glow, a nightclub in Galle Face and finally, Blue

Elephant at the Hilton Colombo. At the Hilton, they were joined by a friend who lived in the same apartment complex as the sisters, Royal Park.

Past midnight, tensions flared. The younger sister's boyfriend became annoyed when he noticed another boy waving at her at Blue Elephant. A heated argument ensued between the young couple, leaving the younger sister in tears. The elder sister quickly stepped in to defuse the situation. Their moods soured, and the couple decided to call it a night. They hailed a Hilton cab and headed back home. Meanwhile, the older sister and her Korean friend returned to Glow. By 2 a.m., the couple had arrived at Royal Park. Forty-five minutes later, the elder sister's car pulled into the complex.

The next morning, only one of the two sisters would be alive.

Yvonne Jonsson was born on 15 August 1985 to Chamalka and Roger Jonsson, a Swedish–Sri Lankan couple living in Colombo. Her younger sister, Caroline, was her best friend and closest confidante. The Jonssons shared a happy, tight-knit home. At the time of her death, Yvonne was a nineteen-year-old fashion student in the US, back in Sri Lanka for her summer vacation.

The morning after Yvonne's and Caroline's eventful night out, Roger Jonsson checked on his daughters around 6 a.m. When he found Caroline's bed empty, he assumed that she was sleeping with Yvonne in her room, which was locked. He asked his wife, and she said that they were probably asleep. As he left their twenty-third-floor apartment for work, he found a note on the front door, written in what appeared to be Caroline's handwriting: 'Wake me up when you come home.' The note struck him as slightly unusual, but not enough to raise alarm. He continued with his day. Later that morning, Chamalka Jonsson went into Caroline's room and found only her younger daughter there. When she asked about Yvonne, Caroline said she hadn't seen her since the night before. She messaged her boyfriend, Jude Shramantha Jayamaha, to check if he knew anything. He didn't. 'She must be still rocking it,' he wrote back, suggesting she might still be out with their friend and neighbour, Khone. It was a reasonable explanation, but Chamalka's maternal instinct told her something was amiss. Yvonne, who let her mother know even if she was going for a swim, hadn't been seen the night before. Uneasy but still hoping for the best, Chamalka left the house to drop Caroline off at a class around 9 a.m.

As Chamalka and Caroline left, Royal Park slowly came to life. Lifts filled with residents as people stepped out for work and school, lunch bags in their hands, the haze of sleep still in their eyes. Sheila Anthony, a domestic worker who was employed by a Korean family on the sixteenth floor, was asked by the lady of the house to go to the nineteenth floor to hand over a few things to someone living there. Since the elevator was taking too long, she decided to take the steps. Just as she rounded the nineteenth-floor stairwell, she saw something that would haunt her for the rest of her days. In a massive pool of blood was the brutalized body of a girl, lying as if she had been 'bent into two'.

Shocked by the gruesome sight, Sheila stumbled down another flight of stairs. Once she recovered, she ran to the building manager's office. Mr Chandrapala joked that she had probably seen a ghost, but the panic and terror on her face and in her voice convinced Chandrapala to accompany Sheila back to the stairwell. When they went back to the nineteenth floor, the sight was just as horrible and outlandish as before. The manager would later say that the body looked like a doll, perhaps because it had been mutilated in a way that human minds struggle to associate with a living person.

The victim's jeans had been pulled down, but not completely taken off her legs. Caught on her ankles, the denim was wrapped around her throat, as if positioned to strangle her. Her head had been brutally smashed using a heavy object, rendering her face nearly unrecognisable. There were splatters of blood on the staircase. Nonetheless, Chandrapala was able to identify the body. It was Yvonne Jonsson.

Meanwhile, on the way to Caroline's class, Chamalka's sense of dread about Yvonne's disappearance grew unbearable. Overcome by the feeling that something was wrong, she asked her driver to turn the car around. When they arrived at their apartment, the entrance was barely visible behind a large group of uniformed officers stationed outside. Mother and daughter were ushered into the apartment and asked to sit down. Then, one of the officers pulled out a picture of Yvonne. In that instant, Chamalka knew her intuition had been right all along – something unspeakable had happened to her daughter.

Around noon, Roger Jonsson received a call at work from a

friend, urging him to rush home. Around 1:30 p.m., he arrived at their apartment, now swarming with police personnel. Inside Yvonne's room, he found his wife and Caroline sobbing hysterically. The distraught father was informed that his Yvonne had been killed – and in an unimaginably brutal fashion. Overwhelmed, Chamalka found herself unable to follow as her husband and daughter went to see Yvonne's body. Even years later, she told the media, 'I did not go to the place where the murder took place, I have no guts and still I could not believe what had happened to my loving daughter.' Roger would later describe the haunting sight of his daughter's head, completely smashed in. Despite his grief and horror, he sat beside her for over an hour. Caroline reportedly did not speak for days after.

The police quickly restricted access to the building and sealed the nineteenth-floor stairwell. The crime scene allowed certain deductions: the vast trails of blood and Yvonne's scattered jewellery on the twentieth and twenty-first floors implied she had run – or been pushed – down the stairs, at some point breaking her ankles. She was subjected to tremendous blunt force trauma, to such a degree that her skull was broken in more than sixty places, her lower jaw was shattered into two and her neck had been squeezed in a deathly grip at least twice. Her jeans had been removed, after which she was strangled with the garment.

As the authorities began their investigations, Caroline shared a crucial piece of information. After recounting the events of the previous night, she admitted that her boyfriend had not contacted her at all the entire day – a detail that struck her as simply unusual. Given how concerned she had been about Yvonne, and knowing that he typically called and texted multiple times a day, Jude's silence stood out. Jude had also attended the prestigious Colombo International School and had once been Yvonne's classmate. He and Caroline had known each other since she was eleven, and though he had pursued her before, they had only started dating in February of that year.

Allegedly, Yvonne had repeatedly warned her sister against dating Jude, citing his issues with drugs and alcohol. Caroline, once a bright and focused student, had seen her grades decline noticeably during her relationship with Jude, reaffirming her sister's concerns. Jude was the scion of a powerful family that owned the iconic Coronation Bar and Restaurant in Colombo, along with several other businesses. But behind the social prestige, the police learned that the Jayamaha household was far from stable. Jude's parents had been at odds since his early childhood and eventually separated. This domestic volatility had left its mark on his upbringing. To investigators, these revelations cast the events of 30 June 2005 in a different light. Perhaps the tangled web of relationships between the sisters and Jude was the missing piece of the puzzle and held the key to understanding what had transpired that night.

The day after Yvonne's body was found, Jude finally broke his silence. He visited the Jonsson home to pay his respects, but the police were waiting. He was immediately taken in for questioning and given the chance to share his side of the story, which sharply contradicted Caroline's. Jude claimed that during the previous night's argument, Yvonne had taken his side – something which Caroline denied. He also alleged that he and Caroline had sex after they reached Royal Park at 2 a.m., while she maintained they argued again and parted ways without any intimacy. What both accounts agreed on was that Jude left the complex around 2:30 a.m. The police began reexamining Jude's story to determine the veracity of his claims, starting with confirming the circumstances of his departure from Royal Park.

At Jude's insistence, his friend, Shafraz Rilvan Mohamed, arrived at Royal Park around 3:30 a.m. to pick him up in a cab. Mohamed was immediately taken aback by how odd Jude looked: he was only wearing a pair of boxers and holding his jeans in his hand. However, as far as Mohamed could tell, there wasn't any blood on his clothing. These details were later verified by the cab driver. Interestingly, the driver mentioned in his statement that at one point, Jude had shaken Mohamed's hand and said, 'Thank you for coming; I will never forget this favour.'

When questioned about his bizarre behaviour that night, Jude claimed that he had gone for a swim before the cab arrived. The prosecution, however, suggested that he had done this to wash off any traces of blood from his clothing. And this wasn't all the evidence stacked against him. Forensic examiners had found a partial bloody palm print near the crime scene – later matched to Jude's. The prosecution theorized that Yvonne's fervent dislike and open disapproval of Jude, and his frustration over her presence disrupting his limited time with Caroline, may have played a role in triggering the murder.

Though the defence presented an alternate narrative – arguing that Jude's shoes bore no traces of blood despite the volume of blood at the crime scene, and that the palm print was inconclusive – the judge was not convinced. Jude was sentenced to twelve years of rigorous imprisonment and fined 3 lakh Sri Lankan rupees. In 2011 and 2012, Jude filed appeals seeking a reduced sentence. But this backfired, and the attorney general of Sri Lanka responded by petitioning to escalate the charge from culpable homicide to murder. In a move that was celebrated by many, Jude Jayamaha – now twenty-six – was sentenced to be hanged. The Jonsson family, at last, felt some modicum of relief since Yvonne's murder.

Soon, the scales of justice tilted. In 2015, Maithripala Sirisena was appointed the seventh president of Sri Lanka, a role which granted him the authority to issue presidential pardons – even to prisoners on death row. On 9 November 2019, Jude Jayamaha was granted such a pardon. The justification given was that he was just nineteen at the time of the crime and was convicted 'over an incident of impatience'. The president also claimed that Jude's release was supported by senior Buddhist monks and a Catholic bishop. He was released from Kuruwita Prison the very same day.

The pardon was met with widespread outrage. Caroline Jonsson published a lengthy statement in response, expressing her family's distress.

> For nearly 15 years we have fought for justice the formal and right way, and their family has consistently tried to bribe their way out of this. This has got to stop. For those who

have taken their money, I want you to know that you've accepted blood money and how you've managed to live with yourself is beyond my understanding.

She rubbished the idea that the murder had been an act of momentary madness, highlighting how Jude had systematically attempted to cover his tracks.

**ARYAAN**
Why would a new president stick his neck out for Jude? Especially since it was such a high-profile case, it's a risky move.

**AISHWARYA**
In true desi fashion, it turns out that Maithripala was related to Jude's stepmother. In fact, President Sirisena suggested that middlemen may have accepted money from Jude's family in exchange for lobbying for his controversial presidential pardon. It just goes to show how fragile justice can be, especially in the hands of those willing to twist it to their advantage.

Even before his release, Jude had benefited from the privileges of wealth and connections while serving his sentence. In prison, he had access to a cellphone and enjoyed an unusual degree of freedom of movement. But the presidential pardon was an even deeper blow to the Jonsson family. On 14 November 2019, days after his release, Jude published an open letter addressed to the Sri Lankan public and the Jonssons. In it, he spoke of his troubled past and outlined his educational achievements, including the PhD he had been working towards while incarcerated. All this was supposed to be evidence of him taking rehabilitation seriously. The most startling part of the letter came when, despite maintaining that he was innocent throughout the investigation and trial, Jude admitted to killing Yvonne.

> Sadly, I know that nothing I can ever say or do will make this go away and make things right for you, although I so wish I could. You knew me as a child, I have been in and out of your house and you have always been so gracious and kind to me. I'm so ashamed for what has happened. I have tried many times to contact you and express my heart; but I was never successful.

On the other hand, Caroline Jonsson claims that Jude has never attempted to apologize to their family.

After his release, Jude Jayamaha fled the country before the end of 2019. This was a final act of betrayal for Yvonne's family, who had not only lost their precious daughter and sister but now were forced to live with the fact that her killer had manipulated legal justice and had gotten away scot-free. When Jude was released, Caroline, lashed out against the verdict: 'I will never return to this country. This country has ruined our lives. I have lost a sister and a home. I will continue to fight till my sister's murderer gets the punishment he deserves.' On the other hand, Roger and Chamalka admitted that they no longer had any hope of justice.

On 6 June 2024, the Supreme Court of Sri Lanka overturned the pardon. Deeming it unconstitutional, the apex body instructed the attorney general to extradite Jude. But he remains at large and is currently believed to be living in Singapore.

# 3

# THE 100 KILLINGS OF JAVED IQBAL

**AISHWARYA**
In 1999, a criminal was unmasked to the Pakistani public who seemed to embody their worst nightmares. This man had spent years committing horrific crimes against children, and his rampage had gone largely unnoticed until he chose to turn himself in. This is the story of Pakistan's most notorious serial killer, whose sole motive in life was to hear the cries of a hundred mothers. This is the story of Javed Iqbal.

On 2 December 1999, Jamil Chishti, crime editor for a popular Urdu newspaper, *The Jang*, arrived at his Lahore office to find a letter on his desk. At that time, it wasn't unusual for editors to receive tips via the post, and he thought little of it as he opened the letter. As his eyes glanced over the first sentence, the seemingly mundane din of a newsroom preparing for the next day's headlines quickly faded into the background. He stood there, frozen in shock. In his hands was a letter written in Urdu, containing the confession of a man who had sexually assaulted and murdered over 100 boys.

The crimes committed by serial killers can often be traced to traumatic childhood experiences. But Javed Iqbal's youth appears to have been exceedingly comfortable and pampered. He was born in 1956, the sixth child (and fourth son) of Mohammad Ali Mughal, a very wealthy Lahore-based trader. His parents and many siblings showered him with love and attention, and he grew up enjoying the spoils of being a child who was denied nothing. In his early teens, he was gifted a 200-cc bike. While an intermediate student at the Government Islamia College, Iqbal's father bought him two villas in Shadbagh. In 1978, he started a steel recasting business in one of these houses and lived there for years with his close male friends. But it wasn't long before these unexpected – and to outsiders, undesirable – guests began to attract scrutiny.

> **ARYAAN**
> But why would living with his friends be suspicious? Many people, especially when they're young, stay with friends, whether for companionship or budget constraints.
>
> **AISHWARYA**
> I agree that it isn't unusual to live with your friends. But it was who Iqbal counted among his friends that was off-putting to those who knew him.

As an adult, Iqbal surrounded himself with much-younger boys; when he was twenty-five, his closest companions were fifteen- and sixteen-year-olds. Almost all his employees at the metalworks workshop were underage, most of them runaways. When the peculiarity of this behaviour was pointed out by his family, he grew defensive – their comments were nothing but unwelcome interference. Eventually, his parents resolved to arrange his marriage as a last-ditch effort to salvage both his and the family's rapidly declining reputation. For many years, he resisted his family's efforts to get him married. Then one day, Iqbal surprised everybody by announcing that he had found a bride for himself, and indeed, he would marry not once but twice. His first marriage took place in 1983; she was the elder sister of one of his boys, and the marriage lasted only a few months. His second wife was the younger sister of another close friend, and the two quickly separated. These were coldly calculated moves; the purpose had always been to prevent the boys from deserting him.

Now twice-divorced, Iqbal decided to start a new business – a video game arcade – the first of its kind in Shadbagh and the perfect establishment to attract young male visitors throughout the day. At the arcade, he would often offer tokens to boys at reduced rates and even for free. Allegedly, Iqbal would throw a 100-rupee note on the ground and wait for a boy to pick it up. Then, he would announce that someone had stolen his money, and he had to search all the customers in the store. Once 'caught', the 'thief' would be whisked away to another room to be punished. Using this tactic, he sexually assaulted and sodomized many boys until word spread, and his business ceased. But Iqbal enjoyed the particular impunity that came with being a powerful, wealthy man. When parents, horrified at the stories that were floating around, stopped their children from going to the arcade, Iqbal went on to open an aquarium, a fair price store and an air-conditioned school. All his ventures, predominantly catering to attracting younger people, quickly failed once his reputation became known.

His actions did not go completely unnoticed by the authorities, either. He was jailed for six months on charges of sodomy. Once he was released, he continued his predatory behaviour. Soon after, he assaulted the son of a notable family in Shadbagh, and the matter caught the attention of the neighbourhood elders. He confessed to his crime before the panchayat at Gol Bagh, where he was made to sign an undertaking on stamp paper, assuring everyone that he would not do this again. Photocopies of the document were distributed among the locals, and Iqbal visited nearly a hundred shops in the market to personally apologize.

**ARYAAN**
Oh, come on. How would a stamp paper stop a serial predator from committing sexual assault again?

**AISHWARYA**
That's just the thing; it didn't.

In 1993, after his father's demise, Iqbal inherited a whopping 3.5 million rupees from the estate. Two years later, he used the money to construct a large, luxurious house with a swimming pool in the backyard in Rana Town, Shahdara, where he once again surrounded himself by his preferred companions: underage boys. At this point, he owned several vehicles and was often seen driving his five-door Pajero with half a dozen boys. Again in February 1998, Iqbal was accused of luring two young boys from the Data Darbar shrine and raping them at gunpoint. As usual, bribery helped him evade the law. It seemed he had truly got the complete freedom he had always wanted. That is, until one of his victims was able to fight back.

In September 1998, Iqbal hired a young masseur, about fifteen years old, to his house, where he was living with a seven-year-old boy. According to the police, Iqbal raped the masseur. In the middle of the night, the masseur (perhaps with someone's assistance) attacked Iqbal, fracturing his skull and injuring his jaw. Iqbal was rushed to the Lahore General Hospital, and his situation was so severe that he remained there for nearly a month. Outside, the authorities charged him with sodomy. The medical bills mounted, and in time, his house, car, store and other assets were sold to pay them off. It was then that Iqbal moved to a smaller house with his aged mother, who nursed him back to health. Devastated by her son's fall from grace, she died a few months later. If his words are to be believed, his mother's untimely loss at one of the lowest points of his life incited his yearning for revenge. In his own words, 'My mother cried for me. I wanted 100 mothers to cry for their children.' It was this twisted logic that led him to commit the most brutal string of killings in Pakistan's history.

Back in his newsroom, Jamil Chishti's office had become crowded. All around him, curious reporters took turns reading the letter that grew more terrible with each line. The writer chronicled how he had preyed primarily on runaways and orphans living on the streets of Lahore – the city's most vulnerable population. He claimed he had strangled the boys with an iron chain, dismembered and dissolved their corpses in hydrochloric acid, before disposing of the remains in a nearby river. He shared names, addresses and intimate details, down to descriptions of the shapes of his victims' faces and the sandals they wore. If the story had to be published, they needed to verify Iqbal's claims. So, Chishti and a colleague headed to an address mentioned in the letter, 16-B, Ravi Road. Little did they know that in late November, Iqbal had turned himself into a policeman who dismissed his morbid confession as a fantasy. It was then that he had sent the incriminating letter and photographs to the *Jang* office.

16-B was an abandoned, nondescript house on a dead-end street. The journalists scaled the front wall, and what they found inside was straight out of a horror film. A stench permeated the air. As described in Iqbal's letter, there were blue plastic canisters of clothes and shoes. Removing one of the lids, they found what looked like half-decomposed human remains in a formaldehyde-like liquid. Using Iqbal's carefully recorded addresses, the journalists confirmed that these boys had indeed been missing. On 3 December, *The Jang* carried a front-page story, publishing the victims' names and fifty-seven photographs. The headline said, 'Claim of Murder of a Hundred Kids'.

As word spread and the media, including international journalists who had arrived in Lahore, began taking an interest in the case, the police went to Iqbal's house. Alongside human remains – including decomposed ankles, a hip girdle and bags of hair – the room was littered with remnants of Iqbal's crimes: large drums containing a mix of hydrochloric and sulphuric acid, sleeping pills, heaps of children's clothing and shoes, empty soft drinks and mineral water bottles and board games for children.

> **AISHWARYA**
> Later, parents whose children were missing gathered at the Ravi Road police station and were made to search through these clothes and shoes to identify their kids, who might have fallen prey to Iqbal. Honestly, I cannot imagine how excruciating it must have been to stand among other parents to search for your child's shoes, knowing that finding them means they would have suffered a horrible death.

Two notebooks had been left behind. One contained the names and ages of the victims, along with the date on which he murdered them, while the other described the murders in detail, at times gruesome and at times terribly clinical. 'In terms of expense, including the acid,' Iqbal had written, 'it cost me 120 rupees to erase each victim.' Iqbal's diaries were haunting, but the most pressing need of the hour was to locate this monster and take him off the streets. The walls of his house were plastered with handwritten posters. On one of them, Iqbal had outlined his plans:

Today, November 25, 1999, I have decided to commit suicide. Yesterday, I killed my employee, Sajid, and incinerated his body in the container so that he could be punished for theft and for disturbing me again and again. Now I can [go] to sleep in the depths of the Ravi[the local river].

It was unsurprising that Iqbal – who had intentionally leveraged damning evidence to bait both police and media – had chosen to take his death into his hands. Pakistani authorities launched the largest manhunt in the nation's history to find Iqbal, but nearly a month went by with no sign of him.

The police were, however, able to locate four teenage boys in Sohawa. Believed to be Iqbal's accomplices who helped him trap innocent boys, they had all shared the three-bedroom flat. Within a few days, one of those boys, Ishaq Billah, died. The official story was that he had jumped out a window, but a post-mortem report indicated that force had been used against him, and many believe this may have been a custodial killing. Hours later, on 30 December 1999, a haggard Iqbal turned himself in; not to the police but to the office of the *Jang*. He was afraid that the Lahore Police would kill him if he was taken into their custody, but at the urging of an editor named Shaheen Quereshi, he began writing a confession. He also spoke to the journalists for an hour, the recording of which was later used in court. In the meantime, over 100 soldiers surrounded the building, and Iqbal was finally brought into custody.

The middle-aged man brought to the police station looked completely ordinary; a paternal face with simple square glasses, thinning hair woven through with grey. His words, however, were evil and unrepentant. With no remorse, he proudly claimed that he could have just as easily killed 500 children; money was never a concern – it was simply his decision to surrender after 100. He criticized the boys he had groomed for being opportunistic and exploitative, and pinned the blame for his killing spree squarely on the masseur who had beaten him up badly. His physical and mental health had been destroyed by the attack, Iqbal claimed, and the loss of his mother had been the final straw.

While Iqbal was awaiting trial, a Pakistani Canadian psychologist named Khalid Sohail travelled to interview him. The man's case had caught Dr Sohail's interest: what had led a seemingly normal boy down such a dark path? The doctor would later write a book about their interaction, *The Myth of the Chosen One*, in which he claimed that a criminal with Iqbal's psychological profile would have been institutionalized, rather than imprisoned or given the death penalty, in Canada. He reported that Iqbal had told him that his parents had always inflated his ego – said that he was a special boy who would go on to do great things, especially after a godman told them that Iqbal had healing powers and was special to God. Even as an adult, this sense of being the 'chosen one' never went away. Dr Sohail linked this to his future crimes, though this remains hypothetical.

When the trial began, under the pressures of an overwhelming media spotlight and great public grief, Iqbal attempted to recant his candid confession. He pleaded innocence and said he had been coerced by the police during the investigation. He claimed that some of the boys he was accused of killing were still alive and were being sheltered by their families, who didn't want them to be publicly known as homosexuals. In a bizarre move, Iqbal even suggested that he had invented the entire story to bring awareness to the sad lives of runaway children from impoverished families and the piles of clothes and shoes were simply purchased from a second-hand market. However, Iqbal's past had finally caught up to him – over 100 witnesses testified to his pedophilic tendencies and abusive behaviour. The evidence that he had so generously left in his home further strengthened the prosecution's case, and on 16 March 2000, Iqbal and his three surviving accomplices – Sajid, Muhammad Nadeem and Muhammad Sabir – were found guilty of their crimes.

Muhammad Nadeem (aged nine or ten) and Muhammad Sabir (aged thirteen or fourteen) were sentenced to serve fourteen years in prison and pay a hefty fine to the next of kin of Iqbal's victims. But the sentencing for Iqbal and his twenty-year-old accomplice, Sajid was unlike any other, causing widespread controversy in Pakistan and outside of it. The verdict described Iqbal as 'Satan in the shape of a human being' and ordered that he be strangled with an iron chain, cut into one hundred pieces and dissolved in acid – a recreation of his modus operandi. The judge ordered that this be carried out in an open place, preferably the historic Minar-e-Pakistan, and 'in the presence of the legal heirs of the deceased children, make it a horrible example'. Sajid was given a similar sentence, though his body was ordered to be cut into ninety-eight pieces instead.

### ARYAAN
Can a judge demand a punishment of this kind? I mean, for this to be the result of a legal trial seems … unusual.

**AISHWARYA**
This verdict was anything but usual. In all of Pakistan's history, there had only been public executions under martial law, when General Zia-ul-Haq was in power in the eighties. Ordering that Iqbal's body be cut up and dissolved in acid was against the law in many ways, and there was a pushback against the verdict from all quarters.

The Islamic Ideology Council, Pakistan's foremost religious body, found the sentence un-Islamic, while the country's Federal Minister of Interior Moinuddin Haider declared that Pakistan, as a nation founded on protecting human rights, could not award such a sentence. Eventually, the brutal execution would not end up taking place, but not because the judge rescinded his verdict.

Allegedly, on 8 October 2001, the guard monitoring Iqbal and Sajid, who were kept at the Kot Lakhpat Jail, fell asleep on duty. When he awoke around midnight, he found that both men had hung themselves in their cells using their shirts. Panicked, he took down their bodies and posed them on the ground, as if they were simply asleep. He then left the prison quietly, telling no one that the most notorious serial killer in Pakistan's history had died on his watch.

According to the warden of the prison, he discovered Iqbal and Sajid – their bodies cold and stiff – only the next morning. In an instant, a man who had caused immense pain and suffering – to his victims, to the young boys he turned into perpetrators and to their families – died on his own terms, just as he had planned. His siblings refused to claim his body – their brother had been dead to them ever since he was revealed to be a pedophile and serial murderer. However, his lawyer suspected that he had been killed, as Iqbal had expressed his willingness to divulge the names of government officials who attended his parties and abused children. Nonetheless, did Javed Iqbal manage to simply evade justice, one last time? Would publicly brutalizing him have been justice at all? Regardless, parents and children in Pakistan may have slept more soundly that night, knowing the cruel phantom that had haunted their streets had been exorcized.

# 4

# GULSHAN KUMAR VS. THE UNDERWORLD

**ARYAAN**

T-Series first captured global attention in 2018 when it famously took on Felix Kjellberg (a.k.a PewDiePie) in an infamous battle for the most-subscribed channel on YouTube. To most Indians, T-Series was already a household name, its red logo a familiar presence on the corner of countless music videos and cassette covers we grew up with. Behind this vast, faceless empire was an ordinary man with no family connections to give him easy access to the entertainment industry. Relying on his faith, relentless work and a handful of cassettes, this man took on the biggest conglomerates - until he was ruthlessly murdered in broad daylight. His murder laid bare the deep-rooted corruption within Bollywood and its entanglement with Mumbai's criminal underworld. This is the story of Gulshan Kumar.

By the 1960s, Daryaganj had already established itself as the commercial heart of Delhi. The air was thick with smoke and dust, pierced by the calls of vendors who were selling wares of all kinds. In one corner of the crowded market, a boy spent his childhood polishing glasses and taking orders at a fruit juice stall. He was Gulshan Kumar Dua, son of Chandrabhan Dua, a refugee from West Punjab. Chandrabhan's family had fled to Delhi after the Partition of India, and by the time Gulshan was born in 1951, they were still rebuilding their lives. This meant that money was scarce in their household, and school was not young Gulshan's only concern. After completing tenth grade, Gulshan was forced to drop out of school and work full-time at his father's stall. But his education continued on the bustling streets of Daryaganj: learning how to strike a deal and attract customers.

But even as young Gulshan helped his father run the stall, something else constantly tugged at his mind: *music*. It drifted from the radios perched on paan shop counters, blared through the loudspeakers outside temples and mosques and poured from vehicles passing by. Songs filled the streets of old Delhi like a second language that everyone seemed to share, and Gulshan noticed how the customers hummed devotional hymns and Mohammed Rafi hits while they sipped their juice. In a city reeling from waves of migration and poverty, music was a soothing balm on lives marked by constant struggle.

At first, music was just background noise in an otherwise monotonous life. But soon it transformed into a business idea. While still in his teens, Gulshan's family added new products to the collection at their shop: records and cassettes. He took charge of this side of the business, which soon became more popular than their juice. Those who knew Gulshan remembered the passion with which he worked. 'Even when other boys played cricket or loitered around, he stuck close to the shop,' one acquaintance said. 'He wanted to understand what made people buy one cassette over another.' Gulshan developed an instinct for what the public wanted to hear – not just popular film songs but devotional music like bhajans and naats. He began sourcing tapes from major labels like Polydor and HMV, and then sold them at reduced prices to local customers – anything that had an audience, if only it was within reach.

Sometime in the mid-seventies, Gulshan began producing cassettes of his own. Working out of a rented room with a few tape decks and blank cassettes, he pirated popular Bollywood songs. The practice was legally dubious, but an extremely common one. Driven by weak copyright enforcement laws and the public's raging hunger for inexpensive music, hundreds of small-time operators across India indulged in the business. What set Gulshan apart was the superiority of his product. He made sure that his recordings were clear and the packaging was simple and distinctive. The prices were kept as low as possible. They were ten or twenty rupees less than the average big-label cassettes, which became the differentiating factor between a family making a purchase or leaving the shop empty-handed. He named this fledgling enterprise Super Cassettes Industries, an ambitious name for what was then a tiny, backroom operation.

### AISHWARYA

Just that name screams ambition to me – to start a project that's dear to your heart with a vision of something grand and important.

**ARYAAN**
I also find it fascinating that the quality of his product made all the difference. As someone interested in that world, it's cool to see the beginnings of an entrepreneur.

By 1977, cassette culture exploded in India as Japanese two-in-one players flooded the domestic market. Portable and affordable, these handy products brought recorded music into their homes, family gatherings and public events. Gulshan, who had been steadily building relationships with wholesalers and street vendors, adapted quickly. If a tape was defective, Gulshan offered to replace it with no fuss. If a seller struggled to pay upfront, he extended credit. In an industry dominated by stiff executives in Mumbai and Kolkata boardrooms, Gulshan stood out as someone you could forge a personal connection with. Those who regularly dealt with him, whether employees or business partners, described him as demanding but equitable. He pushed for quality and speed, but always paid his dues fairly and on time.

Unlike the polished, curated catalogues of bigger labels, Super Cassettes focused on sheer volume. Gulshan expanded his offerings with great care, focusing on devotional music like the 'Hanuman Chalisa' and kirtans. He was quick to recognize that in India, faith never goes out of fashion and older listeners with failing vision often needed an alternative to reading prayers. By the early eighties, Super Cassettes was turning a solid profit. Riding this wave of success, Gulshan rebranded the enterprise. From small-town stores in Meerut and Patna to bustling village fairs, the company, newly coined as T-Series, became a household name.

Having made his mark in the cassette trade, Gulshan took another calculated risk: recording covers of popular film songs. At the time, Indian copyright law allowed re-recordings of music three years after a song's release, as long as royalties were duly paid to the original copyright owners. T-Series aggressively pushed this limit, hiring local singers at low rates to re-record Bollywood songs. In practice, they frequently risked legal action, often flagrantly disobeying the three-year waiting period altogether and flooding shops with these affordable cover albums before the original label had a chance to respond. Rivals were livid. An executive in Chennai reportedly told Gulshan that he was killing the industry. The man behind T-Series simply responded, 'The public decides what sells.' Despite lawsuits and mounting court battles, T-Series, by 1990, dominated the largest share of India's cassette market.

Gulshan reinvested the company's profits into a new branch of the entertainment industry: film production, a notoriously risky and expensive venture. His reasoning was straightforward: if he owned the film, he owned its music. T-Series started with producing low-budget projects like *Bewafa Sanam* and *Jeena Marna Tere Sang*, which flopped at the box office but left behind memorable music. In 1988, *Qayamat Se Qayamat Tak* became T-Series' first major hit, quickly followed by the film that changed everything: Mahesh Bhatt's *Aashiqui* (1990). Its soundtrack, composed by the duo Nadeem–Shravan, became one of Bollywood's highest-selling music albums. With its resounding success, Gulshan's prediction that the future was owning content, not licensing or even duplicating it, started to pay off. By 1997, T-Series controlled rights to thousands of audio tracks and video albums. But not everyone welcomed the meteoric rise of the son of a humble fruit juice vendor. Established music labels accused him of undercutting the industry; new players feared T-Series' dominance and being pushed out altogether. Worse, his growing clout drew the attention of a terrifying threat – the underworld. Gangsters had begun paying close attention to a booming business growing too big and too fast, without paying them any dues.

Gulshan Kumar's business had outgrown Delhi. He decided it was time to trade his modest Noida office for a new frontier: Bombay, the nucleus of India's entertainment industry. But beneath the glitz and gloss of Marine Drive and the star-studded Bollywood premieres was a city controlled by men whose names were only spoken in hushed tones. Dawood Ibrahim, from his base in Dubai, ruled Bollywood's underbelly through a veritable empire of his own with his D-Company. Film-makers received quick cash to finance their films, no questions asked. But this privilege came at an invisible cost. Gangsters dictated casting, summoned A-list stars to lavish parties and flooded the markets with pirated prints before the original films even hit theatres. Some actors quietly left the country when the extortion grew to be too much. Newspapers occasionally carried reports of shootings and unexplained assaults in film studios or upscale neighbourhoods, but most of Bollywood had been swallowed in a culture of fear and silence.

#### AISHWARYA
I've heard stories of underworld dealings in Bollywood for years. I remember Preity Zinta speaking out about receiving threats while filming *Chori Chori Chupke Chupke*. But I don't fully understand the motive. Is it just financial gain?

#### ARYAAN
Money is a driving factor. Bankrolling films is an easy way to invest huge amounts of black money. I do think these figures might have been drawn to the glamour of Bollywood. Maybe it gave them a chance to jump several rungs up the social ladder.

Gulshan's success had always been his armour, but in Bombay, it made him an easy target. He first came onto the D-Company's radar when he refused small but persistent demands that others in the industry quietly met. These included donations to sham charities or investments in phantom films. Most industry veterans complied to keep the peace. Gulshan did not. Friends later said it wasn't pride but faith that doing the right thing would keep him safe. By 1997, the pressure had escalated too much to ignore. Anonymous calls demanding money and threatening his safety were made to his office, prompting him to move with an armed guard assigned by the Uttar Pradesh Police. Beyond that, Gulshan changed little. He lived his life in the public eye: his daily prayers, his business and his relationships were out in the open for everyone to see. He chose not to be sequestered away.

Unbeknownst to him, a larger plot was brewing, with a man named Abdul Rauf Dawood Merchant, known on the city's streets as Raja, at its centre. Raja wasn't a mastermind or crime kingpin; he was a street-level enforcer desperate to prove his worth, which made him all the more dangerous. Allegedly, Raja was acting on instructions from Abu Salem himself – Dawood Ibrahim's trusted lieutenant and his primary link to the world of Bollywood. The top brass had grown accustomed to controlling industry giants like puppets on a string and Gulshan's open defiance was an insult they wouldn't tolerate. Over phone calls and, according to some reports, covert meetings in the D-Company's Dubai headquarters, they decided that they would make an example of Gulshan. For weeks, Rauf trailed his target with help from his brother, Abdul Rashid Dawood Merchant, and another associate. They shadowed Gulshan as he left his Andheri West home every morning, got into his red Opel Astra and prayed at Jiteshwar Mahadev Mandir, a temple he had personally helped renovate years earlier. They noted the temple's exits and surroundings and whether Gulshan was accompanied by an entourage on his daily visits. They watched the armed guard who stuck with him, and the rare moments when he didn't.

In early August 1997, a rumour spread that Gulshan's bodyguard had fallen ill. This was the break the Merchant brothers and their associate had been waiting for – a chink in the armour of an otherwise untouchable man. As a final warning, and perhaps a last opportunity to back down and save his own life, two calls were made directly to Gulshan's number on 5 August and 8 August, demanding extortion money. When he refused to comply, Gulshan's eventual killers were given the go-ahead to carry out their dastardly plan.

On the morning of 12 August, Kumar followed a routine that had become second nature to him. His driver, Rooplal Suraj, drove through the familiar streets of Jeet Nagar, Versova, to the Jiteshwar Mahadev Mandir. The usual third passenger, Gulshan's armed bodyguard, was conspicuously absent. Inside the temple, Gulshan was greeted by the president of the temple trust, Ramchandra Lavangare, with folded hands. He spent about fifteen minutes performing his regular rituals, unhurried, unaware that three men were waiting just beyond the safe and comforting cocoon of incense and chanting. Around 10:40 a.m., Gulshan exited the temple with Lavangare close behind. The car was parked facing Navkiran Road, barely six feet from the temple entrance. Rooplal went to open the door on the driver's side, balancing a canister of water and fruit offerings from the temple in his other hand. For a split second, Gulshan stood by himself, and then the calm was shattered by the sound of gunshots.

Gulshan staggered as the first bullets struck him, before catching sight of one of his attackers, who stepped into his view to fire again. Rooplal tried to shield him but was shot in both legs. A third gunman emerged and continued the onslaught of gunfire. Sixteen shots were fired in total, and most found their mark. The area erupted into panic and chaos. Residents screamed and slammed their doors shut as

Gulshan, wounded and desperate, banged on them for shelter. Satisfied that the job was done, the three assailants calmly fled the scene – first on foot, then by hijacking a taxi at gunpoint some distance away. They ditched the vehicle near Kapaswadi and blended into the crowd.

Back in the temple compound, Gulshan had collapsed in a widening pool of his blood. Lavangare managed to drag him into the backseat of the Opel and hailed a nearby rickshaw driver to take the wheel since Rooplal was too badly injured to drive. Once the car sped off towards Cooper Hospital, the locals began cautiously peering out of their windows. The sudden flame of violence had been extinguished just as quickly as it had ignited. As temple bells swung gently in the breeze, oblivious to what had happened, Gulshan Kumar's life hung by a thread.

When the bloodied, frantic group reached Cooper Hospital, the emergency team was already waiting outside. A police constable who had witnessed the shooting had called ahead to warn them that a critically injured patient was on the way. Gulshan was carried inside, blood soaking through the sheet they had wrapped around him. His eyes were barely open; his breathing was shallow and laboured. His body was riddled with bullet wounds, and despite the best efforts of the doctors and nurses on duty, his injuries proved fatal. 'Brought dead': these words cut through a weeping Rooplal Suraj, who had been shifted to a wheelchair to be treated. At exactly 11:15 a.m., the man who had changed the soundscape of India was declared dead.

The news broke in no time. Soon, national TV channels

were running headlines about the music mogul's death. A crowd gathered outside Cooper Hospital: fans, journalists, curious bystanders drawn to the ruckus. Musicians and producers whose lives Gulshan's work had deeply touched were left shocked by the news, even those who had criticized his business practices. But in Andheri West's D. N. Nagar police station, work was already underway to bring the perpetrators to justice.

Within two hours of Gulshan's death, a formal complaint had been registered. Senior Inspector Rashmi Jadhav started work on case 572/1997 – a homicide investigation unlike any the station had handled before. Under the dusty yellow lights of the station, shell-shocked witnesses gave their first statements. Lavangare, the president of the temple trust, described watching Gulshan collapse, dazed and bleeding, outside the temple premises. Two fruit vendors recalled seeing three men loitering nearby before the shooting, their faces obscured. It was evident that this wasn't a random mugging or a crime of passion. The number of perpetrators and the precision with which they carried out the attack pointed to careful and professional planning. Combined with the extortion calls Gulshan had received, suspicion quickly turned towards D-Company. But the immediate task was to find the gunmen. Gulshan's case was quickly handed off to a rising star of the Mumbai Police, Deputy Commissioner of Police Rakesh Maria.

**ARYAAN**
If you know *Desi Crime*, you know we are fans of Rakesh Maria! In this case, he was joined by Assistant Commissioner of Police Sanjay Pandey and Inspector Nitin Patil, both veterans in the city's fight against its underworld.

After locking down the crime scene, a thorough investigation was launched, which yielded spent 9-mm bullet shells, typical of the weaponry used by low-level gang members in the city. Within forty-eight hours, the Crime Branch's network of informants had produced a name: Abdul Rauf Dawood Merchant, alias Raja.

But by the time police raided a bar in Dongri that Raja was known to frequent, he was already gone. Subsequent raids swept through Dongri, Bhendi Bazaar and Nallasopara, and as word spread, criminals across Mumbai went underground. Raja may not have been a major gangster, but he was allied with those who were. His strong ties to powerful syndicates helped him stay hidden for *years* even after killing a man as influential as Gulshan Kumar. It was only in January 2001 that he was caught from a safehouse in Kolkata. According to a confessional statement later cited in the court judgment, Raja told the arresting officers that 'We had been instructed that Gulshan Kumar must be eliminated. He had refused to comply with demands. His death was to be a message.' And Raja hadn't delivered that message alone.

Police also set their sights on Raja's brother, Abdul Rashid Dawood Merchant, whom they suspected had helped plan and execute the killing. A search of their father's home revealed two pistols wrapped in cloth and hidden under the floorboards. Forensic tests confirmed they matched the ballistics of the bullets recovered at the crime scene. During the interrogation of the two brothers, the police reconstructed the fateful day of the attack. Abdul Rauf had fired the shots, ambushing Gulshan as he approached his car. Abdul Rashid had followed close behind to block any escape, while a third accomplice provided cover. Once the deed was done, they hijacked a taxi at gunpoint to escape, switching vehicles again partway to lose any potential trail. A 400-page chargesheet was filed at the end of the investigation. The fate of Gulshan's killers now rested with the judiciary.

In 2001, the trial began, with the Mumbai Police naming nineteen people as suspects in the conspiracy. Shockingly, famous Bollywood figures like Nadeem Saifee (of the Nadeem–Shravan duo) and film producer Ramesh Taurani were among the accused, both of whom were suspected of having ordered Gulshan's murder over professional disputes. Ultimately, the judge's gavel fell firmly on Raja. On 29 April 2002, he was sentenced to life in prison. All eighteen co-accused were acquitted for lack of evidence. Even under cross-examination, Raja maintained his composure – the expression of a man who knew he had been a small piece in something far greater than himself. According to one report, when asked why he had killed a man like Kumar, Raja muttered in court, *'Hukum toh hukum hota hai'* (Orders are orders). In his final ruling, Judge M. L. Tahaliyani declared, 'Dua's death was not the result of individual grievance, but an organized effort by criminal syndicates to assert control through fear. The accused acted not out of personal hatred, but as agents of a corrupt system that threatened not just individuals, but civil order itself.'

Raja, convicted in 2002, was granted a fourteen-day furlough by the Bombay High Court in 2009. Seizing the opportunity, he fled to Bangladesh. Using forged documents, he evaded Indian authorities for seven and a half years, though he was made to serve a five-year sentence for illegally entering and remaining in Bangladesh. In November 2016, after completing that sentence, he was extradited to India. The case remained dormant until July 2021, when Justice Sadhana Jadhav and Justice N. R. Borkar of the Bombay High Court upheld Abdul Rauf's life sentence, stating that 'in the interest of justice at large, he does not deserve any leniency'. They also quashed Abdul Rashid's acquittal and sentenced him to life in prison, naming him as one of the shooters responsible for the murder. As far as the public is aware, both brothers remain in a high-security prison in Maharashtra today.

In 2006, Bhushan Kumar, who now heads T-Series in his father's stead, told reporters, 'I have done everything possible to get justice for my father, who was brutally murdered eight years ago. Now, I've left it to God. I can't indulge the blame games anymore.' It would take another fifteen years for Gulshan Kumar's case to be considered solved. And yet, the frustrating reality remains that the Merchant brothers were merely pawns in a much larger and convoluted game. The Mumbai Police may have arrested Kumar's shooters, but they have not managed to break through the system that created them in the first place. Abu Salem and Dawood Ibrahim remain at large, protected by loopholes in international law and powerful connections with political and business leaders. Yet even their influence has not been able to overshadow what is most precious about Gulshan's legacy: the music he fought to democratize. Today, T-Series is a colossus in global pop culture, and the company is valued at over 2 billion dollars. Though the internet might occasionally poke fun at the company's penchant for copyright strikes, it's undeniable that Gulshan Kumar has changed the way India and the world listen to music.

# 5

# A ROYAL WEDDING AND A VANISHING: VISHAL MEHROTRA

**AISHWARYA**

On 29 July 1981, 750 million people across seventy-four countries were glued to their television sets, watching a fairytale wedding. In London, nearly 6 lakh people lined the city's streets from the royal residence at Clarence House to St Paul's Cathedral, craning their necks to catch a glimpse of a historical moment. The people's princess, Diana Spencer, was marrying the heir to the British throne in a spectacle costing over 100 million in today's dollars. As the euphoric celebration swept through the streets and over satellite waves, an eight-year-old boy vanished – blocks away from the event of the century and a few steps from his London home. This is the story of Vishal Mehrotra.

Even today, Diana Spencer and Charles III's wedding remains the fourth most-watched television broadcast of all time. At 10:22 a.m., Diana Spencer and her father John Spencer, stepped into a horse-drawn carriage – one of nine in the royal procession – heading to the stunning St Paul's Cathedral. The 3-kilometre journey crawled forward, slowed by the unimaginable number of bystanders peering into the glass windows to catch a glimpse of the young bride. A majority of the city's police force, including 2,200 military officers, had been deployed to secure the event. Sharpshooters were dotted across the skyline, out of sight. Their watchful eyes were affixed not on the wedding procession but the crowd, ready to react at the first sign of trouble.

A select group of spectators had been fortunate enough to avoid the pandemonium – those who had homes or offices that faced the path Diana's carriage would take to the church. One such person was Vishambhar Mehrotra, or Vishu, a young property solicitor who worked on Fleet Street – an enviable, front-row access to watch the procession. His employers had made a day out of the royal wedding. They had a party planned; the partners, employees and their families were all in attendance. By 11 a.m., Vishu was at the office with his young children, Vishal (eight) and Mamta (seven), and their live-in nanny, Joannita Carvalho. It was a hot, sunny day, and the children were dressed for the exciting event. Mamta would later recount, 'It was like the most exciting thing. We had heard about this royal wedding for months, we all wanted to see it … We had our own kind of vantage point, which was safe for all of us, right?'

Her brother was far more interested in playing games with the other children and racing around the desks than watching the royal wedding. Still, everyone gathered at the window when the carriage finally passed by around 12:45 p.m. Cheers erupted, flags waved and the noise from the streets drifted up to meet them. Despite the grand build-up, the moment passed quite quickly. With nothing more to see, the food and drinks were packed away, and the crowd began to thin. Vishu realized that they needed to reach home before Princess Diana and Prince Charles began their return to Buckingham Palace, and the streets swelled once again.

Tired from the day's excitement, the group of four boarded a train from Temple to East Putney, the station nearest to their house. With millions of Londoners either indoors or packed around St Paul's Cathedral, the rest of the city had fallen into an unusually silent stillness, a 'ghost town'. Everyone was quite tired from the excitement of the day, but as they walked home, Vishu remembered he had meant to grab some cough medicine for Vishal. He asked Joannita to take the children to a nearby shop and handed his kids some money to buy candy. Meanwhile, he continued alone and fell asleep almost as soon as he got home.

Halfway to the store, a tired Vishal asked if he could head back home by himself. The chatty young boy took great pride in his independence; he went to school all alone and would often ask his nanny to wait in a different compartment when they were travelling on the London Tube. Joannita refused initially, but Vishal was insistent. He even turned down Mamta's offer to go with him – it was probably safer for his little sister to stay with their nanny. This small battle won, Vishal turned and ran across the street he had crossed countless times before. Home was ten minutes away. He should have been safe. But instead, his life was about to be cruelly snatched from him.

When Joannita and Mamta returned home that afternoon, they immediately noticed Vishal's absence. There was a street party underway in the park nearby starting at 4 p.m., and they assumed he was out enjoying it with his friends. Reassured with this explanation, they drifted off to sleep. But when they woke up and Vishal still wasn't home, Vishu's anxiety began to mount. He checked the park – no sign of Vishal. None of the children there had seen him. At first, he wondered if his son had simply gone somewhere with his friends, but call after call to neighbours and other parents yielded nothing.

By the time darkness descended on Putney, Vishu had contacted everyone he could think of; it was as if his son had vanished into thin air from the quiet, nearly empty streets. Around 7:40 p.m., he called the Metropolitan Police to report Vishal missing. Twenty minutes later, two uniformed officers reached their house. One of them, Jackie Malton, embraced Vishu instead of simply shaking the devastated father's hand. It was a moment of unexpected kindness they would recall even decades later. A physical search was launched for Vishal, including checking neighbourhood homes and outhouses, sifting through dustbins and even opening the freezers of nearby corner stores, in case the boy had got trapped somewhere.

Mamta had been sent to bed before the police arrived,

but that night, she lay awake. At first, she was pleased – she had the room to herself and didn't have to share it with her brother. But that quiet joy quickly curdled into a feeling of unpleasantness. 'I remember the pin drop silence of sleeping in the room without him there,' she described, 'I had never slept a night without him in my whole life. Since the day I was born, I think we had been together every day … my parents weren't there, but Vishal, he was always there.'

The Mehrotra family had undergone several major changes in just a few years. Vishu had met his ex-wife, Aruna, after returning to India after completing his education in the UK. They married, had Vishal and Mamta and the family lived in India for a few years. But after the loss of his father, Vishu decided to move back to the UK in 1978. Their marriage soon unravelled, and Aruna decided to return to India. She began a jewellery business, while Vishu remained in the UK with the children. And now, with Vishal's sudden disappearance, the family stood on the brink of another devastating shift.

The search intensified over the next few weeks – sewers were drained, divers sent into nearby water bodies and search dogs brought in. As time passed, the theory that Vishal may have been kidnapped began to seem more and more likely. Aruna, his mother, became the police's first person of interest. Perhaps, they speculated, this was a family dispute gone wrong. When she flew into London a few days later, she was greeted by officers at Heathrow airport who questioned and quickly ruled her out as a suspect in the disappearance.

The investigation then moved beyond Vishal's immediate circle. The media was given his description: an eight-year-old boy in a blue and white striped T-shirt, black corduroy trousers and blue training shoes who had been last seen outside the East Putney station around 2 p.m. on 29 July. A reconstruction of the disappearance was filmed, but the Indian boy cast to play Vishal, who looked nothing like him, was an oversight which frustrated the family. The boy in the video was as tall as the nanny!

Public tips were encouraged, and tens of thousands of people had the police chasing leads that went nowhere. The media search had proved as futile as the on-ground one. Time passed, and the Mehrotra family was left in the dark, waiting and slowly losing hope that their beloved son and brother would ever be found. Joyous occasions – Vishu's thirty-sixth birthday (four days after Vishal was last seen), Vishal's ninth birthday (two months later in September 1981), Christmas – came and went. But their house remained hollow, stripped of celebration and heavy with the boy's lingering absence. Mamta struggled to adapt, not only to her brother's absence, but to life with both parents under the same roof for the first time in her active memory and to her new identity as the sister of a missing child. Years later, she would remember being scolded by a relative for laughing while watching an episode of *Tom and Jerry* at a time when the family was steeped in sadness. As winter settled over London and blanketed the city in snow, their lives would never be the same, even as they felt stuck in time.

On 21 February 1982, around 6 p.m., two brothers were shooting pigeons in a wooded area of West Sussex called Alder Copse when they stumbled upon something horrific. Near them lay a small human skull. Several feet away was a child's lower jaw. There were more bones – some likely dragged by wild animals, others partially buried in a nearby 2-foot-deep ditch under a large log. On firmer ground, there was a clump of dark hair. The men immediately called the police. Soon, the area was swarming with uniformed officials. Though the remains had not been formally identified, the police called Vishu at his Fleet Street office with the most devastating news: they had very likely found Vishal. He broke down completely; it was the first time Vishu was confronting the possibility that his son was dead. In the hours that followed, clinging to the last strands of hope, Vishu gave an interview, hoping to fuel interest in the case once again and keep the search for answers alive.

Soon after, his worst fears were confirmed. A massive excavation involving thirty policemen unearthed more bones but no clothing, and the remains were transported to London for forensic examination. Using dental analysis, the remains were confirmed to be Vishal's. This was not simply a tragic accident – his body had been discovered 80 kilometres from where he was last seen. Vishal had been murdered, his body discarded in the remote wilderness. With the discovery in Alder Copse, the jurisdiction moved from Greater London's Metropolitan Police to the Sussex Police, a much smaller force who were strapped for resources and didn't have the means or talent to tackle its intricacies. Taking over the investigation seven months after Vishal's disappearance was no easy feat, and the Sussex Police, unfortunately, were overwhelmed with thousands of documents, witness statements and suspect lists. Months passed with no progress.

In May 1982, the family cremated Vishal's remains and submerged his ashes in the Ganga. Aruna stayed back in India, and Vishu returned to the UK. He eventually remarried and had a son in 1992, Suchin. Yet the question of what had happened to Vishal never left the family's minds. Decades passed. The world around them seemed to forget. Finally, in 2019, four decades later after Vishal's disappearance, something reignited their hope as never before.

29 July 1981 was a historic day for Britain and a life-changing one for Vishal's family for a much more tragic reason. It was also, as it turns out, an important day for a police officer named Shaun Keep – it was his first day on the force. By 2019, Keep had had an illustrious career as a Scotland Yard detective and was now travelling the country, advising smaller police departments on challenging cases. As he approached retirement, the Sussex police had invited him to consult on a deeply disturbing case: a nexus of pedophiles who had abused at least eighteen boys at a local boarding school, Muntham House.

While reviewing the case files, Keep came across a chilling detail. One of the predators and the group's ringleader,

Nicholas Douglass, had documented a detailed case study about a young Indian boy, simply titled 'Vishal'. He had finished writing it a year after Vishal's remains were found. Keep immediately alerted the Sussex Police. But to his dismay, little was done to see it through. Although the perpetrators in the Muntham case were questioned, police officials didn't probe any further when they denied involvement. 'I did feel that it was entirely inadequate, frankly,' Keep would say of the police's efforts. 'My personal view on this was that this little boy deserved better than just knocking on someone's door and basically saying, yeah, mate, did you murder someone back in the 80s?'

Keep's only recourse was to involve the media. That led him to give a tip-off to Colin Campbell, a passionate and tenacious journalist at the *BBC*. In the early days of the Covid-19 pandemic, as the world was turned upside down, Colin received a call from Keep, who walked him through the details of Vishal's case. The journalist was instantly intrigued. Born the same year as Vishal, he felt an inexplicable connection with the young boy. He decided to begin by visiting Vishu as a first step. Now a retired magistrate, Vishu had grown jaded over the years. Too many media personnel had come and gone, eager to exploit his son's story. But something about Colin's sincerity struck a chord. Vishu opened up and shared mountains of documentation that had accumulated over forty years. With the support of Keep and Jackie Malton – the officer who had hugged Vishu on the night of Vishal's disappearance and was now a bright star on the force – Colin took on the case. Together, he and Malton visited the site in Alder Copse where Vishal's remains had been discovered. They turned their focus to the boarding school, compiling a list of confirmed victims and potential witnesses who might help provide some long-buried insights into Vishal's death.

Muntham House, a grandiose establishment surrounded by sweeping green grounds, is an idyllic sight. But in 1981, the school's brick walls were concealing a far darker reality. Labelled as 'troubled', boys between the ages of five to eighteen were sent to the school to correct their behavioural issues. Instead of receiving care and protection, many students became victims of horrific abuse. Nicholas Douglass, a popular staff member and a house parent, was meant to provide emotional support and guidance to the boys. Instead, he exploited his close access to them. Under the guise of kindness – inviting students into his home so they could watch TV, drink coffee or smoke an illicit cigarette – Douglass groomed them. When they grew older, many of the Douglass's victims were able to speak out against him and two other predators among the school's staff: James Russell, and a man known only by his nickname, Fat John. While Douglass and John were imprisoned, Russell had managed to flee the country while he was out on bail. Colin spoke to many of their victims during his investigation, now in their thirties and forties. One survivor told him, 'The worst thing he (Douglass) ever did was … [h]e murdered the little boy in me.'

These conversations revealed terrifying details. Many of the boys had been abused off the school grounds and outside term time, suggesting a chilling possibility that Vishal could have crossed paths with these notorious men. Fat John's job was to drive students to and from their homes, and his route may have intersected with Vishal's. Douglass occasionally took his victims to his mother's home, which was twelve minutes away from Alder Copse, the deserted woodlands where Vishal's body was found. As Colin dug deeper, he spotted a pattern: a vast majority of the gang's victims were South Asian. 'The man's obviously got an appetite for an Indian boy,' an interviewee said of Russell, who was suspected to have fled to Sri Lanka.

And then, of course, there was the link that had revitalized the case: Douglass's paper titled 'Vishal'. When he was first investigated for child sexual abuse, the document had simply been quietly filed away. In it, Douglass examined how he had come in contact with an abused Indian boy. The cruel twist in the story? It was Douglass himself who was abusing the boy.

### AISHWARYA
This was a hard-hitting detail. It turns out his victim was one of the survivors whom Colin spoke to during his investigation. While reporting the case, Colin called the boy 'Kabir'.

Unable to use his victim's actual name, Douglass had chosen a pseudonym. But could it truly be a coincidence that he had settled on 'Vishal' – an uncommon name in the UK, and the name of a child who was murdered not far from Douglass's hunting grounds? To answer this question, Colin launched a search for the man himself, who had been out of prison for around fifteen years. Through some online sleuthing, he was able to trace Douglass, now old, frail and living in a remote area of the country. Colin spent hours speaking with him, carefully building a rapport with the well-known predator and recording their conversations. Eventually, he asked the question point-blank. Douglass's response seemed completely mundane: 'It's the first one that came into my head because it had been in the press, massive publicity ... I thought, well, I can't call him Mohammed because he's not a Muslim ... I saw this name, I thought, right, I'll use that name.'

To Colin, this explanation was unsatisfactory for several reasons. By the time Douglass had written the paper in 1983, the news coverage surrounding Vishal's case had died down significantly; the case was cold. Though Douglass claimed he chose the name from the major media and public attention around the boy's disappearance, he seemed oddly evasive when pressed on its finer details. 'I may not have even noticed the news on that, to be quite frank with you,' he told Colin later. He could recall the royal wedding but claimed to have no memory of his whereabouts on that day.

**AISHWARYA**
This is interesting to me. Do you think it's that unusual that he doesn't remember a day forty years in the past?

**ARYAAN**
We've talked about this on the podcast before but, for example, we both vividly remember the day that the Nirbhaya rape case happened, even though we were in the sixth and seventh grade.

**AISHWARYA**
Yeah, I think major events in your immediate surroundings do tend to stick with you …

Crucially, during their discussions, Douglass had revealed himself to be a consummate liar. His obsession with the boys he groomed ran disturbingly deep, and in the 1980s, he had even tried – unsuccessfully – to adopt the boy he had written about in his essay, Kabir. At first, he denied this when Colin questioned him. But when pressed, he eventually admitted it.

Colin used his research to publish a series of stories on Vishal's case and the traumatic histories of the Muntham House survivors. Among them was Kabir's brother, 'Amir', who had been abused by Fat John. For the first time, the two brothers became aware that they had been sexually abused by the same group of men – something they hadn't spoken about for years, silenced by shame and guilt. Colin and the Mehrotras had hoped the newfound media attention would be a renewed call to action for the once callous Sussex police. But they were to be sorely disappointed. The fortieth anniversary of Vishal's death came and went with little more than a cursory police visit to the family. In that meeting, the officials downplayed the link with the Muntham case. They accepted Douglass's explanation for why he had chosen to name the paper 'Vishal' and pointed out that the predators of Muntham, who had such easy and unmonitored access to students to abuse, had no known history of abducting random boys from public spaces.

**AISHWARYA**
I see their logic, but the timing might be relevant here. Schools were off for the summer, and these predators likely did not have the usual access to the boys from Muntham House. Maybe they were seeking other ways to satisfy their perverse desires.

During this visit, the officers gave the family another decisive sign that they had little intention of pursuing justice for Vishal: they attempted to return a few photographs of Vishal, along with a preserved lock of his hair. Vishu and Keep were sceptical; they insisted the evidence remained in police custody in case new developments emerged. But it was a gesture of symbolic defeat – the police were giving up on Vishal.

Colin refused to walk down that path. He began chasing a new thread: James Russell, a convicted pedophile with a disturbing fixated on Indian boys. So deep was his obsession that he had attempted to learn Hindi and visited India on multiple occasions. Though he had served prison time before, Russell had vanished after the Muntham case blew up, evading capture for years. After following numerous false leads, Colin finally received a promising anonymous tip. It was the breakthrough he needed. A man named James Russell, whose biodata matched that of the convicted sex offender, was living in Sri Lanka and still receiving welfare money from the UK government. A local source visited the area where Russell was said to live. Residents described him as an elderly British man who encouraged local children to visit his home for private tuition in English. The source managed to grab a picture of the man, and a facial recognition expert at the University of Bradford confirmed that there was a 76 per cent likelihood that he was indeed Russell.

Armed with a compelling reason to travel, Colin headed for Sri Lanka. He arrived in the country on 29 July 2022, exactly forty-one years after Vishal's disappearance. When he first introduced himself as a *BBC* journalist investigating the case, Colin had anticipated anger, hostility and perhaps the door being slammed shut in his face. Instead, James invited him in and even allowed Colin to record their conversation. Russell denied having anything to do with Vishal's death. He was travelling in India at the time of the royal wedding, though he was unable to provide any evidence. When Colin asked whether he had a preference for boys of Indian heritage, or those with darker skin, Russell allegedly said, 'Yes, I believe they're as beautiful as anyone else ... I have got a thing for them.' He argued that pedophilia was misunderstood, and his behaviour stemmed from a protective instinct that didn't truly harm the boys.

Colin reported James to the Sri Lankan authorities, prompting officials to revoke his visa and force him to fly back to the UK. Upon arrival, he was questioned by the Sussex police. But just a few days later, he died of natural causes. And with him, perhaps, the truth behind Vishal's death. A spokesperson for the Sussex police department defended their inaction. They maintained that extraditing James was not a viable option: 'Based on the information available at the time, it was not proportionate to send a Sussex Police representative to Sri Lanka to try and locate the individual.'

There was one final name to cross off the unofficial suspect list: Fat John. For years, the search for him felt like a wild goose chase. No one seemed to have remembered his full name, his whereabouts or any concrete detail that could help identify him. But Kabir's brother recalled a fragmented memory: once, when he had been taken to Fat John's apartment, he had noticed that the building had an elevator that took them to the ninth floor. That detail, placed next to the timeline of abuse, significantly narrowed the search – high-rise buildings with elevators were rare in the area at the time. A researcher working with Colin eventually identified one John Harper, who had lived on the ninth floor of Churchill Court during the period in question. Sadly, Harper, who had once been a children's entertainer at a hotel, had died of natural causes in 1999. Colin tracked down Harper's family. They confirmed that he was a convicted pedophile who had a proclivity for taking pictures of his victims. Though yet another lead in Vishal's case had ended with a dead man, there was some resolution. Colin showed a picture of Fat John to Amir, mixed in with eleven others. He picked it out immediately. 'You don't know how important seeing that picture is to me right now ... I always came to the conclusion that this would be a story no one would believe,' the man said, finally able to discuss his trauma freely.

As all these revelations came forth, piecemeal and with much lost to time, the Mehrotra family and their well-wishers were left grappling with a painful question: why had none of this come to light during the official investigations? Whether it was Russell's location or Douglass's eerily named paper, they had collated many of these details but done nothing with them. 'I can't forgive them for their inaction,' Vishu said, well aware that his son's case had been treated quite differently from high-profile disappearances of white children. 'I am now convinced that the police's attitude is cover up, cover up, cover up. It cannot be anything short of institutional racism.' His life – and that of his family – had been permanently altered, and the inefficiency of the police investigation – however fervently they denied any prejudiced treatment – had eroded the family's trust in the process. In 2023, Colin and Vishal's step-brother, Suchin, produced a nine-part *BBC* podcast, simply titled *Vishal*. In it, many of these details were made public for the first time, with the care that they deserved.

Over the years, there have been other theories about Vishal's case, all linked his terrible death to wider pedophile rings operating in the Greater London area at the time. Some internet sleuths have speculated about the involvement of notorious child abuser and serial killer, Sidney Cooke. Another theory connected Vishal's murder to the Elm Guest House, a prominent hotel allegedly at the centre of a high-profile pedophile ring. These claims were later disproved. Despite scattered leads, more than forty years on – and two years after Colin's investigation reignited public interest – there have been no significant updates on Vishal's case. For all the tireless efforts of Colin and the Mehrotras, the duty to deliver justice lies with law enforcement and the judiciary, both of which gave up on Vishal a long time ago. Without their support, those closest to the case have done all that they can. For now.

**AISHWARYA**

This case touched upon so many dark topics – not just the murder of an innocent boy but also the world of child sexual abusers and how poorly justice systems all over the world are equipped to handle the complexities of such a crime. Many of the Muntham House survivors had repressed their trauma so deeply that, when Colin approached them, they either couldn't speak or had long accepted that they never would.

The system didn't just fail Vishal – it had been failing for generations. His death was not an isolated incident but the direct consequence of all the people before him; they had been failing for years. Even at the end of some of our worst cases, I've found reason to feel some optimism about the future. This is not one of them. If they haven't already, Vishal's murderer will die soon. And with them, the last hope of uncovering the truth.

# 6

# A CASE STUDY IN CRIME: SAJAL BARUI

**ARYAAN**
The treatment of juveniles – and even the definition of a juvenile – in India's criminal justice system has evolved. However, two fundamental ideas have remained the same: that children make mistakes, and there is an important distinction between the motivations and actions of an adult and a child. The goal is always to rehabilitate a minor rather than incarcerate them and throw away the key. But now and then, a criminal challenges these notions of childhood innocence. This is the story of sixteen-year-old Sajal Barui.

In the early hours of 23 November 1993, an eerie noise pierced through the calm of Subham Apartments in Kolkata's Dum Dum municipality. At first, the residents dismissed it as an animal's cry – perhaps a stray dog yelping after a pedestrian had stepped on its tail, or a scuffle in the street. But one of the homeowners, Dipankar Banerjee, recognized the sound for what it was: a desperate, all-too-human call for help. He immediately phoned the police. Officers arrived swiftly and broke into the fourth-floor apartment from which the cries had originated. Inside, they uncovered a horrifying scene – the seemingly ordinary Barui family had fallen victim to a gruesome crime.

A moment's relief washed over the officers when they realized that the Barui's sixteen-year-old son, Sajal, was still alive. He was tied to a chair near the television in the living room, his voice hoarse from crying out for help. But their relief quickly faded as they moved deeper into the house, Sajal's desperate cries still echoing behind them. In the adjoining room, his mother, Neoti Barui, was also bound to a chair. Her corpse had been hastily bound with rope and a bed sheet. In the next room, Subal Barui lay dead on the floor, his legs marked with deep, bleeding injuries. Nearby, his elder son, Kajal, sat slumped in a chair, bloodied and motionless. What began as a routine call about a possible domestic disturbance had turned into something darker. The Kolkata Police had walked into a scene of familicide. But not quite – one member of the Barui family had survived, though he was in pain and traumatized.

To witness one's family being murdered was an unimaginably terrifying fate, but the police had no one else to turn to. They were forced to question Sajal about the massacre. He told them that he and his mother had been watching TV the previous evening, when seven unknown men (two of them, he said, appeared to be Punjabis) entered their flat, gagged and bound him. This was around 7:30 p.m. They then took Neoti to the next room, where the police now knew she had been tied up similarly and murdered. In shuddery bursts of speech, Sajal recounted how he had become unconscious after this. He had no memory of what had happened to his father and brother. With no other eyewitnesses, the Kolkata Police left a broken Sajal to grapple with his new reality and turned their attention to the investigation. What they didn't know was that they had already interviewed the killer.

Soon, the gaps in Sajal's story began to show. How had he emerged that night with no significant injury or even signs of a struggle? Why would the killers – having so brutally taken three lives – leave behind a witness to the crime? Under police scrutiny, it didn't take long for Sajal to crack. He confessed to what had happened in a disturbingly calm, matter-of-fact way.

On the night of 22 November, Sajal had arrived at the apartment with five of his friends, all teenagers aged between sixteen and seventeen. The boys had purchased a grim toolkit: rubber gloves, coconut rope and lethal weapons that they had sharpened from a shop in the city. Inside, Neoti was alone, watching TV. She never stood a chance as the six boys gagged her, tied her to a chair and strangled her. When Kajal Barui returned home, the boys ambushed him immediately and dragged him into another room. Around midnight, when Subal arrived, he was overpowered by the assailants and tied with a rope. When the strangulation failed, the boys turned to their weapons, brutally hacking the father and son to death. Murder – especially at the hands of amateurs – is a chaotic, messy feat. The entire ordeal took nearly three hours. It's impossible to fathom the sheer trauma of the Barui family's final moments: not just the physical agony of being tortured but the knowledge that their son and brother was the one responsible. Sajal and his cronies were unmoved by screams, and eventually, the noise faded into hollow silence.

What followed was a clumsy cover-up. On Sajal's instructions, they washed the bloodied weapons with mustard oil and water and burnt any incriminating evidence. In a chilling move, they paused to eat biscuits from the fridge and left behind a few coins as payment. Later, Sajal told the police that this was inspired by a segment he'd seen on the TV show, *The World This Week*, where an American murderer had left behind money for a soft drink consumed at the crime scene. Satiated, the boys raided the almirahs in the house, taking money and jewellery to simulate a robbery and mislead the police. As their final touch, they inflicted superfluous injuries on Sajal, tied him to a chair and closed the flat behind them. On their way out, two of them disposed of their gloves and black cloths near an abandoned gate.

#### AISHWARYA
Okay, I need you to tell me why Sajal and his friends did all of this. Why did a mere teenager murder his entire family in such a dispassionate and cruel way? How did he manage to convince five friends to become accomplices to such a vicious crime?

#### ARYAAN
If you believe the prosecution, Sajal had concocted the plan driven by the hope that he could become the sole inheritor of his father's assets.

**AISHWARYA**
I'm not completely convinced about that. The brutal nature of the killings seems to stem from something more personal – a deep-seated hatred for his family.

**ARYAAN**
I have to agree. Maybe, as the cliché goes, to understand Sajal, we need to understand his family history.

Sajal had a somewhat atypical, painful childhood. Neoti was not his biological mother. While Kajal was her son and Subal her husband, Sajal was born out of an extramarital affair. A few years into their marriage, Subal had abandoned his wife and their elder son to live with a woman named Minati. Sajal was the result of that relationship. When he was eight years old, his life was uprooted when Subal abruptly ended the affair and decided to reunite with Neoti and Kajal. He took Sajal with him, and the boy never saw his biological mother again.

During the investigation, Sajal claimed that he had been abused by his stepmother and stepbrother. He narrated harrowing incidents: being burned with a hot iron, scarred by cigarette butts and even having his head jammed inside their refrigerator. This escalating abuse, along with the traumatic loss of his mother, may have psychologically scarred the young boy. The prosecution, however, argued that Sajal had concocted these stories to elicit sympathy from his friends and manipulate them into carrying out the murders. Even if this is true, his deception was compelling enough to push a group of teenagers towards committing an extraordinary act of violence. Perhaps his motive was part financial and part personal, a calculated way to kill two birds with one stone. Or perhaps it was something else entirely. As in most brutal killings, the question 'why' remains the hardest to answer.

Following his confession, Sajal and his co-accused were presented before the additional sessions judge at Barasat District Court. The killings fell under the 'rarest of rare' category. The judge sentenced Sajal to death by hanging, a verdict later commuted to life imprisonment. Reportedly, the boys remained affable and unbothered throughout the trial. Even when the death sentence was announced, they broke into applause and began singing in unison. This bizarre behaviour didn't stop there. Once incarcerated – first at Dum Dum Cantonment, then Midnapore Central Jail and later, Alipore Central Jail – they spent their days singing and dancing along to the latest Bollywood tunes and watching television every evening. It appeared as though prison was just another stage for their fun and theatrics.

In 2001, Sajal was admitted to Calcutta National Medical College and Hospital due to a kidney ailment. Despite his poor health, he orchestrated 'beer parties' with the two officers assigned to monitor him. His girlfriend smuggled bottles of alcohol, and the trio would drink together in the hospital toilets. On 15 September, the routine seemed unchanged. Sajal offered his drinking buddies their usual beer – only this time, they were spiked with sleeping pills. By the time they regained consciousness, Sajal was nowhere to be found. A convicted mass murderer had calmly walked out of the front door of a city hospital crawling with security personnel.

The escape was a major embarrassment for the Kolkata Police. Despite conducting several raids, they were unable to nab the fugitive. Sajal briefly settled in Mumbai, where he married a woman he met there, Silky. However, he was not the kind to lie low and appreciate the joys of his newfound freedom. In mid-2002, Sajal sent his wife to Asansol to stay with relatives and returned to Kolkata. In the city, he sought refuge with a local crime lord named Hatkata Bishu. He adopted a new identity, Kamal, and under this alias, operated a blackmailing nexus that targeted young couples. When 'Kamal' attracted police attention, he changed his alias once again to Sheikh Raju. It was under this name that he was apprehended in February 2003 by the Midnapore Police – nearly two years after his escape – caught in connection with a snatching and robbery case.

Sajal's false identity served him well, albeit for a short period. For three months, the police believed that they had caught only a petty thief, blissfully unaware they had apprehended a notorious killer. But Sajal's arrogance would be his undoing; the attention he and his companions drew made them hard to forget. Though transferred to a different prison, Sajal was soon recognized and blackmailed by a fellow inmate who threatened to expose him. His true identity was confirmed by a jailer who had previously worked at Alipore Central Jail during Sajal's earlier incarceration. Afterwards, Sajal was sent to the Presidency Jail in Dum Dum, and with that, the alias Sheikh Raju died a quiet death.

> **AISHWARYA**
> I'm just thinking Sajal must have been a huge annoyance
> if the jailer remembered him years later, even though he
> had changed his appearance and identity!

Sajal was far from passive in prison. There, he formed a close network with other infamous criminals, including Aftab Ansari, the mastermind behind the 2002 terrorist attack on the American Center in Kolkata, and Debashish Chakraborty, who had killed his girlfriend and attempted to murder his mother. When these risky alliances came to light, Sajal was moved back to the Alipore Central Jail.

> **ARYAAN**
> Sajal seems to have done a tour of most high-security
> prisons in Kolkata. He could have very well left behind
> the life of crime to become a reviewer of prisons, ranking
> their food or living conditions.

Having already attempted to evade the authorities, Sajal chose a different route. This time, he went through the legal system. At the time of his initial arrest, the Juvenile Justice Act applied only to minors under the age of sixteen. As a result, he was tried and convicted as an adult. In 2000, the Act was amended to extend its protection to all juveniles under the age of eighteen. The updated Act stipulated that no juvenile could be held in an adult prison or incarcerated for more than three years. Crucially, the revised law was retroactive, applying to *all* past and future cases, including Sajal's. Recognizing this, the Calcutta High Court ordered Sajal's release on conditional bail.

Finally, in August 2010, Sajal walked out of Alipore Central Jail a free man, nearly fifteen years after he had murdered his entire family. In prison, he had taken an interest in art, and his works were displayed at the Birla Art Gallery and the Kolkata Book Fair. One of his pieces had been sold for 8,000 rupees. As he met the gaggle of reporters waiting outside the prison, Sajal declared that he wanted to exhibit his art soon. It seemed the future was bright. In less than a year, Sajal was arrested again on charges of robbery; he was accused of looting a guest house in Jodhpur Park, taking 1.3 lakh rupees and other valuables. He was imprisoned again until 2017, after which he disappeared completely from the media's eye.

### ARYAAN

Open-ended cases are always bittersweet, and this is an unusual one. I wonder what Sajal is doing now. Did he follow his passion for art or remain a career criminal? Perhaps he's just an ordinary working man like you and me, sitting somewhere in Kolkata, brimming with stories that we haven't been able to uncover in our version of events. I guess we'll never really know.

# 7

# THE GRUESOME MURDER OF SISTER ABHAYA

**AISHWARYA**
Justice delayed is justice denied. This is a foundational principle of every justice system in the world. However, that foundation is plagued with fissures that show through more often than they are hidden. This is the case of a nun from Kerala, whose killers were allowed to roam free for twenty-eight years after her brutal murder. This is the story of Sister Abhaya.

Life in one of Kerala's famed convents promises peace and spiritual fulfilment. For Sister Abhaya, born Beena Thomas on 26 February 1971, that promise seemed to have held true. At the revered St Pius X Convent in Kottayam, the twenty-one-year-old was known for her discipline, devotion and hard work. She approached both her religious duties and her college academics with equal drive. But in the early hours of 27 March 1992, as she rose at 4 a.m. to study for her upcoming exams, Sister Abhaya could not have known the cruel twist fate had in store for her.

When the other sisters rose a few hours later, they were baffled to find the convent's usually orderly kitchen in disarray. The refrigerator's door stood ajar, and water from an overturned bottle had soaked the floor. In the puddle lay a small hand axe – and a single slipper, unmistakably Abhaya's. More disturbing still, the kitchen door had been locked from the outside. A white veil, part of a nun's habit, was snagged on the door. Meanwhile, Abhaya was nowhere to be found. One of the sisters vaguely recalled seeing her head towards the kitchen in the wee hours of the morning. Disconcerted by the strange and troubling scene, the nuns wasted no time and alerted the police. As the police searched the hostel premises, they soon found the slipper's missing pair lying outside, next to the convent's well. They cautiously moved towards it and peered into its depths. A young woman's body was floating in its watery grave.

From the moment Sister Abhaya's body was discovered, the institutions involved appeared hell-bent on obstructing and sabotaging the investigation. The convent publicly described her death as a personal tragedy, but they insisted that she was solely responsible for it. They suggested she may have either fallen into a deep depression and taken her own life, or had accidentally slipped into the well. In fact, soon after Abhaya's death, the convent undertook extensive renovations, drastically altering the layout of the building and erasing crucial elements of the crime scene. The police were equally dismissive of the case. Even though the post-mortem report revealed significant lacerations on Abhaya's shoulders, hips and head, her death was officially ruled as a death by drowning. A crime scene photographer, Varghese Chacko, noticed nail marks on either side of Abhaya's neck, but Dr Radhakrishnan – the doctor who conducted the autopsy – was never allowed to visit the crime scene, so these injuries were absent from the official report. The police also failed to submit Abhaya's clothes, veil and footwear for forensic examination, and their inquest report made no mention of the suspicious wounds she had sustained. As the investigation progressed, the authorities were repeatedly caught destroying evidence and forging signatures on official documents.

**ARYAAN**
We've covered over 100 cases, and the scene you've described, the details in the postmortem report … I would say this was obviously a murder. I mean, there are so many signs of struggle!

**AISHWARYA**
You and I aren't the only ones who found the police's conclusion completely absurd. Thankfully, the public felt the same outrage and decided to take action.

In a rare act of defiance, sixty-seven nuns from Sister Abhaya's congregation spoke out in solidarity. Despite the risks of opposing the official stance of their convent, they refused to remain silent in the face of such a blatant disregard for the truth. Though they had pledged their lives to the service of God, they were acutely aware of the unchecked power the clergy wielded in Kerala – power that bred corruption and complicity. Within a month of Abhaya's death, twenty-three-year-old human rights activist Jomon Puthenpurackal, criticizing the botched police investigation, helped the sisters form the Abhaya Action Council. Together, they petitioned the chief minister of Kerala to recognize Abhaya's death for what it truly was – a murder. At last, the CBI stepped in, and it appeared justice might finally be within reach.

In 1993, the CBI appointed Deputy Superintendent Varghese P Thomas to lead the investigation. From the very start, Thomas believed that the evidence pointed to murder. At first, he meticulously documented his findings and theories in detailed case diaries. However, when Thomas's stance was discovered by the authorities, he was abruptly transferred to a CBI branch in a different state. Not long after, he opted for voluntary – and unusually early – retirement. Before stepping down, he held a press conference where he openly declared that he was leaving the service because the directives he had received from the higher-ups to label Sister Abhaya's death as a suicide, went against his conscience.

In 1995, the newly appointed officer attempted to reconstruct the crime with a life-size dummy of Sister Abhaya's body. The dummy was dropped into the same well from different angles; however, this experiment produced no conclusive results. Over the next fifteen years, the Abhaya Action Council watched in dismay as thirteen different teams of CBI officers probed the case – unable or perhaps unwilling to bring it any closer to resolution. Frustrated by the lack of meaningful efforts from the CBI, the council decided to turn to the masses. They promised a reward of 3 lakh rupees to anyone who could provide credible information on the case.

But even with the incentive to sweeten the deal, no informants came forward.

By 1996, three years after Abhaya's death, little progress had been achieved. When the CBI was asked to submit a report on their investigation, it only stated that they could not determine whether the death was a suicide or murder owing to a lack of medical evidence. The Kerala High Court saw through this – as did the public – and refused to accept the report. A second CBI report produced in 1999 officially labelled the case as a homicide for the first time. However, it said there was no way to identify the perpetrators. Once again, the report was rejected by the court. In 2005 – over a decade after Abhaya's death – the CBI submitted the third report, reaffirming their initial conclusion: there had been no foul play in the nun's death.

Public outrage ensued, and in an uncharacteristic rebuke, the court rejected all three reports. Issuing a scathing statement against the CBI, it accused the agency of having a vested interest in the case and deliberately compromising the investigation to shield certain powerful stakeholders. After prolonged legal wrangling, the filing of a Public Interest Litigation (PIL) in 1997 highlighting non-compliance with court orders and the continuous pressure from the Abhaya Action Council, the CBI finally disclosed a detail that changed the course of the case. They had suspects. These suspects weren't a new discovery; they had been known to the authorities for years.

In September 2008, the investigations were handed over to the Kerala branch of the CBI, and finally, a chargesheet was filed. Not one, not two, but *three* suspects were eventually identified. The lead came from an unlikely source: a small-time thief named Adakka Raju. On the night of the murder, Raju had devised a simple plan to sneak onto the terrace of the nuns' hostel and steal the copper plates contained within the lightning arrester, hoping to sell them at the local market for a modest sum. When he reached the terrace around 3:30 a.m., he noticed two figures at the entrance of the building, as if waiting to be let in.

> **AISHWARYA**
> Now, you might not immediately think this is strange, but
> you have to remember that this was a women-only hostel
> and attached to a cloistered convent at that. Raju sensed
> that there was something unusual about the presence of
> a man in such a private space.

Raju recognized one of the men; it was Father Thomas Kuttoor. However, in the middle of committing a crime, Raju knew better than to linger on what he'd seen. He quickly stole the plates from the terrace and sold them the next day to a local scrap dealer named Shameer. All this while, he tried to put the incident out of his mind. It wasn't until he read about Sister Abhaya's death in the news – and the callous mishandling of her case by the authorities – that he realized the significance of what he had witnessed that night. He had information the world needed to hear.

Within a week of the murder, Raju went to the police – not to save himself, but to tell the truth. He confessed to the theft so he could share what he had witnessed that night and provide his testimony. Alas, Raju's honesty was rewarded not with gratitude but brutality. The police arrested Raju, Shameer and Shameer's brother. For nearly sixty days, the three men were kept in police custody in Kottayam and subjected to inhuman torture. The police prodded Raju to extract a confession from the poor man, and then pressured Shameer and his brother to pin the blame on Raju and falsely implicate him. They were thrashed so badly that Shameer's brother was rushed to a hospital and treated under another name. Despite everything, they held their ground. Even when the cops tried a different approach – offering money, housing, jobs for their relatives and even funds to educate their children – the men refused to give in. They maintained their innocence, and eventually, all three were released.

#### AISHWARYA
Do you understand the magnitude of this, Aryaan? The police had their primary suspect a week after discovering Abhaya's body. And yet they chose to hide it from the public for decades while they did everything they could to cover up the case.

#### ARYAAN
I'm so amazed at Raju's refusal to be bullied into silence. But do we know what really happened that night?

In a casual conversation with friends, Father Thomas had let a damning secret slip: he was having an affair with Sister Sephy, a nun living in the same hostel as Abhaya. He likened their clandestine relationship to a marriage. A cook at the hostel later testified that the priest was a frequent visitor, often accompanied by another clergyman, Father Jose Poothrikkayil. The two men regularly visited Sister Sephy, demanding lavish meals from the kitchen staff. St Pius X Convent was known for its fiercely protective dogs, known to bark at any unfamiliar presence on the premises. But on the night of Sister Abhaya's murder, the dogs had remained silent. The reason was chillingly simple: they knew the murderers. As did Sister Abhaya.

On the night of the murder, Abhaya had unknowingly walked in on Thomas and Sephy in a compromising position in the convent kitchen. Panicked at being discovered by the young nun, Sephy had lifted a small hand axe kept in the kitchen for chopping wood and struck Abhaya, inflicting deep lacerations all over her body. Believing her to be dead, the three carried her body to the well and dumped it inside. They left behind a trail of incriminating clues and didn't even bother to erase them. Fortunately for them, the authorities stepped in to help cover their tracks. Throughout its investigations, the CBI gathered substantial evidence implicating Thomas, Sephy and Poothrikkayil in the murder. The most controversial discovery was documentation showing that Sephy had undergone a so-called 'hymen reconstruction' surgery the day after Abhaya's death, suggesting they wanted to remove any physical evidence of their relationship before the investigation could gather steam. In 2008, under mounting public pressure, the CBI decided to conduct a 'virginity test' on Sephy, claiming that it had proven she was not a virgin. Reportedly, the integrity of the test came into question when the results were tampered with using correction fluid.

**AISHWARYA**
I think it's very important to point out that these pieces of evidence – both the hymen reconstruction surgery and virginity tests – are deeply rooted in a patriarchal lens and fueled by harmful myths. 'Virginity' is a social concept, not a biological one. But there's some insight we can glean here. One, someone was tampering with reports related to the case. Two, that Sister Sephy felt she had something to hide, the day after Abhaya's mysterious death.

Finally, in November 2008, Sister Sephy, Father Thomas and Father Jose were arrested for the murder of Sister Abhaya. The trial that followed marked the culmination of the longest investigation in the history of Kerala. The process was far from straightforward – no less than eight witnesses turned hostile, after allegedly receiving bribes or being pressured by the church. Eventually, however, the court found Thomas and Sephy guilty of the murder of Sister Abhaya, destruction of evidence and defamation. They were awarded life in prison, although Poothrikkayil was acquitted for lack of evidence. In 2023, the Delhi High Court heard Sister Sophy's petition challenging the virginity test she had been subjected to during the investigation. In a landmark ruling, the court declared any form of virginity testing unconstitutional – a violation of both the right to privacy and the right to life. Today, Sephy and Thomas are serving out their terms in two separate prisons in Thiruvananthapuram. The fact that they were allowed to conceal the truth for twenty-eight years stands as one of the most devastating miscarriages of justice in India's modern history.

### AISHWARYA

So many others were wronged in this case and will never get any resolution. Varghese P Thomas was forced into retirement for doing his job honestly; Raju, Shameer and his brother were wrongfully imprisoned and tortured for speaking the truth; and even Abhaya's sisters might have faced consequences for bravely resisting this corrupt nexus of church and state. Like most true crime cases, the justice achieved pales in comparison to the hurt that will always remain.

# 8

# OCCULT SECRETS AND MASS PSYCHOSIS: THE BURARI SUICIDES

**AISHWARYA**
This was the first case we covered on the Desi Crime podcast – one that I was once completely obsessed with. I've spent sleepless nights going back to its details, trying to make sense of them, and I know that I'm not alone in this. The Burari mass suicide captured public imagination in 2018, and even now, most people will have their own opinion of what happened inside that seemingly happy Delhi home. As with most sensational stories, it can be difficult to separate fact from fabrication. But in this case, the truth might just be stranger than fiction.

1 July 2018. Gurcharan Singh, a seventy-nine-year-old resident of Burari, a neighbourhood in north Delhi, set out on a morning walk. As he navigated the densely populated alley outside his front door, he noticed an anomaly: the shutters of the Bhatia family's grocery store were still down. The shopfront usually opened at 5 a.m. on the dot, ready to receive early customers looking to buy their daily groceries.

That day, cartons of milk and bread lay untouched outside the store, left behind by supply trucks that had their schedules to follow. As people started gathering impatiently outside the shop, Gurcharan, a friend of the family, decided to call the Bhatia home. The phone rang and rang; there was no response. Around 7 a.m., he walked to their house, located right across from his own. Just as he opened the unlocked door and stepped into the hallway, he was stopped in his tracks by a sight that many have gone on to describe as nothing short of their worst nightmare. Ten bodies were hanging from a metal frame on the ceiling, like lax puppets dangling off loose strings. The body of the aged matriarch was lying on the floor of the adjacent room. All eleven members of the Burari family were dead.

#### ARYAAN
```
I remember the first time I read about this case, click
baited by some sensational headline. The picture that
accompanied that article was such a shock to my system;
I can't imagine what Gurcharan had felt in that moment.
```

#### AISHWARYA
```
Definitely. Even the first policeman to enter the house,
head constable Rajeev Tomar, later said, 'In my career of
seventeen years so far, I have never seen a crime scene
like this and I hope I do not ever have to.'
```

Though their roots lay in Rajasthan, the Bhatia family had lived for years in Tohana, Haryana, where the patriarch,

Bhopal Singh, was a landowning farmer. Affectionately called 'Daddy' by the entire family, Bhopal was a very respected man and the steady foundation upon which the Bhatia family built their future. In 1989–90, he sold his land and moved to Burari with his wife, Narayani Devi, and younger son, Lalit. Owing to his health issues, Lalit remained an irregular student at a private college in Hisar. He began working at a plywood shop once the family moved. Eventually, he opened a store of his own in Burari, which afforded the family greater financial stability. But a debilitating accident in 2004 left Lalit shaken. He was reportedly pushed under several plywood sheets, which were then set ablaze. The experience was so traumatizing that he stopped speaking for some time. But the event that would truly shatter the Bhatia family would come three years later, in early 2007.

The death of Bhopal Singh in February 2007 was a major blow. Many believe it may have been the inciting incident that sent the family spiralling out of control. Lalit, in particular, was deeply impacted. Ten days after his death, the family organized a ceremony, where one of their neighbours recounted how Lalit's voice suddenly returned to him for the first time since the accident. He began chanting 'Om', and soon after, everyone said, *'Daddy aa gaye'* (Daddy has returned).

**AISHWARYA**
Honestly, when I read about this, it didn't stand out to me as eerie. The death of a family member – especially a parent – can be really, really hard on those left behind. But in retrospect, knowing what was to come, it takes on

new meaning. To understand why, I must introduce you to the rest of the Bhatia family.

At the time of the mass suicide, the three-person family unit had grown manifold. The oldest resident was Narayani Devi, who was seventy-five at the time. Her first child, Pratibha (fifty-seven), had moved into the Burari home with her daughter, Priyanka (thirty-three), after her husband's death. The oldest son of the family, Bhavnesh (fifty), and his wife, Savita (forty-eight), had three children: Neetu (twenty-five), Monu (twenty-three) and Dhruv (fifteen). The young boy was close to his cousin, Shivam (fifteen), who was Lalit's (forty-five) and his wife Tina's (forty-two) only child. Three generations lived under the Bhatia roof, and in one fell swoop, Gurcharan Singh discovered that the entire family had been decimated.

Though the very thought of eleven lifeless bodies is terrible, the scene that met the eyes was far grimmer than anyone could have imagined. The ten hanging bodies were blindfolded and gagged, with their mouths covered with white cloth and surgical tape. They had cotton stuffed in their ears, and their limbs were bound with strips of bedsheet and wire. Narayani Devi's frail body was found strangled to death. The family dog, Tommy, was tied up on the terrace and died soon after being rescued. Constable Tomar would later recount the horrifying sight: 'It was shocking. I stayed only for ten, fifteen seconds before rushing downstairs ... At the time, I noticed nothing other than lots of bodies hanging, just like branches of a tree.' The bodies were all found bound, their feet were oddly close to the ground for hangings and the external circumstances were equally strange. The brutality and abnormality of the scene made both the police and the public immediately presume foul play.

The air of apparent normalcy surrounding the family offered no explanation. On 17 June, merely fifteen days ago, Priyanka had gotten engaged to a successful Noida-based software engineer in a lavish celebration where the family was seen dancing. When interviewed after her death, her fiancé said, 'Priyanka was a normal, simple girl. She believed in living a simple life and was well-educated. If she was about to commit suicide, why would her family get her engaged to me?' In fact, for a few hours on Saturday evening, Dhruv and Shivam were spotted playing cricket in the neighbourhood as a happy Bhavnesh looked on. Their behaviour was completely ordinary, as told to the media by a friend of theirs. What had unravelled in the two weeks since Priyanka's engagement – enough to drive at least ten people to take their own lives? Or in the hours after the youngest Bhatias were spotted enjoying a carefree evening? Something had clearly fractured within.

Speculation was rife. A popular theory floating around was that the family hadn't been murdered by an outsider at all – instead, one of them claimed the lives of the rest. Suspicion fell squarely on Lalit's shoulders, the theory further fortified after investigators delved into his belongings and spoke to those who knew him intimately. Lalit had retreated into himself after his father's death, even as he began speaking again. He frequently visited crematoria, and his phone revealed that he had been consuming hours of YouTube content on paranormal activity, spirituality, afterlife, death and possession. The police discovered eleven diaries and several notes, written in Hindi and spanning the eleven years since Bhopal's death, that seemed to document Lalit's descent into madness.

These diaries contained pages and pages of 'instructions' Lalit claimed to have received from his dead father. They detailed rites and rituals the family would have to perform to exorcize the souls of the dead that roamed their house and attain salvation. One excerpt dated 19 July 2015 read:

> Four souls are still wandering with me. If you improve yourself, these souls will be freed. You feel that by completing all the rituals in Haridwar, the souls achieve salvation. I am accompanied by the souls of others, also.

The Joint Commissioner of Police, Alok Kumar, revealed how the notes mirrored the tragic end of the Bhatia family. These exhaustive diaries contained in-depth instructions on binding the bodies, taping their mouths and placing cotton in their ears. As per the police, the hanging bodies were meant to resemble of the branches of a banyan tree for a ritual called *budh tapasya* or banyan tree worship. A note dated 26 June read, 'Have to meet God on June 30th'; another said 'Using a stool and keeping the hands, eyes and mouth tied up will help attain salvation'. One diary described how the participants were required to tie their hands, only to help each other take off the bindings once the ritual was complete. Evidently, the family had not expected to die. Or perhaps they thought something was awaiting them beyond death.

**ARYAAN**
It sounds like the point of the ritual was to attain salvation - something like Hindu concept of moksha. The belief that what awaits us after death is a cycle of rebirth, and to escape that cycle you must attain moksha. You mentioned that Lalit had an interest in spirituality; is there any chance that there was some kind of self-proclaimed guru radicalizing him?

**AISHWARYA**
The police did look into a proclaimed occultist, Geeta Ma, whose father reportedly was the contractor who built the Bhatia family home. However, nothing came of that lead.

Though Lalit had become the face of the Burari case, those close to him remembered his grounded and positive presence in their lives. His paternal uncle would tell *The Hindu* that he was a teetotaler, while a close friend described him as such: 'He was probably the funniest in our group. But he was a no-nonsense man and he never compromised on principles.' It is difficult to reconcile these kind words with the image that had been pushed forth by the media – of a man who had killed his family and staged their bodies in a gruesome spectacle.

As the investigation proceeded, it became clear that Lalit hadn't acted alone. The diaries were sent for handwriting analysis, and an expert concluded that portions were likely written by Priyanka and Tina, though they may have been dictated by Lalit while he thought he was under the alleged influence of his father's spirit. The CCTV from across the Bhatia residence showed Neetu and Savita carrying a plastic stool towards the house around 10 p.m.; these were found next to the bodies. At 10:39 p.m., Shivam was seen heading to the store, picking up a bundle of wire and walking upstairs. Proof of the family's deteriorating mental state chipped away at the theories of foul play, and the country was convinced that the deaths inside the walls of the home were self-inflicted. The most plausible explanation – and the official stance of the police – is that the family was suffering from shared psychosis or Shared Delusional Disorder.

**AISHWARYA**
This is also known as folie à deux, French for 'folly of two'. It's a rare disorder where two or more individuals share the same, specific delusion.

**ARYAAN**
I have heard about a few cases of this, like Ian Brady and Myra Hindley, the notorious English child killers who murdered five children between July 1963 and October 1965. But I always thought that, as the name suggests, the disorder affects two or three people at most.

**AISHWARYA**
It is definitely unusual to have such a large group experience shared psychosis. But a few common factors for developing this disorder are being isolated and nearby, both of which would have applied to a large, self-contained extended family. Still, it's hard to wrap my head around eleven people ending their lives voluntarily, without trying to fight back.

The police requested the Central Bureau of Investigation's Central Forensic Science Laboratory to conduct a psychological autopsy on the case. After evaluating the textual material found dispersed throughout the house, CFSL's report described the case as 'not a suicide but an accident that occurred while performing a ritual. None of the deceased had an intention to put an end to his/her life'. The report also observed that Bhavnesh may have made an unsuccessful attempt to untie himself and escape, since one of his hands was placed close to his throat, and the rope binding his hands was looser than the others.

Two years after the tragic incident, new tenants have moved into the Burari home. What was once the Bhatia's grocery store is now operated by another family. The three-storey house stands, unassuming, as life continues in the nondescript neighbourhood. And yet, questions linger. How did that night in the Bhatia home truly play out? Was the family's belief absolute? Or did they eventually realize, perhaps too late, that it was death and not salvation that awaited them?

# 9

# THE SCAM CALL THAT WASN'T: THE ADITYA RANKA KIDNAPPING

**AISHWARYA**

It was a quiet Monday in the heart of Mumbai – ordinary in every way. The kind where nothing seems out of place. A boy was at home with his mother, enjoying a peaceful morning. And yet, by the end of that evening, a life would be lost. There would be no signs of struggle, raised voices or shattered windows. This isn't the story of a random act of violence or of strangers crossing paths at the wrong place and time. This is a story of trust misplaced – of the quiet darkness concealed behind the face of familiarity. This is the story of Aditya Ranka.

On 13 May 2013, the bustling neighbourhood of Khetwadi, Mumbai, felt livelier than usual. Summer holidays were underway, and the children living in the area were itching to enjoy their new-found freedom. Even at 11:30 a.m., thirteen-year-old Aditya 'Adit' Ranka hadn't yet shaken off his sleep – he was lazing on the couch in front of the family TV, though he had plans to meet his friends later during the day. Adit's father, diamond merchant Jitendra Ranka, had already left for work that morning, as had his elder brother, Nishit. Suddenly, the shrill sound of the landline ringing filled the room. Adit answered the phone since his mother, Chandrika, was busy with daily chores in another part of the house. An unfamiliar man on the other side of the call claimed to be Jitendra's friend; he needed a quick favour. Could Adit please bring him a set of keys that his father had forgotten at home? He was waiting at the paan shop at the nearby street corner.

Adit, a teenager enjoying his slow morning, had little interest in leaving the house for a random errand. He informed his mother of the call and continued watching television. Shortly after, the phone rang again. This time, Chandrika replied and assured the caller she would send the keys his way soon. The moment she put down the handset, the phone rang for a *third* time. Clearly, her husband's friend was growing impatient. Chandrika, wanting the man to stop calling repeatedly, instructed Adit to run downstairs. The boy hurriedly wore his well-loved red slippers, grabbed the keys and left the house in a rush, eager to get the job done so he could continue watching his show. But time ticked by, and there was no sign of Adit. Chandrika went on with her mundane tasks, expecting her son to return any minute. But he never would.

Across the city, Jitendra's cell phone buzzed with a call from an unknown number. When he picked up, a voice told him something unbelievable: Adit had been kidnapped, and if he wanted his son back, Jitendra would have to pay 30 lakh rupees. Was this a prank? Another moneymaking scheme?

The businessman considered all sorts of probable explanations. He knew Adit was safe at home with Chandrika; he couldn't possibly have been kidnapped in broad daylight from their busy locality. But his paternal instincts superseded all the logic his brain tried to conjure. Jitendra decided to head home immediately to make sure his son was safe.

When he reached home, the situation quickly descended into confusion and panic. Jitendra had never asked anyone to bring him a set of keys – he had no idea who the mystery caller was, nor who had taken his son. Suddenly, the threat was all too real. Soon, the Ranka home was bustling with activity as those closest to the family were informed of what had happened. Himanshu Ranka, Jitendra's twenty-eight-year-old nephew who lived nearby, wanted to offer any form of support he could to get his cousin back home. Even in a state of panic, Jitendra was determined not to simply hand over the money when there was no evidence his son was alive and well. Instead, he headed straight to the Mumbai Police.

#### ARYAAN
That's a sound decision. Many kidnapping victims never make it home, even after their families hand over ransom money.

#### AISHWARYA
That's right. In most of those cases, the victims are killed long before the calls for money are made. We've all heard that the first seventy-two hours after a disappearance are crucial. Immediately involving the police gave them more time to potentially save Adit.

Jitendra and Himanshu headed to the nearby V. P. Road police station to file an FIR, and thankfully caught the officers' immediate attention. They had a solid lead to begin with: the calls the Rankas had received that morning. Four known calls had been made by the kidnappers: three to the apartment's landline, and one to Jitendra's cell phone. The calls did not come from a number registered to a single individual, and the police were able to narrow down the source. They had been made from Sion, a neighbourhood close to Khetwadi. The kidnapper had most likely used a public telephone booth, and the next course of action was to investigate the area, question its residents and obtain any CCTV footage that could trace Adit's whereabouts. But all of this would have to wait for the next day. The Ranka family returned home from the police station without knowing where their son was, hoping that 14 May would bring some news of him. Their wish would come true, but the news wasn't what they were praying for.

The next morning, Chandrika and Jitendra woke up to thoughts of their son. Was Adit safe? Was he in pain? Was he scared? Was he even *alive*? The kidnappers had made no further calls, and the silence was deafening. Jitendra again left for the police station with his nephew. They rode in a Honda City borrowed from Himanshu's friend. En route, Jitendra noticed something alarming: a pair of familiar red slippers in the car's back seat. He had seen his son wear that pair hundreds of times. While it was not implausible that Adit's belongings could find their way to a vehicle that belonged to his cousin's friend, the fact that the boy had been wearing the same slippers at the time of his disappearance raised suspicions. It dawned upon Jitendra that he was no longer in the car with his supportive and reliable nephew – he might be in the company of his son's kidnapper. When they arrived at the police station, Himanshu – who had till then appeared as a pillar of strength for the family – came under scrutiny. Inspectors seized and searched the car and took note of a few suspicious details: the damning red slippers and splotches of blood under the bonnet. They confiscated the contents of the car – including a knife. When Himanshu was questioned, the nervous man quickly revealed the truth behind Adit's disappearance.

Himanshu had recently graduated with an MBA and secured a job that paid over a lakh a month. Everything was coming together. Finally, he had financial security, a loving wife and a supportive family. But when he found himself trapped in the treacherous world of gambling and sports betting, this comfortable life took a dark turn.

**AISHWARYA**
Gambling is heavily regulated in India, though there's some legal ambiguity around online or sports betting since the colonial-era Public Gambling Act of 1867 obviously doesn't explicitly name them. This issue was discussed extensively during the 2013 IPL season, when a massive match-fixing scandal was exposed.

**ARYAAN**
I remember that! There was so much speculation about the IPL being linked with organized crime syndicates. But I'm guessing regular people like Himanshu may have been the biggest - and least spoken about - victims of the nexus.

Like many others, Himanshu found himself sinking astronomical amounts of his savings into the world of illegal IPL betting that had opened up in 2013. And like most others, he never recovered any of it. After squandering nearly 3 lakh rupees that he couldn't afford to lose, Himanshu became frantic. His friend, fellow MBA graduate Vijesh Sanghavi, was in a similar, or even more desperate, boat; Vijesh had lost nearly 7 lakh rupees on bad bets. Together, the men hatched a plan to kidnap Adit. They knew his father was a wealthy businessman and had recently struck a lucrative business deal. Surely Jitendra would be willing to part with eye-watering amounts of money to ensure his son's safety. Vijesh would lure Adit out of the home, kidnap him and demand the ransom, all while Himanshu would keep tabs on the investigation. Once they received Jitendra's money, Adit would be safely returned home.

But somewhere along the way, things had gone horribly wrong. When Jitendra chose to approach the police instead of simply handing over the ransom, Vijesh had panicked. He had bought a knife from a local shop - the owner later verified this in court - after which he drove Adit to Raigad, where he slit the boy's wrists in an attempt to kill him. When Vijesh realized that Adit was still clinging to his life, he drove the dying boy to an isolated spot just off the Mumbai–Pune expressway. There, Vijesh set Adit's body on fire, killing him in one final monstrous act before fleeing the scene. Not long after he was arrested, Vijesh led the police to the location of Adit's mutilated and charred body, forever sealing the case against him in the eyes of the law.

Only ten months after this tragedy, Jitendra passed away due to health complications. The remaining members of the Ranka family – Chandrika and her elder son Nishit – maintain that it was the grief of losing Adit that dealt the final blow. Himanshu and Vijesh were charged with murder, kidnapping, tampering with evidence and extortion. However, four years would pass before they would be presented in court. When the trial finally began, Vijesh was quickly buried under a barrage of incriminating evidence. Two bookies testified that the man had lost huge sums of money to sports betting. The CCTV footage from a telecom store in Sion placed Vijesh and Adit together on 13 May 2013. In October 2017, Vijesh was served two consecutive seven-year sentences before commencing life imprisonment. He was also ordered to pay 9 lakh rupees to Chandrika as compensation, though this meant little in the face of her beloved son's death. Chandrika later told the media, 'Sanghavi deserved the death sentence, but I can live with the life term. When my little son's body was brought back, I couldn't even hug him, because that man had burned him.' The grieving mother was so desperate for an explanation for what had happened that she even attempted to confront Vijesh in court but was restrained by the police.

Himanshu's case was far less straightforward. The man

had a solid alibi during Adit's murder – after all, he was by the grieving parents' side. Still, he was not beyond suspicion. Chandrika testified that she now recognized the second caller's voice on 13 May as Himanshu. Call records revealed that he had been in contact with Vijesh on the day of his cousin's disappearance. However, no CCTV footage showed Himanshu with Adit or Vijesh on that very day. The ten phone calls did not provide any details of what had been discussed between the two, thereby making them entirely circumstantial evidence – indirect evidence that does not, on its face, prove a fact in issue but gives rise to a logical inference that the fact exists. Chandrika may have misidentified the caller's voice, and Himanshu claimed he had only called Vijesh because his family had good contacts within the Mumbai Police, which he thought could help with the case. His father, Jitendra's elder brother Neimchand Ranka, testified that his son had not suffered any significant financial losses that would push him towards such drastic action. Due to a lack of substantial evidence, Himanshu was acquitted on all charges. Principal Judge S. B. Agarwal declared, 'No doubt, there is a needle of suspicion that points to the involvement of Himanshu along with Sanghavi, but there is a settled position of law that suspicion, however strong, cannot take the place of conviction.'

By 2017, Himanshu had spent over four years in prison and maintained his innocence throughout. His wife, sister and parents supported him. When the verdict was announced, he broke down into tears, finally vindicated. Outside the court, he told media personnel:

I was innocent and have been trying to prove this all along. I had nothing to do with this. He was my little brother and I indulged him ... This incident has destroyed my family; I also lost my little brother and my uncle.

Chandrika and Nishit were outraged by the judge's decision. Still convinced of Himanshu's involvement, they resolved to petition the case. Meanwhile, several times, Vijesh has attempted to file an appeal against his conviction. We are yet to completely understand the intricacies of this seemingly open-and-shut kidnapping and murder. Those closest to the case – Chandrika, Nishit, even Himanshu and Vijesh – do not feel justice was served. And until they do, Adit's story will remain a bleak reminder that sometimes, the most terrifying threats might be hiding in plain sight.

# 10

# SNUFFING OUT A RISING STAR: THE MURDER OF QANDEEL BALOCH

**ARYAAN**

In 2013, a short clip went viral on Pakistani social media. 'How I'm looking?' the young woman in the video asks a middle-aged man behind her. 'Tell me, how I'm looking?' He responds with a flurry of affirmations: gorgeous, extraordinary. But when she prompts, 'Sexy?', he hesitates. The woman's words, dismissed by many for being salacious and grammatically questionable, mark a struggle you can only see if you read between the lines: her fight to forge a new life for herself, one shaped entirely by her choices. This is the story of that woman from Pakistan who yearned for more. This is the story of Qandeel Baloch.

On 1 March 1990, Fauzia Azeem was born to parents Anwar Bibi and Muhammad Azeem. Their family of ten – six sons and two daughters – lived on the brink of poverty in the small town of Shah Sadar Din, Punjab. Fauzia was a brilliant spark of a girl; she loved to play outdoors with her siblings, climb trees and shuddered at the thought of covering her head or at the mention of marriage. The earnings from their family-run farm were meagre, which meant Fauzia and her siblings began working in the fields from a young age. It wasn't an unusual childhood in the region where most were engaged in agriculture. Ever since she was a child, Fauzia's driving force had been to alleviate her family's poverty. She envisioned a bright future for herself, one that would empower her to move the family up the socio-economic ladder. But what profession could allow her to do this? The answer came in the form of a new resident in the Azeem household: the television.

Though it has since been overtaken by mobile phones and laptops, the television was a game-changer for children in the nineties. Suddenly, there was a window connecting them to the outside world; a starry-eyed glimpse into alternative lives that looked nothing like their own. At first, the Azeem sisters would sneak over to their friend's house to watch a bit of television. Despite her husband's resistance, Anwar Bibi eventually snuck some money to one of her sons so they could buy one of their own. Their brand-new TV captivated Fauzia; her sister would later recall how she was perpetually glued to the screen. From news reports about the glamorous lives of celebrities to soap operas, Fauzia had finally found her ultimate dream: to be successful on the silver screen!

Fauzia desired the glamour that came with being an actress and singer. Of course, fame and money would follow. But harbouring ambitious dreams around narrow-minded people can be hazardous. Shah Sadar Din was a very conservative town, where women were expected to quietly conform to tradition and fulfil their domestic responsibilities. Anwar Bibi had always advocated for her daughters, insisting they receive education outside of religious instruction, even when her husband hesitated. However, Fauzia's new-found dream was taking it a step too far; the idea that their beloved daughter would move to a big city like Karachi, Lahore or Islamabad to become an entertainer was out of the question. To extinguish the fire of Fauzia's aspirations before they proved troublesome for the family, she was married to her mother's cousin and a small-time farmer, Aashiq Hussain. At just eighteen, she was sent to live with her in-laws. Within a year, she gave birth to a son, Mishal.

> **AISHWARYA**
> This is unfortunately so common for South Asian women. You can dream all you want, but once you have a husband and children, those ambitions cease to matter.
>
> **ARYAAN**
> Definitely. Women are made to feel guilty if they pursue anything for themselves; they're told that it's a selfish pursuit. But Fauzia refused to accept this fate, especially after the abuse began.

'What do you think will happen in a forced marriage? With an uneducated man, an animal ...' Fauzia would later say when asked about her husband. 'The kind of torture he has inflicted on me, you can't even imagine.' She described being burnt with cigarettes, tortured, beaten and threatened with acid. But she was forced to endure it all after the birth of her son, making it even harder for her to immediately flee. Finally, at just nineteen, pushed to her breaking point, she gathered her belongings and fled with her child to a decrepit women's shelter in Multan. Her family severed all ties, leaving Fauzia without any social or financial support. While at the shelter, her son fell extremely sick. With no money or resources, Fauzia was terrified that the child would die. If that happened, her in-laws would drag her to court. Desperate, she agreed to surrender all custodial rights and leave her son with Aashiq. Though she attempted to reconnect with the child years later, her former husband refused to allow it.

### ARYAAN

> This decision has been heavily criticized by those who knew her at the time and later the media, too. But Fauzia was offered an impossible choice, and if that first step towards freedom required such a sacrifice, who are we to judge?

This first step was followed by a journey of 500 kilometers, as Fauzia made her way to the capital of Pakistan. It was in Islamabad that her life began again, and Qandeel Baloch was born.

Qandeel didn't become an overnight star. When she fled her marital home in 2009, she was penniless, had no form of identification and certainly no family connections she could exploit. Her first years in the city were spent trying her hand at various jobs while also pursuing an education. At one point, she worked as a hostess in one of the coaches plying along the

Pakistan highways, reciting prayers at the start of journeys and keeping passengers company. After three years and no sign of success, Qandeel reached out to her parents, who were eager to start afresh. They provided the documents she needed to apply for an identity card, and that allowed her to find better accommodation and audition for high-profile projects. Her big break came in 2013, when at twenty-two, she auditioned for the first season of *Pakistan Idol*.

> **ARYAAN**
> Qandeel's audition went viral at a time when 'going viral' was still a new concept. But the only issue was that it gained popularity for all the wrong reasons.
>
> **AISHWARYA**
> I have a weird obsession with watching failed auditions for *Indian Idol* and shows like it. I can't sing to save my life, and I try not to judge others for it, but when you showed me Qandeel's audition … it's not great, if you ask me.
>
> **ARYAAN**
> Most will agree with you, but that's precisely what's so amazing. In 2013, over a decade ago, Qandeel realized something that social media gurus are still passing off as advice today. That being famous isn't just about talent – it's equally about being eccentric and unforgettable. In her own words, 'To become popular and famous, you need to act strange.'

Qandeel would later claim that the audition was a mere set-up; the showrunners had asked her to act funny and sing badly on purpose to secure airtime. She had agreed, and this decision became the launchpad for a career that would attract much stardom – and infamy.

Qandeel's next viral video came soon after, the one in which she asked a man – her manager – 'How I'm looking?' Hundreds of people made fun of the video, mocking her broken English and bold demands for validation, but the result was undeniable popularity. She continued to push the envelope, making videos and statements that were seen as highly controversial. Brazen and unapologetically sensual, Qandeel's persona constantly invited the ire of conservative Pakistanis. For example, in 2016, Pakistan's prime minister denounced Valentine's Day as a Western construct that did not align with the nation's values. Qandeel's response? She uploaded a video of herself in a short pink dress, wishing her followers a happy Valentine's Day. In her most popular video of all time, Qandeel addressed the Pakistani cricket team ahead of a match against India. She promised that if Pakistan won the match, she would strip before the camera while saying the players' names. Her comment sections were flooded with slurs, abusive language and threats of violence. Even amidst such aggression, the rising star remained undeterred. Junaid Qasi, a social media consultant who worked with Qandeel in the last months of her life, described how carefully she would study 'hot trends' and new events to ideate content. Though her videos may have appeared unplanned, they were far from it.

Qandeel was one of the first women celebrities in Pakistan to embrace her sexuality, shattering the shackles imposed by society. Though many did not see her as a perfect role model, she quickly became a fierce symbol for a new attitude towards self-love and confidence. Other Pakistani women began posting videos impersonating Qandeel's clothing, dancing and singing and talking candidly about their desires. Along with all the hate, there was an outpouring of love. This was the part of her work that most appealed to Qandeel, who told an interviewer:

> So many girls tell me I'm a girl power, and yes, I am ... Being a girl, think yourself, how difficult it is to move around as a woman in this society. How many men do you encounter who bother you? The same way, I have struggled through difficulties to make a place for myself in showbiz ... I want to give my followers a positive message, I want to give those girls a positive message who have been forcefully married, who continue to sacrifice.

By 2016, Qandeel was a frequent sight on national television, invited to talk shows and reality TV alike. She was among the top-searched people on Google in Pakistan; she was making great money and rented a house for her parents in Multan with her earnings. But one chance meeting would soon turn Qandeel's story of triumph into a tragedy.

Mufti Abdul Qavi was a well-known Muslim cleric who headed Pakistan's National Ulema Mushakh Council in 2016. He was regularly invited to TV shows to disseminate his religious wisdom and was humorous and personable, if staunchly patriarchal. When Qandeel and Qavi were invited to the same talk show segment, some feared it would be a recipe for disaster. But the interaction was surprisingly pleasant; the two exchanged jokes and had a spirited conversation. At the end of their segment, Qavi made an offer that would change their lives: to visit Qandeel next time he was in Karachi. She replied, *'Inshallah, khush-nasibi hogi hamari'* (God willing, it will be my pleasure).

Soon after, in June 2016, the two met in a Karachi hotel room, where a series of now-infamous pictures and videos were captured. In one, Qandeel is wearing the mufti's lamb wool cap. In another, Qavi is heard asking which cigarette she would like to smoke. When Qandeel posted these images on Twitter, the outrage was unlike anything even she had faced before. A media storm ensued: headlines on all major news channels demanded an explanation for both Qavi's and Qandeel's behaviour. The holy man's veil of piety had been tarnished; he was suspended from his political party (Imran Khan's Pakistan Tehreek-e-Insaf) and removed from the Council. The consequences for Qandeel were far more devastating.

The death threats that had become all too common for her now metastasized into midnight phone calls from random numbers and violent threats. She held a press conference to tell the media that she feared for her safety and had demanded police protection from Pakistan's interior minister, but to no avail. The situation escalated further when her passport was leaked by a newspaper, leading to the discovery of her true name. With it, her complicated past was thrown into the limelight. Suddenly, Fauzia Azeem, an identity that had been carefully tucked away, was dragged into the public eye for the first time. The people were hungry for blood. Stories about her ex-husband and the child she had 'abandoned' flooded the news, and Qandeel became Public Enemy Number One.

On 14 July, nearly a month after the meeting with Qavi, Qandeel had had enough. She decided to leave Karachi and return to her parents' home in Multan to spend a comforting Eid al-Fitr with her family – in the same home that she had so painstakingly arranged for them. For the first time, she arrived not in her regular pair of jeans but entirely covered in a niqab. It was clear that something was awry but when Anwar Bibi asked her daughter if she was in trouble, Qandeel assured her otherwise. The mood was further soured when her brother Waseem, agitated with her behaviour, threatened Qandeel before storming out of the house. Eager to smooth things over – the pair reportedly been on good terms earlier – Qandeel called him back home with the playful suggestion that she would find him a wife. The next evening, the Azeem family – Waseem included – gathered to celebrate the festival, enjoying delicious food to their hearts' content. After drinking a glass of warm milk before bed, prepared by Waseem, Qandeel fell asleep, finally at peace.

The sun had been out for quite a while when Anwar Bibi woke up on 16 July. She was perspiring, her vision was blurry and her head felt heavy. Holding onto the walls, she headed to the kitchen to prepare breakfast, calling her daughter's name a few times, but there was no answer. Qandeel was still in bed, tucked into her blanket. It was only when Anwar Bibi peeled away the covers that a scream of pure terror escaped her lips. Her daughter was not asleep – she was dead.

### ARYAAN
```
Now, in most cases, this is the part where the authorities
begin the search for a perpetrator. But here, the
murderer wasn't hiding - he was flaunting his kill. And
he was none other than Qandeel's brother, Waseem Azeem.
```

While Qandeel's parents and sisters reeled in shock, Waseem did little to hide his crime. In his eyes, he had redeemed not only the family name but also saved Qandeel from further shame. When Waseem was arrested on the evening of 16 July, he shamelessly declared before the cameras, 'Yes, I killed her last night. Strangled her to death ... I am not ashamed of killing her ... She was doing videos on Facebook and dishonouring the family name ... [And there was] that cleric's issue; our house was sieged by the media. Before, it wasn't like that.'

The cold-blooded murder had been incredibly simple to execute. While the family celebrated the festival and Qandeel's homecoming, Waseem had spiked their glasses of milk with sedatives. When everyone was knocked unconscious, he had crept into her room around 11:30 p.m. and ruthlessly strangled

Qandeel to death. While his sister lay dead – the rest of his family, drugged – Waseem had slept easy, convinced he had done his 'duty'. His willingness to confess the next day was not born of stupidity; in fact, Waseem knew he would most likely get away scot-free. Because of the 'blood money' laws derived from sharia, murderers in Pakistan could be absolved of their crimes if the victim's family agrees to pardon them. As of 2022, hundreds of Pakistani women lost their lives every year to such perceived disrepute brought to the family's honour, and this legal technicality aided the troubling rise of this trend. Perhaps Waseem thought he was going to be the next success story of the law.

**AISHWARYA**
That seems incredibly regressive! This is so blatantly unfair that it's almost hysterical. I mean, in nearly all cases of honour killings, the family commits the crime. Can they simply pardon themselves?

**ARYAAN**
It's a massive loophole that has been taken advantage of by many in the past. But the rarity in this case was that Muhammad Azeem and Anwar Bibi refused to forgive their son. In fact, Muhammad Azeem demanded that those who had killed his daughter be given the death penalty.

In September 2019, Waseem was sentenced to life imprisonment for killing his sister. Though five other men were charged in connection with the crime – including Mufti Qavi – only Waseem was found guilty. Rumours circulated in the airways and social media platforms that Qavi was involved, but these were never substantiated. After her death was made public, however, Qavi made an unsympathetic statement: '[Baloch] said she had 700,000 followers, but when she died, hardly 100 people attended her funeral prayer. This is because people respect muftis, and she disrespected me.'

### ARYAAN
Despite being an active participant in the controversy, Qavi is alive and well today. It just goes to show that both crime and punishment are so deeply gendered, especially in South Asia.

Qandeel's death drew mixed reactions from across Pakistan and the world. Major public figures like Imran Khan, Theresa May and Madonna publicly condemned the honour killing, though several naysayers felt she had got what she asked for, if not what she deserved. Three months after the murder, a landmark bill was passed in Pakistan that ensured perpetrators of honour killings could no longer be pardoned by the victim's family. It seemed Qandeel's death, though it should have never taken place, would not be in vain. However, in a shocking move, Waseem was acquitted in February 2022. No explanation was offered to the public, though Pakistani human rights activists fear his release may have been enabled by the draconian law that had been active at the time of the murder.

In one of her videos, Qandeel claimed, 'When I die, there will never be another Qandeel Baloch.' Indeed, her prophecy has come true in the worst way possible – the world has not forgotten that brave young woman who dared to dream beyond social confines and challenged the rigidity of the country she was born into. Today, she has been immortalized in music, films and books, affirming that though she was killed in the name of honour, Qandeel Baloch died with her honour and dignity intact.

# 11

# A HASTY CONCLUSION: THE CONFOUNDING CASE OF PRAVIN VARUGHESE

**AISHWARYA**

Immigrating to another country is a difficult decision; to leave behind the comforts of home for an unknown land. But along with fear and anxiety, there is excitement. Indians moving to different parts of the world often do so with ambition and hope in their hearts. Such was the case for Lovely and Mathew Varughese, who moved from Kerala to the US in 1990, drawn to the much-coveted 'American Dream' and the promise of a better life for their children. Two decades later, that dream would become a nightmare with a single blow, after the disappearance of their son, nineteen-year-old Pravin Varughese.

On 12 February 2014, Pravin Varughese and his cousin, Ashly Thomas, decided they needed a break from the midweek monotony. They were sophomores (second-year students) at the Southern Illinois University in Carbondale – a five-hour drive from Chicago – and were also juggling part-time jobs. They weren't exactly in a partying mood that Wednesday night, especially since Pravin had just finished his shift at a local restaurant, while Ashley and his flatmate Nate were gearing up for their 11 p.m. shift at a popular club, Stix. Still, when they saw a tweet about a house party at 606 College Street, they decided to swing by around 9:45 p.m.

The next morning, Ashly woke up at 11 a.m. He had overslept, but he gave himself some grace, considering he had been out till three in the morning. Still groggy, he saw that Pravin's bedroom door was closed and assumed his cousin had most likely left for an early class. That was until he got a call later in the day from a mutual friend, Kyle. He was a fellow criminal justice student and a classmate of Pravin's, who had also been out with them the night before. Pravin hadn't shown up for his first class, nor had he answered any of Kyle's calls. Meanwhile, Ashly hadn't seen his cousin the entire day. Pravin's car was still in their apartment's parking lot, which meant he hadn't gone back to his parents' home. The sub-zero temperatures in Chicago in February made it highly unlikely Pravin had just wandered off for a casual stroll.

Kyle and Ashly decided to match notes on what had transpired the previous night. Everyone from their friend group was at the house party, until Ashly had to leave for Stix. At his request, Kyle and a group of his friends headed to the club soon after. But neither of them had any memory of seeing Pravin there. As far as they could tell, Pravin had never left the party. The only other sign of their friend was on his Twitter account. At 11:06 p.m. he had tweeted '99% of the time I have no idea whats going on' and then 'Bloody knuckles... guesss i was in a fight #backdown' at 11:17 p.m.

Panicked now, Kyle and Ashly drove to 606 College Street, hoping their friend had simply passed out there, but he was nowhere to be found. They checked the alleys near the house and even called nearby hospitals, only to come up empty. Not wanting to throw Pravin under the bus, they waited until the last moment to tell his parents. Finally, by 8:30 p.m. on 13 February, nearly twenty-four hours after he had last seen Pravin alive, Ashly dialled 911. Soon after, the Carbondale police would call Lovely and Mathew Varughese, setting in motion a chain of events that would forever change the world they had worked so hard to build and protect.

When Lovely and Mathew Varughese moved to the US from Thekkemal, Kerala, they knew they had the support of Mathew's sister, who had been living there for a few years. The couple settled in Morton Grove, a quaint suburb near Chicago, where they worked as a nurse and a respiratory therapist, respectively. In 1993, their daughter Priya was born, and just seventeen months later, their son Pravin followed. The family would be complete with the birth of a second daughter, Preethi, seven years later. As medical professionals, it was extremely difficult for Lovely and Mathew to balance work with raising their children. Even as the couple worked gruelling shifts – often through the night, in Mathew's case – they were determined to be there for their kids. Lovely would later recount fond memories of her children's growing-up years: Pravin wearing his father's clothes when Mathew was at work or snuggling between his parents when they kneeled to pray. The young boy was an active member of various extracurriculars from a young age, joining the Boy Scouts, singing in the local choir and running cross-country. He eagerly participated in the cultural events organized by the local Indian community and was doted upon by all its members.

The proud parents happily supported Pravin when he decided to move seven hours away for university, especially since he planned to share an apartment with his cousin. Never did they expect that on the night of 13 February 2014, they would receive a call from the police informing them that their son had been missing for over twenty-four hours.

Lovely and Mathew rushed to Carbondale in the icy winter night, arriving around 4 a.m. By then, they had called their son's phone dozens of times, only to receive an automated message telling them it was switched off. They booked a hotel room and were soon joined by Ashly and Priya. When they headed to the police station around 7 a.m., they refused to accept the officers' insinuations that it wasn't unusual for a college-goer to go missing in action, for some time. They knew their son, and he would never disappear without a word. At the family's insistence, the police looked into Pravin's bank account and realized that it hadn't been used since the night of the party.

The last call made from his phone was at 12:33 a.m. to a close friend, Aneeta. She told them that though it wasn't unusual for Pravin to call in the early hours of the morning, something about his behaviour had felt different – eerie, even.

When she had picked up, Pravin had insisted she not hang up. Then all she heard was two male voices arguing, the sound of running and the slamming of a car door. The unknown voice had demanded that Pravin return something to him. Pravin replied that he was only trying to help. After a minute of complete silence, Aneeta had finally ended the call.

It was this alarming account that pushed the police to launch a full-scale search for Pravin, employing helicopters and on-ground search parties. The Varughese family offered a cash prize of 15,000 dollars for any tips that would lead them to their son. Meanwhile, members of the Indian–American community in Morton Grove travelled to Carbondale to support the family and continue to exert pressure on the authorities. Despite their efforts, the progress was slow. The University of Southern Illinois hadn't released a statement about Pravin's disappearance, and the police search lost steam within a day or two. But Lovely and Mathew dug in their heels and refused to leave Carbondale without finding their son. With the support of the lieutenant governor of Illinois, Sheila Simon, the search continued until 18 February, when it ended in the worst way possible.

That day, the dean of Pravin's university had visited the Varughese family to express his solidarity. Soon after, the deputy chief of Carbondale Police came to their hotel room to share a piece of life-altering news. They had received a tip that had led to a gruesome discovery: Pravin Varughese had been found by the side of the highway, painfully close to the hotel where his family was staying. He was dead.

The discovery of Pravin's body shattered the Varughese

family and all those who had known and loved him. The young man had been found wearing only a pair of jeans and a T-shirt in the freezing weather, leading the police to theorize that he had been intoxicated. After consuming alcohol and drugs at the house party, he had simply run into the woods near the highway in an inebriated state. They suggested he had died of environmental hypothermia, having taken off his already-insufficient winter clothing due to paradoxical undressing: a phenomenon where people experiencing fatal hypothermia begin feeling intense heat instead.

> **AISHWARYA**
> I've seen this in a few other major true crime cases, including the famous Dyatlov Pass incident, where nine experienced climbers died in the Ural Mountains – some strangely or completely unclothed. It's a well-founded theory that can sometimes explain odd happenings, but it wasn't the best fit for Pravin's case.

Lovely refused to believe the police's allegations. She was certain that her son had not done drugs, and once that assumption was out of the picture, it seemed bizarre that Pravin would mindlessly run into the woods in the middle of a freezing winter. When the Varughese family asked for the body to be autopsied, the police said the medical examiner would only be available a few days later. Until then, they requested that Lovely identify the body. As the grieving mother walked into the morgue to see her beloved child's body laid out on the cold metal bed, her immediate reaction was shock. Her son's face was marked by shadowy bruises. There were three large ones, surrounded by a constellation of smaller ones. His forehead was red. The police simply dismissed the injuries, claiming they were nothing more than the usual signs of hypothermia. In their eyes, there had been no foul play.

After seeing their child in this heartbreaking, battered state, the family decided to place a cross where the body was found and take Pravin home to Morton Grove, where they would lay him to rest. Soon after, the autopsy results arrived. Jackson County coroner, Dr Thomas Kupferer, agreed with the police's opinion, attributing Pravin's death to hypothermia and his injuries to running through the woods. At the funeral home, the parents were able to see their son's body in its entirety for the first time after the gruesome event: his injuries were more extensive than they had realized. There were defensive wounds all over his palms and arms, large dents on his head and injuries on his back, chest and entire upper body. Lovely, a trained nurse, knew such wounds weren't consistent with hypothermia. On 21 February, the Varughese family had a private autopsy done by a Chicago-based doctor, Ben Margolis. In glaring contradiction to the first autopsy, Dr Margolis confirmed that Pravin's death was a result of a blunt force trauma and that he had experienced a violent encounter. He reported twenty-two injuries on his body, a bruise on his right arm that went down to the bone and four blows to his head and face. Pravin's toxicology report was the final confirmation the family needed: it clarified that he had not consumed drugs, and the only alcohol found in his system was in his urine, which meant he was almost completely sober at the time of his death.

The Varughese family refused to pay the cash reward to the local police until the investigation was reopened. With the support of the Indian diaspora back home, the family formed the Pravin Action Council to sustain interest in the case. Their primary demand: identify Pravin's killer. But so far, not a single potential suspect had been revealed to them. That was until a video was released on a local news channel from a police officer's body cam. The timestamp on the footage revealed it was from the early hours of 13 February. The video shows a police officer pulling up behind a black Dodge truck parked near the same woods from where Pravin's body was recovered, its headlights flashing in the darkness. Moments later, a young white man emerges from among the trees, and the two have a brief conversation. The officer shines his flashlight into the underbrush and exchanges a few more words with the man. Then, they part ways.

The footage left the Varughese family scrambling for answers to new questions: who was the man in the video? Had he been investigated or arrested in conjunction with their son's disappearance? Lovely, along with the members of the Pravin Action Council, lobbied the Carbondale City Council, demanding that they divulge any material that had been uncovered during the investigation. They could no longer accept being left in the dark about what had happened that night. The family had already made a similar request before the police, only to receive paltry offerings like newspaper clippings. Now, with the support of the city council, boxes of material began to arrive at the Varughese home. It was there, in the midst of their grief, that those most devastated by the case began to uncover the truth they had long suspected.

The police material revealed that on 17 February, they had interviewed a man named Jonathan Stanley – the person who had sent in the tip that led to Pravin's body being discovered in the woods. One day before his interview, Stanley was watching TV with his cousin, Gaege Bethune, when the news about Pravin's disappearance came on. Gaege had seemed visibly uncomfortable, even stepping out of the house because he needed some air. Jonathan would later claim his cousin threw up upon seeing the news, but either way, Gaege was disturbed. When Jonathan questioned him, Gaege explained that Pravin was the man he had gotten into a fight with a few nights ago.

In fact, Jonathan and Gaege were together on the night of 12 February. Both had attended a party on College Street, arriving shortly after 8 p.m. Not long after they arrived, Stanley became sick, and his memory of the night became increasingly patchy. At some point, Gaege – who Jonathan claimed hadn't been drinking that night – decided to leave the party. He placed his departure somewhere between 10 p.m. to 1 a.m., a substantial window of time. Jonathan didn't see his cousin again until the next morning, when Gaege had provided an account of the night's events – though, as it turned out, that wasn't the only version he would give.

Gaege had told him that when he left the party and went to his car, which was parked right outside the house on College Street, Pravin had approached him and asked for a ride. Gaege had agreed, but soon grew irritated as the man refused to clearly state where he wanted to be dropped off, leading them in circles. Then, he grabbed twenty-five dollars from Gaege's cup holder. When Gaege had demanded that he return the money, Pravin had tried to exit the still-moving vehicle, which led him to pull over on the highway. Pravin had run into the woods with Gaege in pursuit. When he caught up with Pravin, they got into a physical altercation. Just as Gaege managed to snatch his money, he noticed police lights flashing near his car. He went to speak with the officer, while Pravin had escaped into the woods. It was this encounter between Gaege and the police officer that was recorded on the officer's body cam and made public by the Carbondale media.

However, this version of the story didn't quite match what Gaege had told the officer on the night of Pravin's disappearance when they interacted by the woods. When questioned, Gaege told the cop that a 'black man' had tried to carjack him on the highway. He had noticed the man by the highway asking for a lift and, like a good Samaritan, stopped to see what he needed. Pravin had asked if he could drop him home, and Gaege had agreed, on the grounds that he would pay for gas. Just as he proposed this, Pravin reached into the car and attempted to steal some money. A scuffle ensued, and Pravin had 'run south into the woods'; Gaege had followed him, only to return when he saw the police lights.

#### AISHWARYA

There are major differences between this and the story he later told Jonathan. For one, he labelled Pravin a carjacker who had attacked him on the highway - there was no mention of College Street. In this version, he also claimed Pravin had never gotten into his vehicle.

The ever-winding story became even more convoluted when Gaege was called in by the police after Jonathan's interview. In a new testimony, he claimed that the two had met on College Street, where Pravin had approached him for a ride – likely to Stix, which was just down the road. Gaege had pitied the young man who was wearing just a shirt and jeans in the cold. Thirty minutes went by with them simply going around in circles, Pravin refusing to specify a location. Gaege also told the police that Pravin was on the phone with someone the entire time, attempting to purchase cocaine, which made him nervous. Eventually, Gaege, who lived a little outside of Carbondale, said he had planned to drive home with Pravin still in the car. This caused the young man to panic, prompting him to throw a punch at Gaege. In response, he had stopped the car and demanded that Pravin get out. But he had refused. After turning off his engine, Gaege pocketed his keys and pulled Pravin out through the passenger side. What followed was a physical altercation that, as per Bethune, lasted for about thirty seconds. Once again, the state trooper's lights had drawn Gaege's attention back to the car, while Pravin had vanished deeper into the wilderness.

Gaege admitted that he had been drinking that night. A friend of his had even apparently refused to sit in his car that night because of how drunk he was. Meanwhile, his descriptions of Pravin were strangely contradictory. He claimed Pravin was sober and seemed like a 'well-rounded', decent kid. Later in the same interview, he would change his mind: 'I was scared for my life,' Gaege claimed, 'I didn't know what he was capable of. Definitely wasn't my race, and I'm not used to being around that type of population and those types of people. I'm not used to any of it.'

> **AISHWARYA**
> This must have been a realization of Lovely and Matthew's worst fears. They had suspected they were being treated differently because of barriers of language or racism but this was confirmation that those same biases might have played a part in the death of their son.

As the interrogation went on, many more inconsistencies arose in Gaege's story. He claimed that he had turned off his car before exiting it once the fight began, while the police footage showed his truck was on. His claim that Pravin was on the phone the entire time was immediately disproven by his call log, and in a later interview, Gaege would go on to suggest that *he* was the one attempting to purchase cocaine. However, his callous description of Varughese's beloved son remains one of the most devastating – and telling – details of the case.

State Attorney Michael Carr took charge of the case, and by July 2014, he called a grand jury to review it. This meant the jury's findings were private, and no documents would be made public. In December 2014, the grand jury issued their official recommendation: Gaege Bethune should not be put on trial. On 23 February 2015, Carr made a public statement, reinforcing the theory that Pravin was intoxicated after the party and died of hypothermia – despite the contrary results in the toxicology report. Carr attributed Pravin's injuries to the physical altercation between the men, maintaining that it was unlikely Gaege had killed Pravin on such a busy road and then willingly approached the police afterwards. He also referenced how Lovely Varughese had presented him with over 40,000 signed petitions, but while these spoke volumes about how important Pravin was to his community, they did not change the cold facts of the case.

The findings of Carr and the grand jury were a blow to the family, who enlisted the help of special prosecutor David Robinson. He made new inquests, taking a closer look at the case files and even conducting fresh interviews. A fresh theory was put forward: an intoxicated Gaege had attempted to steal money from Pravin after the two had jointly attempted to purchase cocaine that fateful night. In the argument that ensued, Bethune punched Varughese several times, injuring him so badly that he was unable to find his way out of the forest and died there alone, abandoned in the frigid Illinois winter.

In 2017, three years after Pravin's death, Robinson took his findings to another grand jury. This time, his labour – and that of the Varughese family and their supporters – bore some fruit. The jury recommended that Gaege be tried for two counts of first-degree felony murder. Lovely Varughese told the *Southern Illinoisian*, 'I feel like our son's voice is heard finally ... It's been a long fight, and we wanted someone to look into it honestly and investigate. We believe that's happened and we're so thankful – so, so thankful.' The trial began in June 2018, and the jury's decision affirmed the family's relief: Gaege Bethune was found guilty on one count of felony murder, for which the charge was twenty to sixty years in prison.

However, in a shocking turn of events, Judge Mark Clarke overthrew the conviction in September 2018, due to a language error in the indictment, which he believed posed an 'unacceptable risk of confusion' for the jury. According to the grand jury indictment, 'Gaege Bethune ... KNOWINGLY made a physical contact of an insulting or provoking nature'. The judge believed that the jury could be confused by the word 'knowingly'; so, to give Bethune a fair chance, the case was reset for a new trial.

In December 2014, the Varughese family lodged another wrongful death lawsuit against Bethune, Carbondale Police Chief Jody O'Guinn (the person who questioned Bethune on the night of Pravin's death) and the city of Carbondale itself. Lovely Varughese stated that 'this is the only way we could get some kind of answers from them'.

Today, the case continues to grow colder, and Gaege Bethune seems to have moved on with his life, now with a son of his own. The Varughese family still await the justice that was so cruelly dangled just out of their reach. But their refusal to let Pravin's tragic story be buried in obscurity remains a beacon in the darkness, illuminating the way forward.

## 12

# THE TANDOOR MURDER

**ARYAAN**
Imagine you're seated at a typical north Indian restaurant, perusing its elaborate menu. You'll almost certainly see one word: tandoor. It refers to the clay oven used to make everything from naan to kebabs, a warm presence in the background of so many childhood memories and delicious meals. But what if it was weaponized for something sinister instead – something that would haunt the residents of Delhi for years to come? This is the macabre tale of the Tandoor Murder.

India's capital, New Delhi, is a city that rarely slows down. Bumper-to-bumper traffic, bustling markets and a seemingly endless tide of people fighting for their place – it comes together to form a uniquely chaotic rhythm that can be intimidating. But on the night of 2 July 1995, even the ever-bustling area of Connaught Place was cloaked in an unusual stillness. The sky, for once, hadn't succumbed to the city's notorious pollution. Constables Abdul Nazir Kunju and Chanderpal began their night shift around 11 p.m., patrolling the Janpath area. They weren't expecting anything more than the usual; perhaps a few drunks or minor scuffles. Then, in just thirty minutes, the quiet of the summer Sunday night shattered. The towering Ashok Yatri Niwas hotel was ablaze.

Worried that it would soon turn into a major fire, the duo rushed to investigate. A uniformed guard stopped them at the entrance. He clarified that the restaurant workers were burning some old paper and cardboard near the outdoor tandoor, and there was nothing to worry about. Kunju and Chanderpal retreated towards Janpath Lane but were quickly summoned again by Anora Devi, a panicked vegetable vendor. Nearly 35-feet high flames were licking the night sky. This time, Kunju went past the guards and reached Bagiya Barbeque. They were greeted at the restaurant's door by a man dressed in a long white kurta, the manager Keshav Kumar. Kumar repeated the same excuse as his coworker – that they were just burning some old posters, and the fire was under control – but Kunju would not be convinced a second time.

**AISHWARYA**
I'm glad Constable Kunju didn't buy it. It's very unusual to have a fire burning in the sticky Delhi summer heat.

**ARYAAN**
Exactly, and fire safety was a serious concern in Delhi. The residents hadn't yet forgotten the infamous Siddharth Continental Hotel fire in 1986, where thirty-seven people lost their lives. The police didn't want another incident like that to happen on their watch.

Kunju left Chanderpal near the hotel and immediately called for backup from the Connaught Place Police Station and the fire brigade. By the time Kunju returned to the scene, the fire had grown more intense. The hotel staff tried their best to block access, but the cops scaled a fence on the property and forced their way into the kitchen, where the fire seemed to have originated. Inside, they found Keshav along with another man dressed in a similar milky white kurta, Sushil Sharma. The flames were rising from the tandoor that stood in the centre of the kitchen – an otherwise unremarkable sight. But a matter of immediate concern was the shards of wood and other flammable materials stacked around the clay oven, posing a real risk of the entire hotel burning down. Sushil echoed Keshav's story; he was a Congress Party worker and was simply burning old campaign posters he no longer needed. Kunju, undeterred by the not-so-subtle attempt at strong-arming him, stood his ground. With the support of the back-up officers – Head Constable Majid Khan and Constable Rajbir Singh – they extinguished the fire within minutes.

As they took Keshav to assess the damage from a higher vantage point, a gust of heat rose towards them. The tandoor was ablaze once again, and this time, Sushil was nowhere to be seen. It was clear that there was something sinister about the situation; the smell wafting from the tandoor was sickening and putrid, not the inviting aroma of roasting bread or meat. Once again, the officers went to douse the fire, and that's when Kunju peered inside the tandoor. What he saw wasn't paper or cardboard. It wasn't food. It was a blackened, burnt human body, rendered unrecognizable. The sight was a grotesque perversion of the traditional Hindu pyre – but there was nothing sacred about what had taken place that night. The restaurant had become a mortuary.

Naina Saini was born on 13 April 1966 to Jaswant Kaur and Harbhajan Singh. A bright student, she graduated with top honours from Shyama Prasad Mukherjee College at Delhi University. Her interests went beyond the classroom – she obtained a student pilot license from the Delhi Flying Club and later a private pilot's license in the UK. Though raised in a relatively sheltered environment, Naina was acutely aware of the social and political issues impacting her country. She became actively involved in student politics and was a key member of the National Students' Union of India (NSUI), the student wing of the Indian National Congress. It was through her work as a student leader that she met Sushil Sharma, a fellow NSUI worker. In 1986, when Sushil was appointed president of the NSUI, he nominated Naina to serve as State General Secretary. They were an ambitious pair, but the relationship was strictly professional, as Naina was involved with a man named Matloob Karim at that time. However, facing the social prejudice often directed at interfaith couples, their relationship gradually faded, and in December 1998, Matloob was engaged to a woman from his community, Naaz Gul.

Soon after, Naina's relationship with Sushil blossomed into a romance. By then, he was a prominent – some would say infamous – figure in Delhi's political circuit, with close ties with the city's power brokers. He had earned a brazen reputation, slashing posters of political rivals and carrying a licensed .32 revolver. Their relationship was tumultuous, and when Sushil demanded that Naina withdraw from political life ahead of their marriage, she reluctantly agreed. They were married in May 1993 at the Birla Mandir. No official paperwork was filed, as Sushil preferred to keep their marriage under wraps. His neighbours in Pitampura never saw Naina, and Sushil's father, despite being present at the wedding, often said how he wanted to see his son married. Meanwhile, Naina, barred from pursuing her political ambitions, found herself confined to their apartment on Mandir Marg. She ran a small but successful boutique, yet the venture felt insignificant for a woman who had aspired to conquer the skies and the even-more-treacherous arena of Delhi politics.

Sushil's abusive behaviour soon became apparent. He would come home drunk after work and assault Naina. His possessiveness was suffocating – he jealously prevented her from interacting with other men and subjected her to constant suspicion. Meanwhile, Ila Jhunjhunwala, a woman Sharma had a long-standing relationship with before their marriage, disclosed to Naina that their affair was still ongoing. Ila also revealed that Sushil had developed a reputation as a womanizer; she was far from his only extramarital partner. All the while, his marriage to Naina remained a closely guarded secret. Naina's pain bled into a letter she wrote around this time.

> I know you hate me and cannot adopt me. Do not waste your time. Take care of your life. Forgive me. Leave me to

my fate. Do not suspect me. I know I do not deserve you. Do not say anything to my parents. They are innocent. Inflict any punishment on me you deem fit.

The last line is a haunting premonition of what was to come.

As her marriage deteriorated, Naina turned to Matloob for support. She confided in him about the abuse she was enduring at the hands of her husband and sought his help in obtaining an Australian visa, so she could emigrate and set up an export business. On 2 July 1995, she called Matloob around 7 p.m. for an update on the visa. He assured her he would pick it up from the travel agent's office in Jor Bagh. Satisfied, she poured herself a drink. At 8:15 p.m., Sushil's car pulled into their apartment complex, and he joined his wife. As usual, his ever-present insecurities resurfaced. Suspiciously, he redialled the last number Naina had called. A deep, familiar voice answered on the other side – one that was all too familiar. It was his wife's former lover.

To Sushil's mind, Matloob's voice was a confirmation of everything he had suspected and accused Naina of during their marriage. He disconnected the call, stormed into their bedroom and confronted Naina, who held her ground as best she could. Her answers were acidic; Sushil had no right to question her about her private life and dealings. The conflict only escalated. Emboldened by the alcohol and driven by pure rage at his wife's behaviour, Sushil fired his service revolver three times at point-blank range. Two bullets were lodged into Naina's head and neck. The third missed her and hit a piece of plywood. She died almost immediately.

Having committed cold-blooded murder, Sushil was suddenly confronted with the reality of his actions. Sushil's white kurta was drenched in blood; their bedroom now a crime scene. Amid the rising tide of panic, fear – and perhaps even regret – Sushil's primal survival instinct took over. He hauled her corpse down the stairs and into his car. He had to dispose of Naina's body before he was discovered. Initially, he considered dumping her in the nearby Yamuna, but as he approached the ITO bridge spanning across the polluted river, he realized that the plan was unworkable. It was past 9:30 p.m., the area was teeming with traffic and the Delhi Police Headquarters plaza was uncomfortably close. Abandoning his idea, he shifted the gears in his white Maruti, took a U-turn at the end of the bridge and drove towards Ashoka Road, reaching Bagiya Barbeque around 10:15 p.m.

Parking the car inside the main gate, Sushil rushed into the restaurant. Drawing Keshav, the manager, aside, he confessed his crime and pleaded for his help in covering his tracks. Keshav was terrified as the gravity of the situation sank in. Yet, torn apart by guilt and loyalty, he hesitated – Sushil had been a good friend to him over the years, and he wouldn't desert him now. When questioned by the police after Naina's body was discovered, Keshav could only say, *'Unn ke mujh par kaafi ehsaan hain'* (I am highly indebted to him).

Customers at the restaurant were hurried through their dinner, and the staff were handed twenty-five rupees to compensate for the complimentary meal that was usually provided at the end of their shift. Around the tandoor, a makeshift pile of scrap wood and paper was assembled. Naina's lifeless body, wrapped in a plastic tablecloth, was placed inside. The pair used four slabs of butter to help ignite the fire. All this while, Sushil murmured repeatedly, *'Yeh maine kya kar diya? Yeh mujhse kya ho gaya?'* (What have I done? What did I end up doing?) But when the police arrived shortly afterwards, only Keshav was arrested – his face blackened with soot – while Sushil managed to flee the scene.

The body was taken to Lady Hardinge Medical College, and since the investigating officer suspected it might belong to Naina, her parents were called to identify it. At the sight of the charred body in the mortuary, the devastated couple simply wept and were unable to identify their daughter's remains. Later, on 5 July, Matloob was the one who confirmed it was her. Her limbs had been severed from her body, and the doctor who conducted the first autopsy suggested that the burns had been inflicted post-mortem. Meanwhile, the investigating officers had searched Sushil's Mandir Marg flat and found five empty cases of used cartridges and traces of blood on the mattress in the bedroom. Based on their findings, the authorities requested an X-ray of Naina's body to ascertain if there had been a firearms injury. However, the X-ray machine at Lady Hardinge was reportedly out of order at the time.

While the lives of Naina's loved ones had been irreversibly shattered, Sushil was on the run. Known for his unscrupulous reputation, he leveraged the extensive network he had built through deep ties in party politics. With the assistance of these friends in high places, he evaded capture for days after he became a wanted man. On the night of the murder, he took refuge at New Delhi's Gujarat Bhawan. Then, he fled to Bombay. As news of the gruesome crime captured national headlines, he travelled to Madras, where he secured anticipatory bail – a direction to release a person on bail, issued even before the person is arrested – from a sessions court. However, the Madras High Court later revoked the order at the request of the Delhi Police. Despite the furore surrounding the case, Sushil managed to travel to Bangalore, where he was finally arrested. On 11 July, police officers from Delhi arrived to take him into custody.

At the time of his arrest, Sushil was carrying a briefcase that contained a .32 Arminius pistol and live bullets. Following a request of the lieutenant governor of Delhi, a second autopsy conducted on 12 July by a team of doctors changed the course of the investigation. They found bullets in the body's head and neck region, confirming that Naina's death was caused by firearm injuries. DNA testing verified the identity, and the blood found in the flat and inside Sushil's car matched Naina's blood group. As evidence mounted, Sushil and Keshav were charged on multiple counts, along with three men – Jai Prakash, Rishi Raj Rathi and Ram Prakash Sachdeva – accused of harbouring Sushil during his flight. All five men pleaded not guilty. At various points in the investigation, Sushil even denied that he and Naina were married, and they merely lived together, though this was rubbished by several witnesses, including her family.

On 7 November 2003, Sushil was sentenced to death by the trial court, while Keshav received seven years of rigorous imprisonment. The High Court reaffirmed Sushil's death sentence on 19 February 2007, describing his act as one that 'reflects extreme depravity'. The gruesome manner in which Naina was killed and her body was dealt with 'must have shocked the conscience of the community at large'. However, his sentence was later commuted to life imprisonment.

**ARYAAN**
The twist is that in India, life imprisonment doesn't mean you have to spend the rest of your days in prison. And on 21 December 2018, the Delhi High Court ordered that Sushil be released from prison after serving twenty-three years.

**AISHWARYA**
I understand that our legal system is built with a purpose, that there's a reason why cases are reopened, even after a conviction. But after everything you've told me today, it's hard to accept that Sushil walked free.

The years of incarceration were harrowing. Sushil struggled with suicidal thoughts and adapting to the cut-throat world of prison. It wasn't until a fellow inmate introduced him to spiritual practices and Hindu scriptures that he began to find a sense of inner balance. In an interview after his release, Sushil told *The Hindu* that he was grateful to be reunited with his ageing parents before their passing. He even mused how things may have unfolded differently had he undergone counselling before getting married. Whether or not one believes that Sushil deserves a second chance at life, he is a free man today. Even Ashok Yatri Niwas has emerged from the shadow of the controversy better than anyone might have expected. The once government-owned hotel was taken over by an award-winning international chain. Only Naina's story was irrevocably cut short, twice over – the moment she married Sushil, and the moment he murdered her.

# 13

# NOT-SO-JOLLY JOSEPH

**ARYAAN**
What's in a name? In India, some astrologists will tell you that two syllables might even alter your destiny. In any case, names hold great meaning across most cultures, often representing traits like kindness, strength or beauty – a symbol of parental hopes for children. But what if your name is at complete odds with who you are? The protagonist of this story epitomizes this cruel irony. How someone's name can be completely misleading, and just how deceptive appearances can be. This is the story of Jolly Joseph.

October 2019. Jollyamma Joseph was being escorted to her family home, surrounded by the police and amidst the angry, albeit inquisitive, cries of onlookers. Ponnamattam, a pastel pink, two-storey home in Koodathayi, Kozhikode, belonged to an idyllic dreamscape. But the picture-perfect house had allegedly become the scene of a crime spree. Some threw sexual innuendos and insults in Jolly's direction, while others expressed their confusion at how their warm and welcoming neighbour, whom they called 'Jolly', had found herself in this position. A *CNN* crew was present at the scene, capturing footage that would be broadcast to thousands across the world. But what could have possibly gone down in a small Keralan village to prompt this level of outrage and interest? As with most cases, the answer lies in a story that began many years before.

In 1997, at an unassuming gathering of friends and family, twenty-five-year-old Jolly was introduced to her future husband, Roy Thomas. This chance meeting at Roy's uncle's housewarming would change the lives of their families forever. A romance blossomed between the two well-educated and good-looking individuals, and less than a year later, Roy declared his intention to marry Jolly. Jolly, who hailed from Kattappana, was a first-generation college student in her family of cardamom farmers. Marrying into the Thomas family seemed like a step up; the Thomas's possessed generational wealth, education and even though they were among the handful of Christian families in a predominantly Muslim neighbourhood, enjoyed great popularity in the village they called home. Roy's father, Tom Thomas, was a senior clerk in the education department. His mother, Annamma, was a teacher; his siblings, Renji and Rojo, were ambitious young adults. When the couple married in 1997, Jolly's parents were satisfied that their daughter was in good hands.

### ARYAAN

In most true crime stories, this would be the point where I would say something like, 'But little did Jolly know that she was marrying into a family that would treat her horribly' … But this was not the case.

After Jolly became her daughter-in-law, Anamma proudly told anyone who'd listen that the beautiful, college-educated girl was a perfect match for her son. According to Renji, her mother had always wanted Jolly to be more like her. As a former teacher who understood the value of independence and having a career, Anamma encouraged Jolly to further her studies and enter the workforce. Her advice would become more pressing when Roy lost his job in Hyderabad, prompting the couple to move to the family home in Koodathayi. Tom and Annamma were in their fifties by this time, sustained by their careful savings and a meagre pension. Nonetheless, they welcomed their prodigal son with open arms, along with his wife and their son, Romo.

The family grew even closer when, in 1999, Jolly requested her in-laws' support to pursue another degree and eventually follow in their footsteps to become a teacher. They happily agreed – an incredibly open-minded approach for the time. Their show of faith paid off, as Jolly became a breadwinner for the family and Roy continued to while away his time and invest in failed business ventures. By 2000, Jolly had managed to find a job at the prestigious National Institute of Technology (NIT), Kozhikode. She was continuing her in-laws' legacy as an educator, but very soon, a tragic series of events would make her its sole keeper.

In August 2002, Annamma was sitting in the living room. She had been unwell and had been served a bowl of mutton soup by her daughter-in-law to soothe her stomach. Suddenly, she was overcome with nausea; she fell to the floor, convulsing, frothing at the mouth. A shell-shocked Jolly somehow gathered her wits and rushed Annamma to the hospital. But it was too late – the fifty-seven-year-old woman died en route of a heart attack. All her life, Annamma had kept the home front buzzing; she managed the family's finances, cooked for friends, mentored the neighbour's children and hosted vibrant Christmas parties. A neighbour who lived across the street, Mohammed Bava, commented, 'There was no happiness in the house like how there used to be when [Annamma Thomas] was alive.'

His wife's death left Tom devastated. Jolly took on Annamma's role as the family's backbone, gradually winning Tom's trust, especially after the birth of her second son, Roland, in 2004. He insisted she upgrade her scooter to a Honda City so she could easily commute to NIT. At the same time, Roy's descent into alcoholism worsened the situation. Soon, Tom sold a few acres of property at Manimunda and transferred 18 lakh rupees directly to Jolly's account. Then, on 22 August 2008, six years after his beloved wife's death, sixty-six-year-old Tom fell unconscious on the bathroom floor, vomiting violently. Jolly called Mohammed Bava, who rushed Tom to the hospital. He had succumbed to a heart attack. The second untimely death in the Thomas family was eerily similar to the first ... but surely it was all just a coincidence? At that point, no one felt the need to order a post-mortem for these seemingly natural deaths.

The grieving family gathered for Tom's final rites: Roy and

Jolly, their two sons and Roy's siblings, Rojo and Renji. Also present was Mathew Manchadiyil, Annamma's brother, at whose house the couple had first met. Almost immediately, Jolly produced a will, typed in Malayalam and accompanied by Tom's photograph and signature. The document stated that he had made Roy and Jolly sole heirs of Ponnamattam. Tom's wishes were clear; the turmoil that may have accompanied the sudden death of the family patriarch was avoided. But it wasn't easy to restore normalcy after another pillar of the home had collapsed; the once tightly knit Thomas family dispersed into the wind. Roy fell deeper into the trenches of alcoholism and unemployment. Rojo and Renji returned to the US and Colombo, respectively. Jolly was left raising two children by herself while balancing her job at NIT. Despite this, she didn't seem to be facing any financial difficulty. Those who knew her assumed that her job and Tom's inheritance gave her enough security. Three years passed in relative peace.

On 30 September 2011, the family was struck by yet another tragedy. After a morning spent in the town, Roy returned to Ponnamattam to have lunch. He ate around 3:30 p.m. and then busied himself with household chores. In the evening, Jolly prepared their dinner and went to put the children, then aged thirteen and seven, to bed as Roy entered the bathroom, presumably to wash his hands for dinner. But the man was not afforded even the luxury of a last supper.

Jolly heard a commotion and rushed downstairs to find that her husband, who was clearly in distress, was trapped inside the locked bathroom. Once again, Jolly called Mohammed Bava, who helped her break open the door.

They found Roy unconscious, covered in putrid vomit and frothing at his mouth. He was rushed to the nearby Santhi hospital and, just like his parents, died on the way. At forty, Roy Thomas became the third member of his family to die in nearly identical fashion.

**ARYAAN**
This is just bizarre to me. You could attribute this to some kind of genetic predisposition, but three family members dying due to unprecedented cardiovascular events? It seems as unlikely as lightning striking you twice.

**AISHWARYA**
What I find even more unlikely is that no one had become suspicious of Jolly yet! Though she was present for every death, no one questioned her involvement.

**ARYAAN**
Don't worry, that will change soon.

Unnerved by the decade of ill-luck that had struck his family, Mathew Manchadiyil demanded an autopsy of his nephew's body and an inquiry into his death. The post-mortem exam was conducted at Kozhikode Medical College, and though the anatomical analysis seemed normal, the toxicology report revealed the presence of a substance in Roy's body that would later become synonymous with Jolly Joseph. Cyanide. Moreover, though Jolly claimed that Roy's final meal had been lunch, the autopsy showed that he had last eaten around 8:30 p.m., a dinner of rice and chickpeas curry she had prepared.

The holes in her story exposed, Jolly was forced to pivot. Her husband hadn't died of a heart attack, she admitted to close members of the family, he had died by suicide. Addiction, debt and the sudden loss of his parents had driven Roy into a depression which he could not overcome. Unable to handle the crippling sense of loss, he had killed himself. Jolly begged the family not to take the inquest further; her husband was dead, but her two young sons would be severely impacted by a police investigation and the knowledge that their father had killed himself. But this uncharacteristic subservience would not last long. Shortly after Roy's death, Jolly presented another version of Tom's will to Rojo and Renji. According to this document, the house (including 38 cents of land) had been given to Roy and Jolly. For the remaining 50 cents, the three children had equal shares. As Roy's widow, Jolly would inherit his portion of the land. Rojo and Renji refused to accept this, as it wasn't signed by witnesses and didn't have a date. Not long after, Jolly produced yet *another* will, this time signed by two witnesses – complete strangers to the family. Additionally, none of Tom Thomas's close friends knew of this will's existence.

Even under Rojo and Renji's increasingly watchful eyes, the aura of death and destruction that surrounded Jolly only grew darker. In 2014, Mathew, who had pushed for the investigation into Tom's death, died after a sustained period of ill health. He had recently undergone an angioplasty, so his death did not raise any suspicions with medical practitioners.

Once again, Jolly found his body. By this time, she had also reportedly begun a romantic relationship with Tom's cousin, Shaju Sakhariyas, who was married to and had two children with a woman named Sili Shaju. Shaju, unlike Roy, was a quiet, well-off teacher. On 3 May 2014, Sili and Shaju's daughter, Alphine, died after choking on food at a christening ceremony where Jolly was in attendance. Two years later, on 11 January 2016, Sili passed away after suffering from acute breathlessness while she and Jolly were headed to a dental clinic. Allegedly, Jolly had offered Sili a capsule before her sudden death. Doctors at the Santhi Hospital Omassery, where Sili's body was taken, suspected that there might have been some foul play. How had a young woman in her forties, otherwise in perfect health, suddenly died? However, Shaju vehemently opposed this line of questioning and signed a document requesting that a post-mortem not be conducted. A year later, in 2017, Shaju and Jolly were married.

Renji later told an interviewer that 'first, had Jolly not been adamant about the fake will she prepared, and two, had Jolly not married Shaju Sakariya, our first cousin', she and her brother might not have pursued the case so fiercely. But Jolly's flagrant disregard for basic propriety was the final straw. In 2018, Rojo travelled to Koodathayi to file a series of RTI requests that would blow the case open. His appeal to the revenue department revealed an alternate version of Tom's will – signed and with witnesses present – which was structured very differently than the one Jolly had shared. Tom had *not* left half of Poonamattam to Jolly and Roy; in fact, his will required that Rojo and Renji be its sole inheritors. It was also revealed that Jolly had forged the property transfer papers, and the police received information that local political leaders and revenue officials had helped her fake the will without Tom's signature.

Armed with indisputable evidence that their family's case had not been properly scrutinized, Rojo and Renji were able to demand a reinvestigation. The case was transferred from the Thamasseray Police – who had till then maintained the deaths were due to natural causes – to the Kozhikode Rural Police, who were better equipped to approach the convoluted case with a fresh perspective. Superintendent K. G. Simon created a team led by Superintendent Haridasan, who began their investigation in August 2019. After decades of impunity, Jolly Joseph was finally taken into police custody on 5 October 2019.

Like any good storyteller, Jolly made sure to build her lies on a foundation of truth. She was indeed born to a comfortable, though simple, family in Vazhavara, a small, rainy village in the foothills of the Western Ghats. Her parents, K Joseph and Thresiamma, owned a humble spice farm and operated two ration shops. Jolly was the fifth of six children, and her family would later describe her as a 'sweet and cheery' girl. Her academic drive prompted their father to send her to undertake a BCom degree at a private college, M. E. S. Nedumkandam. While she was there, Jolly was accused of stealing a gold bangle from a classmate. Her father punished her dearly for the misstep, but still supported her when she decided to pursue a master's degree at another college in Kattappana. Little did he know that the incident of the bangle was only the beginning of his daughter's prolific career in deception.

Jolly told her family that she had completed the degree with flying colours when in actuality, she had dropped out in the first year. When she met Roy, it seemed she had found her perfect match. Not only was he from a well-established family, but he shared her propensity for lying. After the ill-fated couple met at his house, Mathew had dissuaded the Josephs from marrying their daughter to Roy. His nephew had poor eyesight and was unemployed, which, to him, made Roy a poor prospect. On the contrary, Roy claimed that he was indeed employed and earned between 25,000–30,000 rupees a month. When Jolly supported his story, her parents acquiesced, and the marriage went forward.

By 2000, Jolly was leading an alarmingly duplicitous double life. Her family and neighbourhood had celebrated her employment at NIT; for them, she was a young woman accomplished enough to earn a place at one of India's premier institutions. But the truth was that Jolly had *never* been employed at NIT.

**AISHWARYA**
But didn't she go to work every day? Tom even helped her purchase a car to commute to Kozhikode!

**ARYAAN**
The farce went deeper than you can even imagine. Façade upon façade, and it was all coming to the surface now.

Later investigations revealed that Jolly would travel to NIT nearly every day, only to spend an inordinate amount of time at the college canteen. She had acquired a fake employee ID card, but this could not cover up the fact that none of her professed colleagues recognized her. The college registrar confirmed to officials that there was no record of a Jolly Joseph or a Jolly Shaju on the staff. But how did these compulsive lies escalate into what many believe was a killing spree?

Though the Josephs were Christians – and thus, their bodies could be exhumed post-burial – years of decomposition made it very difficult to derive forensic evidence. Kerala DGP Loknath Behra commented, 'Extraction of DNA is a difficult process, especially on older remains.' The police could only speculate about what may have led to Jolly's actions, but when it came to Annamma and Tom, Jolly's motivations were somewhat evident. They hypothesized that Annamma had uncovered her web of lies – indeed, Rojo had suspected that Jolly wasn't an NIT employee as early as 2012, but the family refused to believe him. Poisoning her mother-in-law would allow her to both preserve her secrets and assume Annamma's role as the social and financial nucleus of the family. Jolly's growing closeness to Tom proved fruitful at first. The trusting old man became a steady source of money and resources, but his son's dire financial situation ultimately led him to declare that Roy and Jolly had no further claim on the rest of the property. The police theorized that this led to Jolly serving her father-in-law poisoned tapioca on 26 August 2008, causing his death.

If Jolly's alleged poisoning of Annamma and Tom was

motivated purely by greed, she may have had other reasons to kill Roy. Not only was her wastrel husband a drain on her resources, but some have also speculated that Jolly's relationships with other men – and later Shaju – may have prompted her to lace his curry with cyanide. The subsequent deaths appear to fit naturally within this convincing line of reasoning. Mathew had voiced his suspicions about the deaths in their family and prompted the autopsy of Roy's body. Sili had come in the way of Jolly's relationship with Shaju, and as callous as it may sound, so had little Alphine.

> **AISHWARYA**
> It's upsetting to hear these tragic events laid up in such cold detail. But I'm struggling to wrap my head around how Jolly could have possibly pulled all of this off. I mean, it isn't that easy to get your hands on cyanide in India, is it?
>
> **ARYAAN**
> That's a great question, Aishwarya, and it allows us to talk about the other people who may have been involved. In fact, Jolly's elder son Romo, who has sided with Roy's siblings throughout the legal proceedings, told a major Malayalam newspaper, 'My mother could not have committed all the murders alone, including that of my father. I suspect help from outsiders.'

Cyanide is a controlled substance in India, and Jolly would have needed a supplier to carry out the crimes she has been accused of. Enter M. S. Matthew, Jolly's friend – and by some accounts, lover – who worked at a local jewellery store. Potassium cyanide is used by jewellery stores for several mundane activities, especially treating metal. Matthew allegedly plied a goldsmith named Prajikumar with 5,000 rupees and two bottles of liquor to provide Jolly with cyanide. When they testified in court, Prajikumar claimed he was told that the poison was for 'personal use', while Jolly told Matthew (as he claimed in his statement to the police) that the cyanide would be used to kill a stray rat which was causing her a great deal of trouble in her house.

Another figure who has ignited some suspicion is Shaju Sakhariyas, Jolly's second husband. Many have questioned his refusal to have Sili's body autopsied and his quick remarriage, while Romo has claimed that he seemed unaffected by the deaths of his wife and child. However, Shaju continues to maintain his innocence. He claims that Sili's family encouraged him to remarry in the interest of his children, though Romo has disputed this. Shaju has also said he suspected Jolly neither of harming others nor of having an affair with Matthew during their relationship. In 2021, he told *The Hindu*, 'Now I realise how perfectly she acted, leaving nothing that will expose her lies. I would have been her next victim if she had not been arrested now.'

Since her initial arrest, Jolly has spent all her time in and out of police custody. In a major development after two months of intense police scrutiny, K. G. Simon announced at a press conference in October 2019 that she had confessed to all six murders. Despite this, Jolly – along with the Joseph family and the rapt onlookers – awaits a final verdict on the case. Her father has told reporters that her birth family has disowned Jolly and will not be supporting her legal battle.

In the meantime, Jolly's story has taken on a life of its own in media and public memory. Shaju is not the only one whose version of events and opinion of Jolly have oscillated wildly. Her neighbours have alternately condemned her for tarnishing the reputation of their humble locality while also recounting her kindness and generosity. Many remembered her as a devout Christian, often seen at the Lourdes Matha Church. At the same time, Reverend Joseph Kizhakkepurakkal told a journalist that 'Jolly was not a frequent visitor here, nor did she have anything to do with the activities of the church.' A massively popular documentary on Jolly's case was released in 2023, though many, including Shaju, feared it would influence public opinion. As of now, we are certain that Jolly was completely corrupted by her drive for money and power. If a judge confirms what the police and public already believe – that her greed wiped out an entire family – Jolly Joseph will be remembered in the bloody corridors of history as one of India's few, and most infamous, female serial killers.

# 14

# MISSING SINCE 9/11: SNEHA PHILIP

**AISHWARYA**

On 11 September 2001, Al-Qaeda targeted four significant buildings in the United States, including the Twin Towers of the World Trade Center in New York. In all, 2,977 people died as a result of what is considered the deadliest terrorist attack in world history. In its aftermath, global geopolitics redefined 'national security' and the United States initiated their highly controversial War on Terror, an American-led military campaign to 'seek out and stop terrorists across the world'. Not many know that 250 people of Indian origin lost their lives in these attacks. This is the story of an Indian-American woman who was on the streets of New York that day. Until she simply ... vanished. This is the story of Sneha Philip.

Sneha Anne Philip was born on 7 October 1969 to Ansu, a computer professional, and Dr Kochiyil Philip in Kerala. Sneha, the only daughter of her family, was cherished for all that she was — a loving and artistic girl interested in music, writing and academics. She had an elder brother, Ashwin, and a younger brother, Kevin, whom she doted upon. When

Sneha was a young girl, her family moved to upstate New York; first to the Albany area and then to Duchess County. Like many immigrant families, their move to the US opened up a world of opportunities for the young woman, and she embraced them all. Sneha completed her undergraduate degree from the prestigious Johns Hopkins University and decided to study medicine, like her father. After graduating in 1991, she attended the Chicago School of Medicine. It was there, in 1995, that she met her future husband, Ron Lieberman.

The young lovers mirrored each other in many ways; both were aspiring doctors who had creative pursuits outside of their academics. Sneha decided to take a year off from college to graduate at the same time as Ron (who was a year behind Sneha in medical school). During that time, Sneha travelled across Italy, sampling some of the best experiences the world had to offer. In 1999, the couple completed their degrees and were thrilled to be placed in New York for their residencies: Sneha at Cabrini Medical Center in Manhattan and Ron at Jacobi Medical Center in the Bronx. With their futures secured, the couple decided to take the leap and get married. They held an intimate wedding in May 2000, close to Sneha's home in Duchess County. The ceremony beautifully blended their cultural traditions – Jewish–American and Christian–Indian. In a heartfelt gesture, Rob gifted his bride a minnu, a traditional teardrop-shaped Syrian–Christian wedding pendant worn by Malayali brides. The couple moved into a one-bedroom flat at 225 Rector Place, Battery Park, to begin a new phase of life together as 2001 came around. Their home was only a few blocks away from the iconic World Trade Centre.

On 10 September 2001, Sneha had a rare day off, which she planned to use to prepare for an upcoming visit from her cousin, Annu. After breakfast, Ron kissed her goodbye and headed out for work around 11 a.m. Around 2 p.m., Sneha started a conversation with her mother on Instant Messenger, and the pair exchanged messages until 4 p.m., after which she ended the call and left to run her errands. The security footage from the lobby showed her leaving around a quarter past five.

That night, Ron came back home to an empty and silent apartment. He wasn't concerned – after all, it was not unusual for Sneha to visit bars with her friends and then spend a night at their house. She also occasionally stayed over at her brother's or cousin's apartment as they both lived nearby. However, she usually called to let him know beforehand. But he hadn't heard from her. Past midnight, after having somewhat soothed his anxiety in the calming presence of their cats, Figa and Kali, Ron fell asleep. The next morning, the ill-fated 11 September 2001, he woke up for work at 6 a.m. There was still no sign of Sneha. Annoyed that his wife hadn't bothered to call or leave a message, but under the impression that she would be back that very night, Ron headed out to the Bowling Green subway station. His meeting at the Jacobi Medical Centre was scheduled to start at 8 a.m.. A few short hours later, the streets of New York City descended into unimaginable chaos. An hour later, Ron left his meeting and saw his colleagues gathered around the television. The imposing twin towers had been hit by an American Airlines flight and a United Airlines flight in quick succession.

> **ARYAAN**
> I've read that people had no idea it was a terrorist attack until much later. At first, many just thought it was a terrible fire or an accident. I can imagine it must have felt like the apocalypse, especially once other reports from across the US started trickling in.

Ron had to immediately get a hold of his wife – that small seed of worry gnawing within him since the last night had now snowballed into a full-blown panic as the city collapsed on itself. But this was 2001; Sneha, like most people, did not carry a cellphone. He called the house and got the machine. Thousands were making frenzied attempts to contact their loved ones, fighting for what little bandwidth was available, as one of New York's largest cell towers had been destroyed at the World Trade Center. Desperate, Ron called Sneha's parents, but Ansu and Philip had no idea where their daughter was. He also called her brother, and he didn't know where she was either. At that point, Ron couldn't think of a reason for Sneha to be in the Trade Center. But other horrifying scenarios flash through his mind: what if she had been in an accident? What if she had been kidnapped? Or crossed paths with a wrong stranger at a bar? While the city's grid failed, Sneha's family, too, was left floundering in the dark.

Around 3 p.m., Ron decided to stop waiting for the list. He left his office building and began walking towards their apartment, the streets stifled with thick smoke, blaring ambulances and reporters rushing to the scene. He managed to hitch an ambulance ride, but even that took six hours as people fled Lower Manhattan in hordes. Around 9 p.m., Ron, still in his scrubs, managed to convince the police to let him enter the cordoned-off Tribeca area, raced past scenes of carnage and finally reached their Rector Place apartment. Alas, city-wide power shortages had disabled the automatic locks of the twenty-three-storey building. He ran around the building screaming Sneha's name, begging someone to let him in, but there was no response. When a neighbour answered, Ron asked him to knock on their apartment door, but there was nothing but silence. Having exhausted all avenues that might lead to his wife, Ron spent the night at a friend's house and was able to enter their building the next day, on 12 September.

The distressing scene that greeted Ron was devoid of the familiar warmth of home. The couple's apartment was blanketed in ash and dust that had drifted for miles from the towers, seeping in through open windows – a haunting reminder of the devastating tragedy that had unfolded. Amidst the chaos, Ron was grappling with a crisis of his own. The one small advantage of the soot-covered surfaces was that any footprints were visible. There were paw prints tracing small, looping trails left by their cats ... but none that belonged to a human. Sneha had not returned to the apartment. Two days had passed since she was last seen.

When Ron contacted his in-laws again, Ansu was hit with a terrifying realization. During their last conversation, Sneha had told her mother that she intended to visit the Windows on the World restaurant in the North Tower. An old friend was set to host her wedding event there in the spring, and Sneha wanted to take a look at the venue. She hadn't specified when she was planning a visit to the location, but was it possible she had been lost in the devastating attack?

Sneha's family made their way to the police station to file a missing persons report. Ron even went to the 9/11 help centre at Lexington Avenue to drop off flyers. But this was the day after a historical catastrophe. Of the 2,977 people who lost their lives in the attacks, 40 per cent remain unidentified even today. On 12 September, rescue workers had only just begun the grim task of searching through the rubble. Sneha's disappearance was one among thousands – and there was no evidence she had been on the scene at all. Her family tried to draw attention by putting up fliers, hoping to spark public interest. But the media quickly moved on once it became clear she might not have been at Ground Zero and had been missing since 10 September.

As a last resort, Sneha's brother Ashwin concocted a lie that would inadvertently derail the investigation. Creating a scenario of her final moments, Ashwin told the police, 'I was on the phone with her, and she told me she couldn't leave because people were hurt. She said, "I have to help this person," and that's the last thing I heard from her.' With that, Sneha was added to the growing list of people being searched for among the rubble, and her picture began showing up on the news. For a moment, it may have felt like a breakthrough. But in truth, Ashwin had unintentionally misdirected the police search. By placing Sneha at Ground Zero, he had narrowed the scope of the investigation despite having no real idea where she was. It could have been entirely possible that Sneha needed help, but she was somewhere else in the city – so the trail would grow cold while the cops chased a false lead. As investigators dug deeper into the circumstances surrounding her disappearance, Ashwin's lie quickly began to unravel.

The police were able to confirm certain details of the day of Sneha's disappearance. She had logged onto her computer to speak to her mother for two hours, following which CCTV footage showed her exiting her building. She was dressed in a brown, short-sleeved dress and her hair in a ponytail. What followed was a series of mundane errands. She dropped off some dry-cleaning and then headed to a nearby store, Century 21, where she used Ron's American Express credit card to buy a dress, pantyhose, lingerie and bed linen just after 6 p.m. An hour later, around 7:18 p.m., she was seen buying three pairs of shoes at the next door shoe annexe. This video footage, along with the credit card transactions, was the last indication of Sneha's whereabouts.

When Ron learned these details, he asked his friends to drop off flyers at other Century 21 branches (the one downtown being closed). Later that week, he received a call from a clerk at Century 21, Sonia Mora. Sona recognized Sneha as a frequent customer and claimed she had been there on 10 September with another young woman, dark-skinned, in her early thirties and possibly of Indian descent. Ron spent three weeks in a windowless room, reviewing the store's security footage. He did find a video from an hour earlier that captured Sneha shopping alone. The other mystery woman never made an appearance. As Ashwin's concocted account began to unravel, the authorities began prioritizing confirmed victims of the 9/11 attacks once again. But Ron wasn't ready to let the investigation go cold. He decided to hire a private investigator and former FBI operations agent, Ken Gallant. Starting from scratch, Gallant managed to uncover intriguing leads. He scoured Sneha's favourite hangouts, interviewed her colleagues and people at the bars she frequented, took photographs and went through hours of surveillance footage outside the couple's apartment building. Minutes before American Airlines Flight 11 crashed into the North Tower, someone who resembled Sneha walked into the building. She briefly stood in front of the elevator, then turned around and exited – never to be seen again.

Though the woman's clothing did look similar to what Sneha had been wearing, the woman in the footage wasn't holding any shopping bags. This raised unsettling questions. Some believed that Sneha, a trained doctor, rushed out to help the victims of the attacks after hearing the sudden commotion. But if that was indeed her, what happened to the Century 21 shopping bags? If she left them at a friend's place, why didn't that person come forward after she was reported missing?

Sneha Philip's disappearance remains a bizarre case – one that has captured public attention despite coinciding with such a significant day in US history. The intrigue surrounding her final hours has given rise to several theories about what might have happened to her. The most widely circulated theory suggests that Sneha Philip simply used the chaos of 9/11 and its aftermath as an opportunity to disappear voluntarily, walking away from her life and never to return.

> **ARYAAN**
> She was a successful doctor with a loving family. Why would a perfectly ordinary person do something like that?
>
> **AISHWARYA**
> Sure, Sneha's life may have been pretty ordinary, but that doesn't mean she was doing well. That perfect exterior was hiding a less-than-ideal life.

It wasn't a coincidence that Sneha had a day off on that fateful day. In fact, she hadn't been employed for a few weeks at that point. Citing tardiness and 'alcohol-related' issues, the director at the Cabrini Medical Center had refused to renew Sneha's contract in the spring of 2001. For a medical intern, this decision was as serious as getting fired. Sneha had a different version of the events. At an evening out with her colleagues, she claimed that she had been groped by an intern at a bar. She filed a criminal complaint, but after an investigation, the Manhattan D.A.'s office dropped the charges against the intern. Since she had no evidence of her claim – as is often true for sexual harassment cases – the investigating officer dismissed it and instead charged her with false reporting – a misdemeanour under New York law. The prosecutor offered to drop the charge if Sneha recanted her complaint, but when she refused, she was arrested and spent a night behind bars. These problems resurfaced on the day of her disappearance. On the morning of 10 September, Sneha had a court date where she pleaded not guilty to filing a complaint and was formally arraigned. A police report stated that Sneha and Ron got into a 'big fight' about her actions at the courthouse. Then, she stormed off, leaving Ron behind.

After losing her job, Sneha secured a new position at St Vincent's Medical Center on Staten Island, under the condition that she would regularly attend meetings with a substance abuse counsellor. However, after missing several of these meetings, she was dismissed once again. Having lost her second job, the NYPD claimed she began frequenting many local LGBTQ+ bars, often leaving the bars with women she met there. One report even claimed that Sneha had been found in a compromising position with her brother's girlfriend. Her brother denied this. In fact, Sneha's family firmly rejected many of the NYPD's assertions, including reports of the argument at the courthouse and the speculation about Sneha's sexuality. Still, for some, these claims offer a potential explanation for her movements on the night of 10 September – for the fact that despite possibly spending the night at someone's house and leaving her shopping bags there, the person she was last with refused to come forward.

Another popular theory is the suspicion that Ron had

something to do with his wife's disappearance. Some speculate that tensions in their marriage – stemming from Sneha's reported struggles with alcohol and her sexuality – resulted in a violent confrontation, causing Ron to act out in a fit of rage. Interestingly, Gallant's investigations revealed that although Ron was the only one home on the night of 10 September, a call had been made from the home phone to Ron's mobile phone at 4 a.m. on 11 September. This would mean someone – most likely Sneha – entered the house and called Ron's phone while he was sleeping in their only bedroom. Ron claims he doesn't remember receiving a call, though he may have briefly woken and sleepily checked his voicemail.

### AISHWARYA

```
If this call really happened, it is definitive proof
that Sneha returned to and left the apartment, never
to be seen again. It's a baffling lead that doesn't get
mentioned enough. But why would he spend all that time
and effort digging into the case, even hiring the private
investigator who uncovered this clue?
```

Ron has consistently maintained his innocence, and his actions in the aftermath of Sneha's disappearance align with the image of a devoted, devastated husband. He also denied the allegations about Sneha's sexuality, explaining that while she did frequent gay and lesbian bars, it was to avoid harassment from men. Though her mental health had suffered greatly after the incident at work, he firmly denied that she was having an affair or had any reason to flee from what he saw as a happy and settled home.

Gallant dismissed the theory that Sneha used the chaos of 9/11 to intentionally escape an increasingly troubled life. After looking through her belongings, he found no evidence to support such a plan. Her passport, driver's license, credit cards and a hard drive had been left behind. In fact, the only thing Sneha had with her on the day of her disappearance was Ron's American Express card, which was never used after 10 September. Gallant also emphasized the strength of Sneha's family ties, especially her relationship with her mother. They had spoken on the day of her disappearance, and Ansu hadn't reported anything out of the ordinary in Sneha's behaviour. For years, the case remained entangled in a frustrating 'they said, they said' back-and-forth between the NYPD and Sneha's family. All this while there was no news of the missing woman.

By 2003, the search turned cold, and the NYPD decided to close the investigation, having concluded Sneha had simply run away. Her family refused to accept this and filed a petition in the New York County Surrogate's Court to have her officially declared a victim of the 9/11 attacks. This would also make them eligible to claim from the federal September 11th Victim Compensation Fund. However, the case hinged on concrete evidence placing Sneha on Ground Zero – evidence that was lacking. Ron and the Philips could only speculate: that, as a first responder, Sneha would have rushed to the scene, or that she had plans to visit the Windows on the World restaurant. On 29 June 2006, Judge Renee Roth ruled that the available evidence was insufficient. She officially declared the legal date of Sneha's death as 10 September 2004, three years after she had been reported missing. As a result, Ron's claim to the memorial fund was denied.

Her family appealed the court's decision. On 31 January 2008, a five-judge panel overturned the original ruling. The court accepted the explanation that Sneha had likely died while trying to help others caught in the attack and dismissed the NYPD's report as being based more on conjecture than concrete evidence. But by 2008, payments from the September 11th Victim Compensation Fund had ceased; the families of victims identified after 2003 were no longer eligible for financial compensation. Still, Sneha's name was added to the National September 11 Memorial at Ground Zero, inscribed on panel S-66 of the South Pool. Her family buried an urn containing ashes from Ground Zero at a cemetery near their home, and a memorial was established in her honour at Duchess Community College, where her mother worked. Ron has since remarried and remains close with Sneha's family. Her body was never recovered, joining the thousands of Americans whose families wait for some fragment of their lost loved ones – a piece of clothing, a shoe, an errant earring – to hold onto.

### AISHWARYA
Though authorities have long since given up on Sneha's case, internet sleuths have not. There's an online community called PostSecret, where people mail their secrets on home-made postcards. In 2012, they received an anonymous confession that some believe was Sneha. The postcard was etched with a pencil sketch of the twin towers burning, with a single sentence above it: 'Everyone

who knew me before 9/11 believes I'm dead.' Could this be proof that Sneha did indeed leave everything behind in the rubble and start a brand-new life? Or was she indeed the 2,751st victim of the ghastly terrorist attack that changed the world?

# 15

# THE TALE OF TWO VISHWANATHS

**ARYAAN**

Puttur, Karnataka, may appear to be a small, sleepy town. But like most parts of India, regardless of geographical size, it has a thriving cricket culture. The day this murder investigation broke open was like any other. A crowd of boys, many barefoot, ran around chasing leather balls in an empty field that doubled as their cricket pitch. An older teen went up to bat. He was lanky, focused; he was the kind of boy who had earned a reputation. Whose name the audience cheered. Unbeknownst to him, one of his fellow players was a constable on the hunt for a clue. While everyone waited with bated breaths for a six, an officer was chasing a lead so tenuous that it had taken the police thirteen years to track it down. A lead that would finally bring closure. This is the story of Vishwanath Rai and Vishwanath Shetty.

At the turn of the millennium, two men began to gain recognition in Puttur and the surrounding towns of Dakshina Kannada. Vishwanath Shetty and Vishwanath Rai. If you were in the area and needed a loan or were looking to invest in a small-time financial scheme, chances are that you had heard of Shiv Finance. Founded in 1999, the company did not run its business in grand glass buildings or sprawling boardrooms. Instead, they operated out of their humble homes. Still, Shetty and Rai had built a reputation for being efficient and dependable – the traits that mattered most when entrusting someone with your hard-earned money. Customers liked them, and money kept coming in. But a business partnership, no matter how solid it seems, is ultimately a marriage of convenience. And as their success grew, the cracks in their relationship slowly began to reveal themselves.

Despite sharing the same first name, Shetty and Rai had very different personalities. Shetty was quieter, more reserved; he was the kind of man who tended to keep to himself. Rai, on the other hand, was described as outgoing by some and flashy by others. He had a fondness for the finer things in life and owned multiple homes, including a house near Gandhi Park in Uppinangady, Mangaluru – 11 kilometres from Puttur – solely for business purposes. Aside from meetings, Shetty and Rai often met there to deliberate on major decisions. Perhaps it was inevitable that the Gandhi Park home would become the place where things crumbled for their once-flourishing enterprise.

By early 2001, financial disagreements between the partners began to simmer. There were a few stray signs of unrest – whispers among colleagues, a growing unease between the previously friendly duo – but they managed to keep up appearances. The tension finally reached a boiling point on 7 June 2001, though the day began like any other. That morning, Rai told his wife, Mallika, that he and his business partner were headed to Mangaluru for a meeting. Then he left, headed to the Gandhi Park house to discuss finances with Shetty and a younger associate, Subhas Chandra. Mallika had no way of knowing that this mundane, fleeting exchange would be the last time she saw her husband alive.

The next morning, Mallika began to worry when Rai, who had promised to call her, failed to do so. When she finally got through to his phone, another voice greeted her. Vishwanath Shetty. He told her they were in Talapady, 23 kilometres from Mangaluru. It was nowhere near where she expected them to be. When she asked to speak to Rai, the call was abruptly disconnected, and the phone switched off. At first, Mallika held on to the hope that her husband had simply been caught up at work. But as two days passed in silence, those hopes gave way to dread. On 9 June, Mallika reported her husband missing at the Puttur Rural Police Station.

Within a day of the report being filed, a lead arrived from 100 kilometres away: a male body had been found in Honnavar, in Uttara Kannada district. Decomposed beyond recognition and lacking any identification, the corpse might have become just another unclaimed body, buried quietly by local authorities. But one key detail stood out: a clothing tag on the shirt's collar that read 'Sindu Puttur 21376'. Gibberish to most, the tag became a crucial clue once the Puttur police were alerted. Sindu Tailors was a well-known local shop in Puttur, and the number was a customer reference. Investigators traced it back to Vishwanath Rai. Mallika was called in. When she confirmed that the body was her husband's, the missing persons case now had a dead body to account for and officially became a homicide.

The obvious person of interest was Shetty. The man had been with Rai on his final night amongst the living – and even answered Mallika's call the next morning, by which time Rai was likely already dead. But Shetty was long gone; his phone switched off, his home locked. His Maruti Zen car was found abandoned near Kadri Park in Mangaluru. The police deduced that he had absconded, taking 1 lakh rupees with him.

The only other person who might have known the true chain of events that unfolded on 7 June was Subhas Chandra, the third associate present at the meeting. Tracking him down wasn't easy. Some reports claimed he came forward voluntarily, encouraged by his lawyer; others say he had to be brought in by force. Either way, Chandra confirmed that something had gone wrong that night. There had been a heated argument, and raised voices had escalated into a violent altercation. Allegedly, he told police that Shetty struck Rai with an iron rod, possibly delivering the fatal blow, and then took the body away in his car. Chandra said that he had been threatened into silence. But with one man dead and the assumed perpetrator missing, silence was no longer an option. The police had an eyewitness, but his testimony, while invaluable, was not enough to move the case forward.

Search parties scoured the coastal districts for the runaway killer and tracked Shetty's phone, but the trail went cold quickly. Over time, the file with that tailor's tag was buried under stacks of newer, more pressing investigations. Officers who once led the case had moved on. Witnesses forgot details. Locals stopped discussing the strange end of Shiv Finance and its quarrelling owners. As the seasons changed, from one monsoon to the next, so did the news cycle. The story of two men named Vishwanath – one dead, one vanished – remained idle for over a decade, slipping away from public memory.

In September 2012, Inspector Suresh Kumar P was transferred to Puttur, bringing a fresh eye to the town's older, unresolved cases. Soon after, Udipi Superintendent of Police S. D. Sharanappa encouraged his team to revive cold cases wherever possible. Motivated by the directive, Kumar revisited the Vishwanath Rai file. He found that the original investigating officers had done their part thoroughly – collecting witness testimonies, examining the crime scene and conducting state-wide searches. Still, despite having a prime suspect with a strong motive, the case had remained unresolved. Eleven years on, it seemed unlikely that any new lead would answer questions that had haunted the closed file for over a decade. And yet, there was one question that no one had ever dared to ask: why had there been no hue and cry from Shetty's family?

The disappearance of a close relative can forever alter a family's fabric. But Shetty's wife and child had not done any of the things one might expect in the years since he had vanished. They hadn't filed any reports or contacted the media or raised queries; they hadn't approached the media or demanded answers from investigators. This glaring gap in an otherwise rock-solid case was exactly the break Kumar needed. '[W]hat was suspicious was that Shetty's wife and son continued to live in Kodimbady village in Puttur taluk and never tried to contact the police to know whether he was arrested or traced,' Kumar said. He began digging into the Shetty family. They were still in Puttur, and by some accounts, Shetty's wife worked in a court canteen, but they had never approached the authorities with information or questions of their own. Their silence spoke volumes, but it wasn't enough to find the man they were looking for. For that, the cops needed a lead, and it would come to them from an unexpected source.

Rai's son, now eighteen or nineteen, was quiet and unassuming, though he had become something of a local legend for his cricketing talent. He often participated in regional cricket tournaments and was the envy of many young players in Puttur. On one such morning, as he stepped out to bat like he had so many times before, he had no idea how he was inadvertently leading the police to his fugitive father.

An officer in the crowd watched as the boy stepped away from the pitch and pulled out a cellphone. The device was not one his friends were familiar with, but a smaller and older handset. He checked something on the screen and returned the phone to his bag. In that fleeting moment, he had unknowingly brought a decade-long manhunt to an end. You see, a police investigation in such a small community often runs on more than just evidence – it is fuelled by local gossip. Inspector Kumar worked with a police constable who played cricket in the same circles as Shetty's son. He knew the boy and had noticed something odd: although the son had shared only one number with his teammates, he regularly used two phones. This detail raised suspicion. The police pulled phone records for both numbers registered in the boy's name, one of which told an intriguing story. The number was only used once every two or three months, but when it was, the calls lasted for hours. Shetty's wife had also been seen using that secret phone, and those calls lasted for twenty to thirty minutes. All the calls came from a single number, always from Tamil Nadu. But the question remained: who was on the other side of the phone?

From that point on, the police began methodically tracing the mystery number. Its location shifted now and then, bouncing between Erode district and the border town of Chamarajanagar. These weren't large cities where one could disappear in a crowd. But their heavily forested outskirts and transient populations offered a special cover. The number was not registered to Shetty. On paper, it belonged to someone named Raj Tambi. The name was unfamiliar; the persona, however, was not. 'Raj' had arrived in the area a few years before, claiming that he worked as a driver for a private hospital. Over time, he had quietly built a small-time financing business registered in Sathyamangalam, Erode. He ran chit funds and offered modest loans, carefully avoiding banks or the use of national IDs.

Confident they were on the right track, Puttur police travelled to Sathyamangalam in August 2014. They chose not to alert the local authorities; word couldn't be allowed to spread, not when a fugitive who had evaded them for years was finally within their reach. For three days, they studied Raj's movements from a distance. On the fourth, they closed in on him. The confrontation, years in the making, wasn't really much of a confrontation at all. There was no chase, no standoff. When police arrested 'Raj', the man offered up no resistance. It was almost as if he had been expecting them – it was only a matter of time. Though he insisted that he was Raj Tambi, a fingerprint test identified him beyond any doubt as the absconding Vishwanath Shetty. Thirteen years after the death of Vishwanath Rai, they finally had the man most assumed was responsible in police custody.

When Shetty was brought back to Karnataka, there were no flashing cameras, hungry journalists or large crowds waiting outside the station. Even in an intimate community like Puttur, public memory is fickle. Only Mallika Rai and perhaps Shetty's own family had waited thirteen long years for the day to come. Now, Mallika stood face to face with the man who had once been a friendly and familiar presence in her house. The man who had called her so calmly the morning after her husband's murder and then vanished without a trace. The man who may have killed him.

The case was formally reopened, and fresh charges were filed. Subhas Chandra was contacted once again for his crucial eyewitness testimony. Though older, he had not forgotten the violence he had witnessed on that ill-fated night. What followed was a trial that crawled through procedural delays. Evidence was reviewed. Witnesses were cross-examined. For a time, Shetty was even granted bail and briefly returned to civilian life. Through it all, he firmly maintained his innocence. Finally, in December 2021, the Fifth Additional District and Sessions Court in Puttur announced its verdict. In the eyes of the law, Shetty was guilty. He was sentenced to life imprisonment for murder, five years for destroying evidence and three years for threatening a witness. He was also ordered to pay 95,000 rupees in fines, 60,000 rupees to Mallika Rai and 20,000 rupees to Subhas Chandra.

### ARYAAN
It makes you wonder about the cost of a human life – can that 95,000 rupees make up for the loss of Mallika's husband, or for the trauma and threats that Subhas Chandra endured? Perhaps not, but they might be able to rest easy knowing Shetty has now paid for his crime, in more ways than one.

# 16

# BURIED ALIVE: THE GRISLY MURDER OF SHAKEREH KHALEELI

**AISHWARYA**
Did you know that one of the most common fears in the world is being buried alive? Many of us have at some point woken up after a nightmare where we found ourselves entombed in the ground – drenched in cold sweat, screaming for help, unable to escape. For some, this dark scenario becomes a reality. Such was the case for a beautiful socialite from one of India's most influential families. This is the story of Shakereh Khaleeli.

In 1991, twenty-four-year-old model Sabah found herself looking at a familiar face on a bustling market street in Delhi. Pictures of socialite Shakereh Khaleeli were often splashed across the news, but Sabah knew her as more than just a pretty woman who made a frequent appearance on the tabloids. She knew her more intimately, even if she hadn't seen her in six years. Six years may not be too long to reunite with an old friend or a former colleague. But how about your mother? After a series of unfortunate decisions had driven a wedge between them, Shakereh's and Sabah's paths had long diverged. Yet over time, the mother had yearned to reconnect with her children, and the chance meeting in Delhi was the perfect opportunity to begin mending what had been fractured. They began talking multiple times a day and meeting often. It seemed things were looking up for their relationship, until one day ... radio silence.

Shakereh Khaleeli was born on 27 August 1947, just twelve days after India's independence from the British. She was a descendant of two illustrious families from South India that had left a mark on the nation, long before India as we know it came to exist. Her mother, Gauhar Taj Begum, was the youngest daughter of Sir Mirza Ismail, a prominent Persian statesman who had served as the diwan of the princely states of Mysore, Jaipur and Hyderabad. Shakereh's father, Gulam Hussain Namazie, came from a notable Iranian merchant family. Her childhood was idyllic and sheltered, as her parents' diplomatic and business ventures took them all around the world.

In 1965, eighteen-year-old Shakereh, also known as an elegant singer, was considered eligible for marriage. Her parents arranged the match with her first cousin, Akbar Mirza Khaleeli, a keen sportsman, lawyer and diplomat. Akbar had joined the IFS in 1954, and his early postings took him from Baghdad to Colombo to Paris, and through it all, Shakereh remained by his side. In time, the couple had four daughters:

Zeebundeh Khaleeli was born in 1966 when Shakereh was just nineteen, Sabah Bakache in 1967, Rehane Yavar Dhala in 1969 and Essmath Khaleeli in 1972 when Shakereh was twenty-five. Theirs seemed like a perfect diplomatic family, loving and nurturing despite the constant relocations and new additions. But there was tension bubbling under the surface.

In 1983, the family moved back to India, and that very year, they paid a visit to the erstwhile nawab of Rampur in Delhi. While on that trip, Shakereh and Akbar met a man who would change the course of their lives: Swami Shraddhanand. Born as Murali Manohar Mishra, he had refashioned himself into a self-proclaimed godman. The son of a small-time school teacher from Sagar, Madhya Pradesh, Mishra had dropped out of high school to work as an errand boy to a royal family in Kanpur, eventually evolving into a fixer who assisted them with tax and property matters. Somewhere along this colourful journey, he had adopted the persona of a white-robed holy man.

At the time, Shakereh was actively involved in real estate and had begun managing the numerous family properties she and her siblings were set to inherit. Meeting Shraddhanand, who was introduced to them as someone who specialized in urban landed estates, felt fated. The swami quickly became her advisor on far more than financial matters. Shakereh shared her deepest thoughts with him, especially her desperate desire to have a son – a dream that seemed to grow further from her reach as the years passed. Soon after, Akbar was appointed as the Indian Ambassador to Iran, amidst the Iranian Revolution. In those days, Iran was not a family station, and for the first time in their decades-long marriage, Shakereh did not accompany her husband. Instead, she stayed back in India and invited Shraddhanand to move into her Bangalore residence on 81 Richmond Road. Now with unrestricted access to her time, the scheming godman was able to chip away at her resolve. He began assisting her in matters of property, and above all, convinced her of his occult power and that her only chance to have a baby boy was to have sex with him.

**ARYAAN**
As if Swami Shraddhanand could control that!

**AISHWARYA**
It may sound ridiculous, but somehow, he got Shakereh to believe this. In fact, he led her to upturn her entire life.

Two years passed, and in 1985, when Akbar returned to India, his wife asked for a divorce. A few months later, on 17 April 1986, Shakereh defied all societal norms and resistance from her family and friends to marry Shraddhanand. Their marriage was registered under the Special Marriage Act. After their wedding, Shakereh slowly lost all contact with her parents. Her distraught children chose to support Akbar.

Incidentally, Shakereh's mother, Gauhar Taj, filed at least ten cases against her daughter during her second marriage over various pieces of property. Shakereh distanced herself from her daughters as Shraddhanand placed ultimatums on her relationships. All this while, he was preying on her copious financial assets. According to the Khaleeli family's friends, he earned over 100 million rupees by selling portions of their properties. He convinced Shakereh to grant him a general power of attorney over her estate and executed a testamentary will in his favour, making him both part and, in some cases, sole owner of her assets. She opened many joint bank accounts and issued bank lockers in their joint names. In the event of her death, Shraddhanand would stand to inherit an estate valued at over 6 billion rupees.

Six years into their marriage, Shakereh had realized that her second husband had exploited and isolated her. Their inherent differences had started setting off frequent quarrels. Her reunion with Sabah was the first opportunity she had to revive her frayed ties to the rest of her family. They spent an enchanting month together, and Shakereh seemed overjoyed to rebuild her connection with her daughter. She discussed the possibility of reconnecting with her family, making her sudden disappearance even more suspicious.

Though Sabah had spent years with little contact with her mother, she could sense there was something unnatural about her sudden silence. When in Bombay, Sabah would call her mother a couple of times during the day. Then, she stopped abruptly. Every time she attempted to call Shakereh, she would hear from the swami instead. He would insist her mother was in Surat for a wedding, travelling to Hyderabad or lying low after a tax issue. Once, when she attempted to call her mother's landline, Shraddhanand informed her that

Shakereh was pregnant and was refusing to speak to her family to avoid any bad luck. Sabah rushed to meet her mother in Bangalore, but she was not there. Shraddhanand told her that she was being treated at the Roosevelt Hospital in New York. A contact at the hospital squashed this claim. When Sabah confronted Shraddhanand about the false information, he told her Shakereh was in London and had wanted to keep her whereabouts under wraps. The ruse completely fell apart when, just a few weeks later, Sabah spotted her mother's passport in Shraddhanand's hotel room. One glance through it, and it was confirmed that her mother hadn't stepped out of the country.

In 1992, Sabah visited Bangalore, bringing with her a beautiful pale-yellow chiffon sari embroidered with sequins. While dropping off the gift, Sabah noticed that many of her mother's expensive saris were missing from her wardrobe. It had been months now since anyone had seen her in public, but Shraddhanand had continued to host lavish parties at their Bangalore residence. The backyard of 81, Richmond Road shimmered with fine lights and pulsed with music as guests danced and dined to their heart's content. Everyone knew where the money for these events was coming from: Shakereh's inheritance. Even the house belonged to Shakereh. Still, whenever a guest asked about his wife, the consummate storyteller always had a new tale ready.

At a wedding performed by the swami in Bombay, Sabah was flabbergasted to see an unfamiliar woman dressed in one of Shakereh's most beloved saris. By then, Sabah had stopped buying into his excuses. She began to frequent events where she knew Shraddhanand would be present, hoping to catch a glimpse of her mother. In August 1992, Sabah visited the Bangalore residence again, leaving behind two saris and a birthday card for her mother. When she returned a few months later, the yellow sari appeared to have been worn, and the birthday card was on display. Shraddhanand explained that he had given Shakereh the gifts in London but brought back one of the saris and the card, since he was fond of the sentiment written inside. On 10 June 1992, Sabah decided to register an official complaint at the Ashok Nagar Police Station.

The cops arrested Shraddhanand, and though he was able to obtain anticipatory bail, he had to submit a written promise to show up at the station every Monday for the next three months. In fact, he had even declared complete innocence in his petition, stating that constant legal issues with her family had pushed Shakareh to depression, and she had run away in a fit of anger while he was away from home. During the first few meetings with the police, he continued to spin the same tall tales. But the cracks in his excuses – the same ones Sabah had noticed – began to shine through. Finally, on 28 March 1994, the swami broke down during an intense session of interrogation and made a statement that would shatter the Khaleeli family once again:

> If I am taken I will show the place where the wooden box was prepared and the person who prepared it, the persons who transported the box and the people who helped in digging

out the pit and the crow bar, spade, pan used for digging pit, the cement bags and the spot where Shakereh is buried. I will exhume her dead body and show you. The statement what all I had earlier given to Ashok Nagar police was a false statement given intentionally just to escape myself.

As the police sat him in their car, Shraddhanand began spouting directions. Their quick journey past winding roads and traffic lights ended right in front of 81, Richmond Road. The repellent man had buried Shakereh Khaleeli in her own house.

#### AISHWARYA
```
If at this moment you're not having flashbacks of the
dancing and partying in the backyard I mentioned some
time ago, I haven't told this story right.
```

Shraddhanand was handed a piece of chalk and asked to mark the body's location. He walked to the centre of the backyard and drew a line on the ground. A minute into digging the loamy earth, the metal spades struck something solid. Slowly, the exhumation team unearthed a 2x7x2 wooden box, resembling a casket. When opened, it revealed a nearly entirely decomposed body; only its hair and bones remained. A thin mattress, a sleeping gown, a pillow and bed sheets cushioned the corpse. Most haunting of all, one of Shakereh's hands appeared to be clutching the mattress beneath the box, and scratch marks lined the inside of the box.

**ARYAAN**
Wait. Does that mean she was buried alive?

**AISHWARYA**
All signs seemed to indicate that's what happened, though the heavy decomposition makes it hard to say anything for certain. Apparently, if you're buried alive in a coffin, you can survive for up to five hours if you remain calm. Just the thought of her there for five hours, desperately trying to find a way out …

Dr Nissar Ahmed, who oversaw the exhumation, had the entire process filmed. For the first time in the history of the Indian judicial system, footage of an exhumation was submitted as evidence to the court. Gauhar Taj was called to identify her daughter's body, and she recognized a red stone ring and two black rings. A domestic worker identified the gown. The teeth and hair were compared to Shakereh's parents' DNA to confirm that the corpse belonged to her. This was the first time DNA testing was used to identify a victim in India.

The trial against Shraddhanand began in late 1997. In his statement, he described how, on 25 May 1991, he had asked for tea to be prepared for the two of them. Unbeknownst to Shakereh, he had laced her tea with a heavy dose of sleeping pills. Once she passed out, he dragged the mattress she lay on into a long box he had commissioned under the pretence of transporting furniture. He lightly covered the spot with dirt, and the following day, he hired wage labourers to cover it up.

The police suspected Shraddhanand would not have been able to carry her body alone, and soon, half a dozen domestic workers were questioned as accomplices. On 21 May 2005, the Civil and Sessions Judge B.S. Totad sentenced Murali Manohar Mishra to capital punishment by hanging – a verdict he reportedly received with little emotion. Today, Mishra is still alive, after his death sentence was commuted to life imprisonment in 2008. Meanwhile, though Shakereh lost her life when she was only forty-four, her memory is preserved by the daughter who fought so fiercely to bring her justice.

## 17

# THE SICKLY-SWEET SMELL OF MURDER: THE JOSHI-ABHYANKAR MASSACRES

**AISHWARYA**

Between 25 June 1975 to 21 March 1977, Indian democracy faced one of its gravest tests. Prime Minister Indira Gandhi's declaration of Emergency suspended civil liberties, weakened the judiciary and imposed mass censorship of the press. To speak our generation's language, India was a hot mess for a hot minute. Despite the political crackdown, daily life for most Indians went on much as before – and the laid-back city of Pune was no exception. That changed abruptly when a murderous rampage brought the city to a screeching halt. Safe spaces and ordinary homes turned into a killing ground. This is the terrible tale of the Joshi-Abhyankar murders.

On 15 January 1976, Sundar Hegde, a hotel owner, returned home to find his wife anxious – she hadn't heard from their son, Prakash, all day. At first, the couple tried to remain calm. After all, he was a young college student in a city with a blossoming nightlife. But as the hours passed, their unease only intensified. Then came a note, in their son's handwriting.

He wrote that he was leaving home of his own accord and needed 25,000 rupees from his parents. No explanation, just a final 'goodbye, forever'. It didn't add up. Prakash was a caring son and a dedicated student at Abhinav Kala Mahavidyalaya, the local arts college. His parents couldn't believe he would disappear with nothing more than a note. Their gnawing suspicions deepened when Sundar noticed how the note had been signed: 'Prakash'. At home, they always called their son Devdas, not Prakash. They knew, with certainty, that something was very wrong.

**AISHWARYA**
```
Honestly, Aryaan, I completely understand their alarm.
Everyone who knows me personally calls me Isha. If I
were to leave my parents a note and sign it 'Aishwarya',
they'd freak out.
```

The Hegdes showed the police the note when they reported Prakash missing, but the unusual sign-off – very significant in their eyes – failed to convince investigators that Prakash hadn't simply run away. Over time, his case was buried under a pile of more pressing files, and his parents were left waiting in vain, hoping against hope for a son who would never come home.

While the Emergency consumed national attention, most headlines were captivated by the government's everyday violations of India's democratic institutions. It wasn't surprising when, amidst the political uproar, an unrelated incident in August 1976 went unnoticed by the media. In Kolhapur, a nearby city, an oil businessman named Arvind

Kashid was attacked by four men in his home. Though their robbery attempt proved unsuccessful, the assailants escaped unscathed. This incident was quickly dismissed as another petty crime, and its link to Prakash's disappearance would remain hidden until much later.

Two months later, the police were confronted with another seemingly unrelated crime. But this time, it was too gruesome to look away. On 31 October 1976, in Pune's Vijaynagar area, three bodies had been discovered: businessman Achyut Joshi, his wife Usha and their son, Anand. Each body had pieces of cloth stuffed in the mouths, limbs bound together and necks strangled with blue nylon rope. The teenage boy was found completely naked, an unsettling detail that stood out to the investigators, led by Assistant Commissioner of Police Madhusudan Hulyalkar. Inside, the house reeked of perfume, its scent too overpowering to be pleasant. The family's belongings had been ransacked: money was gone, silver idols had been stolen and the cupboards had been stripped of valuables, including Usha's mangalsutra and Achyut's luxury watch. Although the operation required more than one person, no fingerprints or traces of DNA were found at the scene. Whether this was a result of police oversight, careful planning by the killers or simply the limitations of forensic science in the seventies remains unclear.

The gruesome Joshi murders had already put the entire city on red alert when the next incident occurred. On 22 November 1976, a panic-stricken Yashomati Bafna rushed to the Pune police. Four men had broken into her home on Shankarsheth Road and tried to rob her, but her staff had fought them off. Amidst the mayhem, she noticed that three of the men were deferring to a fourth man they called 'Boss'. Bafna's complaint was duly noted, but once again, the police failed to connect it to the growing pattern of violence in their jurisdiction. Just a week later, this lapse would prove fatal once again.

On 1 December 1976, the police were called to a sprawling bungalow named 'Smriti' on Bhandarkar Road. The beautiful home of the Abhyankar family, members of Pune's intellectual elite, had become the scene of a massacre. Eighty-eight-year-old Sanskritist Mahamahopadhyaya Kashinath Shastri Abhyankar had been brutally murdered, along with his wife Indirabai (seventy-six), their house-help Sakhubai Wagh (sixty) and two grandchildren: twenty-year-old Jui and nineteen-year-old Dhananjay. The children's parents had returned around 10 p.m. after an outing only to discover the bloodied remains of their lives. Just as in the Joshi case, the victims' hands and feet were bound, blue nylon rope cinched around their necks and cloth forced into their mouths. Again, money and valuables worth more than 30,000 rupees had gone missing, and no forensic evidence remained. And once more, the sickening scent of perfume greeted the horrified investigators as they found young Jui's body, stripped of her clothing. Pune had become a hunting ground for a band of serial killers, with a specific modus operandi and no trail.

After the Abhyankar murders, fear and hysteria gripped Pune. People stopped leaving their houses after sunset and refused to open their homes to strangers. Movie halls ran shows to empty halls, and restaurants sat deserted. The Pune police called in the Central Reserve Police Force (CRPF) to help patrol the streets. If India was already in a state of national crisis, Pune was now facing an emergency of its own. Despite the state's heightened vigilance, the murderers struck again.

This time, on 24 March 1977, a young man's body was found tied to a metal ladder leading into the Mula-Mutha river. Weighed down by boulders, the corpse had still managed to fight its way to the surface. Unlike the others, there was no gag or bound limbs – only the now all-too-familiar blue nylon rope. That's when Inspector Manikrao Damame noted another overlooked detail: the knot used was identical to the Joshi and Abhyankar murders. The victim was soon identified as Anil Gokhale, whose brother Jayant was a student at the Abhinav Kala Mahavidyalaya.

**ARYAAN**
Where have I heard that name before?

**AISHWARYA**
Right at the beginning of our story. Prashant Hegde was a student at Abhinav Kala Mahavidyalaya. That's the common link that finally broke this case open.

Anil Gokhale's post-mortem report indicated that he had died within twenty-four hours of being found. This meant that the killers likely hadn't fled the area yet. That wouldn't be the case for long; the police didn't have much time. They decided to pursue their most solid lead so far: Abhinav Kala Mahavidyalaya. The list of suspects was further narrowed when a group of infamous students of the college – Rajendra Yallappa

Jakkal, Dilip Dnyanoba Sutar, Shantaram Kanhoji Jagtap and Munawar Harun Shah – took an unusual interest in the investigation. The boys visited the station repeatedly, inquiring about the progress in the case and disrupting police work.

When police questioned their fellow students on campus, it was confirmed that Jakkal was the last person seen with Anil – the two were riding his motorcycle the day Anil went missing. Officers found Jakkal near the college gate and took him into custody. When questioned about his whereabouts at the time of the murder, Jakkal claimed he had been with his three friends: Sutar, Jagtap and Shah. Overnight, the four became prime suspects. The group's lack of preparedness was evident from the fact that none of their stories quite added up, yet none would confess. ACP Hulyalkar knew that he needed to break through to one of the men and learn the truth. He focused on Jakkal, the apparent ringleader of the operation. In a quiet moment, he offered Jakkal a cigarette, lighting it himself with his lighter. Then, he continued the interrogation. Though the young man refused to name the perpetrators, he divulged something shocking: that he believed Anil Gokhale's death was connected to the *murder* of Prakash Hegde.

**ARYAAN**
Wait a second. Do we know for sure that Prakash was dead? I know you implied it, but hadn't the police called it a missing person case?

**AISHWARYA**
Exactly! Jakkal's casual comment prompted them to go back to Prakash's case, and as it turned out that no one

> – no news channel, not the police, not his parents – had ever publicly called it a murder. I mean, his body was never found.

Another important piece of evidence was the final confirmation that Hulyalkar needed: reportedly a bottle of perfume that matched the one used in the Joshi–Abhyankar killings was found among Jakkal's belongings. But with the four friends refusing to cooperate with the investigation, the Pune police were forced to let them go, for the moment. But they weren't ready to abandon the case. Plainclothes officers shadowed the suspects day and night. During the surveillance, they overheard the men reassuring each other that 'Boss' would take care of the police for them. The name struck a chord: Yashomati Bafna described the same figure during the attempted robbery. Another piece had been added to the ever-expanding story.

Meanwhile, as the police interrogated other students at the academy, a timid young man named Satish Gore came forward. He admitted that the four men had frequently bragged to him about the murders. According to Gore, there was a fifth member of the group: Suhas Chandak. The investigators decided to give the 'divide-and-rule' strategy another try. They brought Chandak into custody and told him they could link him to the murders, but if he cooperated and testified, he would be offered protection as a state witness. Chandak instantly broke down. He confessed where Prakash Hegde's body had been hidden and events of the night of his murder, though he maintained he had no part to play in the remaining nine killings.

Using Chandak's statement, the police were able to arrest all four accused on 20 March 1977, seven days after Anil Gokhale's murder. At the time of their arrest, their ages spanned from twenty-one to twenty-five. After hours of questioning, suffocated by the realization that they were truly caught, the full story came spilling out.

The four first bonded at Abhinav Kala Mahavidyalaya, drawn to each other by shared vices and a reputation for trouble. On campus, they were notorious for being heavy drinkers, eve-teasers and generally ill-behaved troublemakers; the university administration had tried more than once to discipline them. The men were desperate for money. Unlike many of their privileged classmates, they came from disadvantaged households with fewer resources and limited financial support. At first, they started stealing cycles and bikes parked outside the university and selling their parts. Soon, small thefts became inadequate. They decided to plan and execute a larger burglary, one whose spoils would sustain them for a longer time. Prakash Hegde, the son of a wealthy hotel owner whose popular restaurant was right across from the college, was their golden ticket.

They enlisted Suhas Chandak's help to lure Prakash to a shed owned by Jakkal, a place where the group often gathered to get drunk in the evenings. In a display of bone-chilled cruelty, the group had forced Prakash to write his ransom note and killed him soon after. A terrified Chandak fled the scene, having signed up for nothing more than a kidnapping. But this was cold-blooded murder. He vowed that he would never tell anybody about what had happened. The others put

Prakash's corpse in a metal drum, weighed it down with rocks and threw it into the nearby Peshwe Park lake. What they hadn't anticipated was that Prakash's parents would sense that something was wrong with the note they had received and refuse to pay the ransom.

After Prakash's murder, the group changed tactics. Now they began breaking into houses, burglarizing and killing their residents. Though their first attempt at the businessman's house in Kolhapur had failed, they robbed and finished the Joshi family soon after. Usha and Achyut Joshi were spending a quiet night at home when the gang forced their way into the house, armed with knives. While they were tying up the couple, their teenage son Anand entered and was instantly overpowered. They killed his parents in front of him, then stripped him naked and demanded he reveal where the family stored their valuables. A frightened Anand complied. They stuffed cloth into his mouth, strangled him with blue nylon rope, and sprayed perfume throughout the house, hoping to throw police dogs off their scent.

#### ARYAAN
Do we have any idea why they stripped Anand while leaving his parents clothed?

#### AISHWARYA
The gang thought that making the last surviving member strip would make them hesitate to run outside for help. The logic seems twisted to me. I know it's just hypothetical, but rest assured, if my parents had been killed in front of me and I was about to die, that wouldn't stop me.

After the failed robbery at Yashomati Bafna's house, they set their sights on the Abhyankars, and this time, they succeeded. They simply rang the bell and walked in with knives. Following the same modus operandi, they forced young Jui to watch as her grandparents, younger brother and their house-help were killed before her eyes. She was then stripped and murdered in the same brutal fashion. The public outcry after the Abhyankar killings made it impossible for the men to repeat their past actions. Anil Gokhale was simply a victim of circumstances. The younger brother of one of their classmates, Jayant Gokhale, Anil had accepted a lift from Jakkal, a familiar face. He took him to the same shed where they had killed Prakash Hegde, murdered Anil and dumped his body, stealing the little money that he had on him.

Having confessed, the four men were sent to prison to await trial. Prosecutor Shamrao G. Samant argued the case in the Pune Sessions Court, and in just over four months, they were sentenced to death by Judge Waman Narayan Bapat. The verdict – classifying the case as 'rarest of the rare' – was widely accepted as a fitting punishment for their brutal reign of terror. However, even as the residents of Pune and the victims' families experienced some semblance of relief, the convicted men requested a presidential pardon. When denied, they appealed to the Supreme Court, asking to be executed via the electric chair rather than by hanging.

#### AISHWARYA
Their argument was, and try not to die of irony here, that hanging was unnecessarily painful. Can you believe

> that? These men had brutally strangled ten people but were afraid to face death themselves. They were seeking sympathy when they had shown their victims none.

Medical and legal experts from across the country were contacted to resolve this issue, though many thought the men were just buying time. Eventually, it was unanimously agreed that there was nothing uniquely painful about hanging. In fact, electric chairs were considered more inhumane and have been banned in many countries across the world. So, on 27 November 1983, seven years after the murderous rampage began, Rajendra Jakkal, Dilip Sutar, Shantaram Kanhoji Jagtap and Munawar Harun Shah were hanged at Yerawada Central Jail.

Till the very end, they displayed little remorse for shattering the lives of four families, and in many ways, tearing apart the fabric of Pune itself.

# 18

# A DEADLY VIRAL VIDEO: THE KOHISTAN KILLINGS

**ARYAAN**
Do you remember the videos shot on Nokia phone cameras in the 2010s? Highly pixelated, nearly unusable in the dark, yet many of us preserved precious memories, however blurry they were, because of them. In 2012, an innocent video taken on a two-megapixel Nokia camera sent shockwaves around the world. It had originated in the isolated region of Kohistan, Pakistan. To someone unfamiliar with the case, the video may appear to capture a joyful moment, and perhaps it was. But what followed once it went viral was far from happy. This is the story of a moment caught on video that resulted in eight deaths. This is the story of the Kohistan video murders.

Kohistan lies at the juncture of the Himalayas, the Karakorum and the Hindukush, tucked away in Khyber Pakhtunkhwa (KPK), Pakistan. Surrounded by snowy mountains and rich in ecological diversity, the region is a beautiful sight. However, a bird's-eye view can never truly capture the lived reality of a place and in Kohistan, this contrast is all too stark. Just 175 kilometres from Islamabad, Kohistan feels worlds apart from the capital. It has the lowest human development index in KPK, reflecting the region's limited life expectancy, poor access to education and low gross income levels.

In Kohistan's steep, rocky terrain, one quickly notices a conspicuous absence of women in public spaces. The region's location makes it difficult for Pakistani authorities to administer or even reach, meaning national laws have little impact on the ground. In this deeply patriarchal society, that relative autonomy from centralized power rarely works in the favour of Kohistani women. Education and paid work are tightly controlled, limited mostly to tending family land or domestic tasks. Moreover, their freedom of movement is heavily restricted. In 2010, a single video directly violated all spoken and unspoken rules of this insular community, and its consequences were devastating.

In May 2012, over a year after the video was recorded, an MMS began circulating rapidly through Kohistan, spreading like wildfire. It showed a moment from a wedding held in the village of Gadaar. Four women – later identified as Bazeegha, Siran Jan, Begum Jan and Amina – were singing and clapping along. The bright young girls were dressed in traditional clothing, their heads covered in colourful patterned scarves. Across from them, a man named Gul Nazar was spinning in graceful circles, a traditional dance movement. Off-camera,

Gul's brother, Bin Yasir, was recording the scene, alongside a fifth girl, Shaheen.

When this video was made public, it provoked outrage among local menfolk, who saw the mingling of unmarried women and unrelated men from another tribe as a grave transgression of local customs. In Gadar's hyper-patriarchal environment, this was viewed not only as a violation of the honour of the women in the video but as an unforgivable disgrace to their families and the community. All four women who were captured on film were soon held captive by members of their families in a single, cramped room, and a jirga was called to decide their future.

**ARYAAN**
```
A jirga is essentially a quasi-legal tribal council,
composed exclusively of male elders in the community.
Their decision, especially in a close community like
Kohistan, where formal law enforcement has little sway,
was binding.
```

The elders in the jirga declared that everyone involved had breached their community's honour. The council ordered the execution not only of the four women who were seen on the video but also of Gul Nazar and Bin Yasir. The brothers, members of the smaller Salehkhel tribe, now faced retribution from the dominant Azadkhel tribe to which the girls belonged. The latter held a 75 per cent majority in Gadaar. But the two men had a small window of time to escape, and they took it. They fled their village, leaving behind their ancestral home and family history for a chance to keep their lives. Several Salehkhel folk followed, recognizing that the dispute had snowballed into a raging inter-community conflict. The women had no such opportunity, but they *did* find an unlikely supporter.

Afzal Kohistani, Gul Nazar's and Bin Yasir's elder brother, lived in Gadaar with his wife and brothers. Despite the deadly repercussions of his actions, Afzal risked his life to raise his voice against the jirga's immutable decision. He defied the council's ruling and reported its members and the girls' families to the police, hoping that their deaths could be prevented. But the local authorities proved to be powerless. After enduring thirty days of inhumane torture, all four women were reportedly murdered on 30 May. Four precious lives, finished before they could truly begin, for no greater crime than enjoying a moment of celebration.

Refusing to let their story die with them, Afzal travelled 145 kilometres to the northwestern city of Abbottabad, where he spoke at a packed press conference, vehemently criticizing the barbaric punishment inflicted on his brothers and the four women. On the same day, 4 June 2012, the story was broadcast across Pakistan. Within hours, the country's Supreme Court ordered police personnel in Kohistan to investigate, and just as quickly – perhaps a tad *too* quickly – the local police reverted with a report. They rubbished Afzal's claims, insisting that no jirga had been conducted, and none of the women had been murdered. Unconvinced, Chief Justice Iftikhar Muhammad Chaudhry ordered that the women be brought to Islamabad the very next day. In a shocking show of defiance, Kohistani officials refused, arguing that appearing in court would dishonour the women and violate the rules of purdah. The same rigid beliefs that had justified the deaths of the victims were now thwarting the course of justice.

### ARYAAN
```
This is a frustrating theme that keeps reappearing in
this case. The perpetrators hid in the dark shadows of
tradition to protect themselves from scrutiny. But as
with all oppressive power structures, there were voices
of dissent fighting back. In this case, those bravely
speaking out against blindly obeying tradition changed
everything.
```

Around the same time, the National Commission on the Status of Women (NCSW) had filed a petition before the Supreme Court for constitutional safeguards against illegal practices in jirgas – a system long linked to the bloody trail of honour killings and acts of violence against Pakistani women. Several notable women's rights advocates were present in Islamabad to support the petition, including feminist activist and scholar Dr Farzana Bari, who had been keeping a close eye on the developments. Noticing her presence in court, Chief Justice Chaudhry recommended she accompany Interior Minister Rehman Malik in visiting Gadaar to provide an objective and independent assessment of the situation. Bari invited fellow members of NCSW: Shabeena Ayaz, Dr Fouzia Saeed and Riffat Inam Butt. Within an hour, the impromptu fact-finding delegation gathered outside the Islamabad Marriott and boarded a helicopter bound for KPK.

### AISHWARYA

Honestly, I'm a little surprised at how swiftly the case seems to be moving. The Supreme Court's adjudication and even the creation of the task force were so quick. I'm so used to hearing about cases being mishandled by an inefficient early investigation.

### ARYAAN

I felt the same while doing my research. Prompt action was key to ensure the perpetrators would not have time to stage the scene in their favour. But when the delegation landed in Kohistan, they realized that those who held power in the local system had no intention of allowing a fair inquiry.

The Kohistani landscape can be hostile for outsiders. When the visitors flew into the Kolai-Palas area, they could not land directly in Gadaar since the village was on a high cliff. Instead, they were dropped off at a remote valley below the village. Though locals had been informed of their visit, only Maulana Mohammad Javed Azad, who was allegedly involved in the jirga, came to meet them. Refusing to acknowledge any wrongdoing, the cleric would later deny not only being involved in issuing a fatwa (decree) calling for the executions but also ever having watched the video in the first place.

The trek to Gadaar was arduous. After what felt like hours of walking, the group was met halfway by a girl draped in red clothing. She was introduced as Amina. She claimed that they had never consented to being filmed, a statement that subtly shifted some of the blame away from the women in the video. This perspective may have protected the girls at one point, but it only served to mislead the investigators now.

**AISHWARYA**
```
I'm not so sure I believe that either. It's obvious in the
video that Gul Nazar wasn't hiding the camera. If that
had been the case, surely the girls would have noticed
and reacted.
```

**ARYAAN**
```
It's definitely strange, but there was no way to disprove
her, especially in the presence of a male elder who enjoys
considerable power in the community.
```

When the committee members asked for the three other women in the video, Maulana Azad gestured towards the distant hills. Despite their shared ties to the same closely knit community, he claimed the girls had moved to three separate areas in the mountains and were unavailable to meet the committee. Having collected next to no evidence and barred from entering Gadaar, local authorities pressurized the researchers to return to Islamabad. Their sole finding – that Amina was alive – was shaky at best.

Snubbing the unchecked power of Kohistan's cabal of male elders, a second task force was formed, this time headed by District and Sessions Judge Munira Abbasi. Dr Bari returned as the only women's rights advocate, and she was joined by KPK Information Minister Mian Iftikhar Hussain and politician, Bushra Gohar. On 16 June, the Munira Commission travelled to Kohistan. Despite assurances of an impartial and well-trained translator and adequate security arrangements, neither promise was fulfilled. Instead, the translators provided were members of the girls' families – far from an unbiased party. Inside a tent, the men had brought two young women with them, whom they claimed were Siran Jan and Begum Jan.

> **ARYAAN**
> I've seen the footage from this meeting, and the fear in the girls' eyes is palpable. They look like lambs awaiting slaughter – they know perfectly well that the smallest misstep might prove fatal.

The two young women were questioned, filmed and had their photographs and fingerprints taken. When asked about Bazeegha, the men said she was pregnant and could not travel, a completely different explanation from their earlier story. Bari remained sceptical. She requested special permission to stay another night so she could visit Bazeegha's home herself. In response, she was bluntly told to proceed at her own risk. For a lone woman, seen locally as an outsider and an agitator, this wasn't an option to pursue in a place like Kohistan. Instead, when the committee submitted its findings, Bari wrote a 'dissenting note', making clear she did not entirely endorse the conclusions put forward by Abbasi. With no definitive evidence of the murders, the chief justice closed the case, although he allowed it to be reopened if new evidence came to light, acknowledging Bari's unresolved doubts.

> **AISHWARYA**
> And was it?
>
> **ARYAAN**
> It certainly was.

On 3 January 2013, three of Afzal's brothers were viciously murdered in their home in Gadaar. A group of men raided their house and unleashed a fury of bullets. None of the victims had appeared in the controversial video. Nor had they been involved in the legal struggles that had unfolded since then. Unlike many Salehkhels who had fled, they had chosen to remain in Gadaar, with the faith that it was their home as much as anyone else's. It was a conviction for which they paid with their lives. The murder of the three men was widely construed as an act of revenge by the still-enraged families of the women; a message to Afzal and his community that the hatchet had not been buried.

Six men were convicted for the killings in 2014, but their sentences were later overturned. By then, the once-impressive momentum of the investigation had stalled; the case was declared closed, and both the media and judiciary had largely stopped paying attention. Afzal, however, refused to let the injustice be forgotten, even if the public had moved on. The only other person who was still fighting alongside him was Katharine Houreld, a *Reuters* correspondent he had met at their Islamabad office back in 2012, when he was desperately searching for someone who would hear him out.

#### ARYAAN
We reached out to Katharine while writing this, and she took us through the facts of the case, from an insider's perspective. Her on-ground reporting made her familiar with the ground reality in Pakistan, where violence against women and honour killings are systemic issues. In fact, Pakistan has the highest number of documented

honour killings in the world, even today – around 1,000 each year. And those are just the official numbers.

Katharine candidly told us how her 'binder was crammed with cases of women pounded to death, girls strangled, pregnant women shot, sisters and daughters drowned and beaten … Honour killings were so common – several each day – we could rarely cover them … Too frequent. Couldn't get it past the desk'. But like Afzal, she refused to give up on this case.

Katharine managed to track down the headshots of the women taken by the Munira Commission in 2012. Meanwhile, an anonymous source from Kohistan provided her with national identity cards of Begum Jan, Siran Jan and Amina, which included their pictures and fingerprints. Examining closely, Katharine immediately noticed a subtle but significant discrepancy. In Begum Jan's identity card photo, she had a small, raised mole above her left lip, while the photo taken by the committee showed a flat mole in a slightly different spot. Though intriguing, this evidence was not compelling enough to reopen a case that the government had so painstakingly investigated. So, Katharine and Afzal opted to send the pictures to a British company for facial recognition analysis. The results were striking: Begum Jan's identity card photo and a screengrab from the original video were a 49.5 per cent match, solidly confirming her identity. In contrast, the ID card and the picture taken by the second commission were only a 17.4 per cent match. The discrepancy was damning.

Armed with this new evidence, Afzal submitted a petition requesting that the women be brought to the court so their fingerprints could be studied. Their families contested his petition in the Peshawar High Court, arguing that a related hearing was already pending in the Supreme Court. The High Court sided with the families. Undeterred, Afzal took his petition to the Supreme Court with the support of the NCSW. Once again, Gadaar locals said that their traditions forbade them from presenting women in court. Justice Ejaz Afzal Khan rejected this justification and called for another commission to visit Kohistan and verify whether the girls in the video were alive and well.

When the commission arrived, a few local girls were brought before them, but the team was not permitted to photograph them. One member of the committee, Kohistan's District and Sessions Judge Shoaib Khan, later reported that the girls seemed extremely nervous and their words were controlled by the elders around them. They appeared noticeably younger than the women in the video would have been, given the years that had passed. Khan also claimed that the girl introduced to them as 'Amina' had had her fingerprints burned off, making any attempt to verify her identity impossible.

Yet another investigation unfolded in July 2018 in which Bari played a key role. Finally, the team was able to conclude that three of the girls, Begum Jan, Siran Jan and Bazeegha, had certainly been murdered. Amina might have survived, though the previous commission's allegation that her fingerprints had been burned off stank of foul play. Eight tribesmen were arrested and charged in connection with the killings. In September 2019, Bazeegha's father, Begum Jan's brother and Siran Jan's father were convicted of murder and sentenced to life in prison. After years of waiting and the crashing waves of unimaginable loss, justice had finally been attained, in some capacity. However, it had come too late, not just for the women in that video but for their greatest champion.

On 7 March 2019, Afzal was in Abbottabad for a court hearing. On days when he had to travel into town for hearings, he was most vulnerable: his location was public, and his movements became conspicuous and easy to track. Despite repeated requests to the police for additional security, given the constant threats and harassment he and his family faced because of the case, his requests were denied every time. On that fateful day, his worst fears came true. He was publicly assassinated, shot dead in broad daylight on a busy shopping street.

This was a man who had struggled for years to tell a story that he could have easily ignored and let go, who had lost nearly all his family to a seconds-long video. At one point, his home had been firebombed, and he had only moved and continued his work. After Afzal's death, Katharine wrote,

> I was angry with all the people who failed him, who hadn't returned his calls and messages, who were honour-bound and bloody well paid to support him in his fight and who had chosen to watch from the sidelines. I was mad I didn't try harder to write his story ... I was sad to think that he was one of many who died in vain. I am sad that I won't see his bright white smile again.

### ARYAAN

Katharine's words remind me of something Afzal said after his brothers were murdered: that he would give his life if it meant they would be brought to justice and that their story would not be forgotten. In the end, that's why this story was so important to us, too. This is our small attempt to remember Afzal and his brothers, Bazeegha, Siran Jan, Begum Jan and Amina, and the hundreds of others across South Asia who are killed every year in the name of honour.

# 19

# GONE WITHOUT A TRACE: THE SUDDEN DISAPPEARANCE OF THE CHOHAN FAMILY

**AISHWARYA**

The prospect of simply disappearing into thin air is more common than we might want to accept. Parents often caution their children, concocting scary tales to warn them against strangers or straying too far from home. Most of the time, these stories are about children or young women going missing, like the tragic story of Geeta and Sanjay Chopra - siblings who were kidnapped and later murdered in 1978 - that shook the country. However, in this case, three generations of an entire family vanished overnight. They went missing without a trace. This prompted one of Scotland Yard's most complicated manhunts, spanning four countries, 4,000 documents and a ten-million-pound trial. This is the story of the Chohan family.

On 15 February 2003, journalist Onkar Verma woke up in his New Zealand home with a growing sense of unease. For two days, he had been calling the landline at his sister's house in Hounslow, suburban London, but no one had answered.

The siblings had moved from India to different countries, and it had been nine years since they had seen each other. But even with Nancy heading to the UK, they continued to be very close and spoke often. Nancy had recently given birth to her second son, Ravinder, and she regularly sent pictures of her newborn and his older brother, Devinder, an eighteen-month-old toddler. Their mother, Charanjit Kaur, who had stayed with Nancy throughout her pregnancy and was now supporting her daughter through the chaotic early days of motherhood, had also been completely silent. Onkar felt every mile of the 7,000 that separated them – and he had reason to be worried.

Just two days ago, Nancy had faced the same crippling anxiety. Her husband, Amarjit Singh Chohan, a successful businessman twenty years her senior, had suddenly vanished. He hadn't come home after work or answered her calls and text messages. Running his company, CIBA Freight, took up much of Amarjit's time and kept him very busy. Even then, it was highly unusual for him to leave Nancy in the dark as to his whereabouts.

When she had called the office to check in with him, an employee reassured her that nothing was wrong. Amarjit had simply flown out to the Netherlands for work. It still seemed bizarre that he would leave the country without telling her, but the CIBA team was close-knit, and their calm answers eased her nerves for the moment. Soon, she realized something that made her stomach churn. Amarjit couldn't have left for the Netherlands, or anywhere outside the UK, since the couple had recently submitted their passports to the UK Home Office to process their British residency permit. So where was her husband? Just days earlier, he'd been at home, filming home videos with her and their children. Later that day, Nancy thought she had finally had an answer when she received a voicemail from Amarjit's number. Relief washed over her, until she pressed play and heard her husband's voice: 'Hello Nancy. Don't panic. I'm OK. I'll be back tomorrow.'

### AISHWARYA

```
This may sound like a perfectly normal message, but
Amarjit always spoke to his wife in Punjabi. This small
discrepancy was enough to make Nancy reach out to her
brother in panic. Onkar assured her that things were
probably fine, unaware of the eerie turn their lives
would soon take. Soon, Onkar too would be in a similar
spot, left fumbling in the dark after both his sister and
mother suddenly stopped all communication.
```

After waiting a day with no word from his sister or mother, Onkar wrote to the London Metropolitan Police, requesting an inquiry into his family's mysterious disappearance. Officers made a brief visit to the home, only to find it empty. Neighbours hadn't heard or seen anything suspicious, and to the police, it seemed perfectly plausible that they had simply gone away. In 2003, international calls were expensive and difficult – perhaps Nancy just hadn't had the time to inform her brother. To them, that seemed more likely than an entire family vanishing with an explanation. The cops informed Onkar that they weren't going to launch a search for the family yet. Onkar didn't accept the lukewarm response. Unconvinced, he applied for a UK visa, and on 5 March 2003, landed in London and headed straight to his sister's house.

As Onkar stepped into the Chohan's home, nothing seemed amiss at first. It looked ordinary, exactly as the police had suggested. But the normalcy itself grew more disturbing the longer Onkar walked through the silent rooms. It felt as if the family had simply vanished mid-sentence, leaving life frozen behind them. Toys were scattered all over the floor; the refrigerator, stocked with food, was still running. The washing machine was still loaded with clothes. Onkar also found his mother's flight ticket back to India. But the date had passed. Most troubling of all, Charanjit's Guru Granth Sahib lay on the table, untouched. She never left the house without her holy book.

Onkar went back to the police, and this time, they searched the house thoroughly and interrogated friends, neighbours and colleagues. When they spoke to Amarjit's employees, they uncovered a key detail that even Onkar had not known. CIBA Freight had been sold on 17 February, only days after Amarjit had gone missing, followed by the rest of his family. An employee named Kenneth Regan had broken the news to the rest of the team and introduced a woman named Belinda Brewin as the company's new director. Although the staff were sceptical at first, they recalled Amarjit mentioning plans to retire and return to India. Perhaps he had just acted sooner than expected and simply seized the first opportunity that came his way. When Kenneth showed them a signed document from Amarjit confirming the sale, the employees accepted it as genuine.

> **AISHWARYA**
> I've just introduced two new characters in this story. Kenneth Regan and Belinda Brewin. Who are they? How were they related to each other and the Chohan family? And why were they the only two people who seemed to know about the company being sold? To answer these questions, we need to go back to the year 1996.

In 1996, Amarjit, who often cut corners in business, was charged with tax evasion and spent nineteen months in prison. After he was released, he divorced his first wife and turned a new leaf. Soon after, he founded CIBA Freight, and he fell in love with Nancy and the couple was married in 2000. With the births of Ravinder and Devinder, Amarjit's efforts at a fresh start had culminated in a beautiful family. But just as meeting Nancy had changed his life for the better, crossing paths with Kenneth Regan would destroy it.

In 2002, Kenneth Regan approached Amarjit for a job at CIBA Freight. A career criminal, Regan had a long history of money laundering and drug-related crime and was known on the streets as 'Captain Cash'. In 1999, he was convicted of dealing heroin and injuring a police officer while trying to escape. He was sentenced to twenty years in prison but served only three after trading insider knowledge of London's high-profile drug-smuggling circles, which led to the arrest of a dozen associates and gangsters. That was when he crossed paths with Amarjit. The businessman saw something of himself in Regan: another person trying to rebuild his life after losing his way. Regan had no money and no assets, and after his time in prison, he was forced to share a cramped apartment with his father. Amarjit wanted to help, and he hired Regan to operate several of CIBA Freight's trucks.

Before his prison time, Regan had been introduced to a beautiful socialite at an upscale bar in London, Belinda Brewin. She lived the kind of starry life Regan craved to experience through his criminal activities. He quickly became obsessed with her, even telling his friends that she was his girlfriend. Though according to Belinda, they hardly knew each other. She had found his behaviour alarming, and his conviction may have come as a relief. But by 2002, out of prison and working at CIBA, Regan was back to his old ways, this time pursuing Belinda even more aggressively.

In February 2003, Regan called Belina with a business opportunity. Belinda had two children. She had a daughter studying in an expensive private school, and they had recently moved into a sprawling, 50-acre farmhouse in Devon, South London, leaving her with more liabilities than assets. Despite her lack of relevant experience, Regan offered her the position of the managing director of CIBA Freight with an immensely generous salary of 6,000 pounds a month and a two-day work week. The lucrative offer, despite her reservations about Regan, was too tempting to pass. Meanwhile, Regan told Amarjit that he had found an interested buyer for CIBA Freight. Nancy had been encouraging him to retire; she wanted them to return to India and raise their children. Amarjit agreed. The two parties were set to meet at Stonehenge on 13 February to finalize the details of the sale. Belinda, oddly enough, was not at the meeting.

> **AISHWARYA**
> Now, isn't that a fishy location for a business meeting? It's like Mukesh Ambani meeting a stranger under the Qutub Minar to sell off his business empire.
>
> **ARYAAN**
> Very odd. Belinda's absence is weird, too. If not her, who did Amarjit meet?
>
> **AISHWARYA**
> For the longest time, this remained a mystery, even to Belinda. All investigators knew at this point was that two days later, the rest of the Chohan family vanished. And on 17 February, Regan announced that Amarjit had left the country and introduced Belinda to the CIBA Freight team as their new boss.

The new position gave Regan unrestricted access to Belinda's time and her home. He suddenly took an unusual interest in her property, constantly suggesting improvements like installing electric gates, constructing a border wall and clearing the overgrown vegetation. Belinda tried to brush off his attention, but his fixation was slipping beyond her control. On 19 February, her second day as CIBA's managing director, Belinda felt sick and decided to head home early. Driving up to her house, she spotted an unfamiliar, battered Jaguar parked outside, instantly putting her on alert. When she got out of her car, Belinda was alarmed to find two strange men in her field, using a large truck to carve a large ditch across her land. When she questioned them, they told her they were friends of Kenneth Regan. When confronted, Regan brushed it off in his characteristic heavy-handed way. He simply told Belinda he thought she would appreciate his help. She demanded that the two men leave her property but chose to drop the matter.

Despite the tension with Belinda, Regan was living the life he had always wanted. He controlled CIBA Freight, the woman he was obsessed with was now working under him and he had inherited a multi-million-dollar business at the cost of nothing. But there was one factor that Regan had not anticipated: Onkar Verma.

Once the police became aware of the dubious circumstances under which the transfer of power had been executed, they quickly narrowed down on Regan as their prime suspect. When he was called in for an interrogation, the man spun a fine yarn and denied any culpability. He claimed that Amarjit had been in deep financial trouble, which was believable, considering his record, and that he had fled the country to evade the law. According to Regan, the office had received a typewritten letter from Amarjit. He was lying low in France with his entire family, waiting for the right time to return to India. The only glaring loophole in Regan's story was that Nancy and Amarjit's passports were still at the UK Home Office.

The police also traced the last location where Amarjit had used his phone, triangulated through nearby cell towers.

It wasn't France, as Regan claimed, or even the CIBA office or his home. It was Stonehenge, the location of Amarjit's meeting with the potential buyer. Conveniently, the iconic structure was not far from Regan's father's home in Salisbury. When they checked Regan's phone records, it revealed that his location had coincided with Amarjit's on the day of his disappearance. All roads seemed to lead to the police's initial suspect: Kenneth Regan.

The next logical person to question was Belinda, who had technically purchased the company and appeared, to an outsider, to be closely linked to Regan. Regan was outraged when he learnt the authorities were planning to speak to her and pressured Belinda not to meet them on her property. Coincidentally, before they could interrogate her, the police were contacted by Regan's friend and associate, William Horncy. He was one of the men who had trespassed onto Belinda's land a few days earlier. Horncy claimed he had recently spoken to Amarjit on the phone and insisted that he was not in India or France, but in Wales. Amarjit had asked Horncy to organize fake passports for his family, which would enable them to flee the country. They had scheduled a meet-up on Easter Monday, 21 April, next to a famous bronze statue of a pig on Newport, Upper Dock Street, where Amarjit was supposed to collect the forged documents.

The police decided to prioritize the chance to locate Amarjit and postponed their interview with Belinda. Oddly enough, Regan later called her to confirm whether she had spoken to the cops. That Saturday, he visited her farmhouse, offering to finish some repairs to her property. She agreed and took her children into town, leaving the land in Regan's hands. When she returned, the road was gravelled and levelled, just as she had wanted.

When Easter Monday arrived, the police cautiously monitored Horncy's meeting with Amarjit. As they waited with bated breath ... nothing happened. Amarjit was nowhere to be seen. Eventually, Horncy received a call, and his agitated movements made it amply clear that something had gone wrong. He told the police that Amarjit had realized the police were involved and had refused to show up for the meeting. The phone number that had made the call was unregistered and couldn't be traced, and the trail went cold once again.

On 22 April, a father and son duo, Dave and Carl Chapman, were canoeing off Bournemouth pier when they noticed something floating in the water. Though bloated and waterlogged, Dave knew with chilling certainty that he was looking at a human corpse. While Carl called 999, his father stayed in the water with the corpse, hoping a rescue team would come quickly. But three hours would pass before emergency services arrived on the scene. The body was transported to a nearby mortuary, and on 29 April, it was identified as Amarjit's. The post-mortem revealed that he had been struck on the back of his head, and brown duct tape had been wrapped around his face and the wound. The cause of death was likely a combination of blunt force trauma and suffocation. Onkar was immediately notified, and

the investigation, now officially a murder case, gained new urgency.

Belinda Brewin was the police's last hope. At first, she seemed she have no new information to offer them; it was the same old account about Amarjit handing over the company with Regan's help. But when she mentioned Regan's inappropriate behaviour, particularly his repeated encroachment on her land despite her objections, the investigating officers knew they had to look closer. The drainage ditch that Regan had dug on the property seemed the obvious place to start. A team was put together to exhume the site, and the search began on 30 April. It took five days and was documented in full as the police knew they were unearthing evidence that might have to be legitimized later. No bodies were found; there were several signs that the ditch had served as a temporary burial site. Forensic teams recovered clumps of hair confirmed by DNA analysis as Amarjit's, and burnt remnants of what appeared to be baby clothes. The sheer size of the ditch seemed to indicate that the entire Chohan family had been buried within. Ash and char around the area suggested it had recently been set on fire.

What had started as a missing person's case was now a brutal multiple murder, and the culprits were clear as day. But just as the police finished building their case against Kenneth Regan and William Horncy, the two men disappeared. A few days later, Belinda reported that Regan and Horncy had turned up at her farmhouse, asking her to get in their car. Despite the fear and anxiety she must have felt – standing across from potential murderers – Belinda excused herself to grab something from her shed and called the police. But by the time they arrived, the duo had fled. Regan and Horncy's escape drove them out of the UK, first to France and then to Spain.

But there was a third perpetrator who hadn't yet revealed himself: Peter Rees. He, too, had fled the scene of the crime but had stayed hidden within the UK instead of escaping abroad like Regan and Horncy. One day, while seeking refuge in Gloucestershire, Rees allegedly confessed to a local that he was on the run because he had been accused of disappearing and killing an 'Asian family'. He argued he hadn't killed anyone; he had only helped hide the bodies. Regan was the real murderer. The horrified listener alerted the authorities. Finally, on 14 May, Rees was arrested from a pub in Coleford, Gloucestershire, but refused to provide any useful information to the police. Regan and Horncy remained at large.

On 15 July, fishermen off the Isle of Wight found another body caught in their nets. Nancy's remains had decomposed so badly that police offered Onkar the option not to view them. But this was his final chance to see his sister, after nine years apart. The brother who had dropped everything to pursue his family's case performed one final selfless act: he identified Nancy, ensuring her death would not be in vain.

After the gruesome discovery of Nancy's body, the case began to move forward. On 2 August, Regan was captured at a campsite in Belgium. Exactly a month after, Horncy voluntarily surrendered at Dover, tired of living on the run. All three perpetrators were in police custody. Days later, on 7 September, another body washed up on the Isle of Wight. This time, it was identified as Charanjit Kaur. As all the final pieces fell into place to reveal a truly monstrous picture, the police completed their investigations. By tracing Horncy's and Rees's phones, they confirmed that both men had accompanied Regan to the meeting at Stonehenge. Then they all travelled to Regan's house in Salisbury, 3 Forge Close.

After abducting Amarjit on 13 February, that unassuming house became their base of operations. At least one of the men was always present on the premises, leading investigators to hypothesize that Amarjit was held there until his death. The 'official' documents that Regan had used to convince the CIBA employees that their boss had sold the company overnight were all signed by Amarjit under great duress. It was likely that Regan had simply kept him alive just long enough to sign blank sheets of paper, which Regan then used to execute the hostile takeover he had planned.

However, once Amarjit had served his purpose, the men were not content with killing him. They had to destroy his entire family to ensure that no one could challenge their claim to CIBA. With this twisted logic, a plot to commit five murders was formulated. As Detective Inspector Andy Rowell would later state, 'These murders meant as little to Regan as changing his shirt.' On 15 February, the day that Nancy, Charanjit, Ravinder and Devinder disappeared, Rees stayed at 3 Forge Close. Regan and Horncy went to the Chohan family home in Hounslow, London, where they remained for several hours. Police believe that this was where and when the rest of the murders took place, although there was a lack of conclusive evidence. The trio then hired a van to transport the bodies to a temporary location in the West Country before burying them on Belinda's farmland on 19 February, the same day Belinda had caught the men excavating her land without permission. When the risk of discovery became stronger by the second, they bought a boat, and on 20 April, dumped the Chohan family's bodies off the Dorset coast.

Regan had tried his best to cover their tracks; when the police searched his house, they found it had been hastily renovated to remove any forensic remnants. Even so, two key pieces of evidence proved vital when the trial finally began on 8 November 2004, with all three men pleading not guilty. First, a drop of blood was found on the garden wall, later identified as Devinder's. Second, investigators found a clue intentionally left behind by Amarjit – a dated letter tucked into his sock at the time of his death. It had survived the severe water damage because it was tightly folded, with the ink protected inside. Initially overlooked by the forensic scientists who examined Amarjit's body post-mortem, when investigators took a closer look, they realized that the letter was sent to Regan and his father on 12 February. As Prosecutor Richard Horwell told the jury, 'The contents of the letter are unimportant; the date, however, is significant ... It could not have arrived at 3 Forge Close before February 13 at the earliest – the date that Anil [a.k.a. Amarjit] Chohan disappeared.' This was the final proof that Amarjit had been taken to Regan's home after he had gone missing. While Regan claimed that the letter had been planted, the prosecution maintained that Amarjit had saved it intentionally, knowing that it would one day tell the truth he perhaps would not live to say.

Finally, on 1 July 2005, the Chohan family case, one of the longest and most expensive murder trials in UK history, reached its conclusion. Peter Rees, who had attempted to distance himself from his co-accused as the trial proceeded, was convicted of assisting an offender and sentenced to twenty-three years in prison for Amarjit's murder. Kenneth Regan and William Horncy were both given five consecutive life sentences, for each of the lives they had so callously ended in cold blood. Onkar told the media that '[t]he deliberate, premeditated slaughter of my innocent family is akin to me being given a life sentence – a life with no laughter, no happiness and no joy.'

Having fought to ensure his sister and her family were given the justice they deserved, Onkar returned to New Zealand and was forced to come to terms with the crushing trauma that he had endured. He had never gotten the chance to meet Nancy's children or her husband; he had never visited their home that she had so lovingly built for herself. And when the time came, it had been mutilated into a mausoleum. Yet he knew, from the beautiful traces left behind in photographs, videos, his memories, that his sister's life had been filled with love and joy. Though fleeting, it would have to be comfort enough.

## 20

# TO BE HANGED UNTIL DEATH: THE CASE OF HETAL PAREKH

**ARYAAN**
Where do you feel safest? For most of us, the answer is within the four walls of our home. The certainty of knowing that the sound in the next room is someone you know; that the bell ringing at 10 p.m. is likely just a guard asking you to move your car. So, when Yashomati Parekh left her daughter home alone on 5 March 1990, she could never have imagined returning to a scene so gruesome that it would eventually lead to the first judicial execution in Independent India. This is the story of Hetal Parekh and Dhananjoy Chatterjee.

The Parekhs were a quintessential nuclear family living in Paddapukur, Kolkata: Nagardas Parekh, a sixty-three-year-old shopkeeper, his fifty-three-year-old wife Yashomati Parekh and their two children, Bhavesh (nineteen) and Hetal (eighteen). They lived in a three-bedroom flat on the third floor of a gated building, Anand Apartment. Bhavesh had recently joined the local Bhawanipur Educational Society College to study commerce, and Hetal attended a prestigious all-girls Catholic school, Welland Gouldsmith, in the bustling Bowbazar of central Kolkata. On the morning of 5 March 1990, Nagardas and the children were dispersed across the city: he had gone to open his shop in Bagri Market, Bhavesh was at college and Hetal was appearing for one of her ICSE board examinations. Around 11:30 a.m., Bhavesh briefly came home for lunch and then went to help his father at the shop. On the other hand, Hetal headed back to the flat at 1 p.m., having finished her exam.

Hetal and her mother spent a quiet afternoon together. At 5:20 p.m., Yashomati left to carry out a daily ritual of her own: visiting the nearby Laxminarayan Mandir. Around half an hour later, she returned to some unsettling information: the lift operator, Ramdhan Yadav, told her that one of the security guards of the building, Dhananjoy Chatterjee, had gone into her flat to make a phone call. This information made Yashomati visibly anxious and annoyed.

On multiple occasions, Hetal had complained to her mother that Dhananjoy had been harassing her as she travelled to and from school. He had even tried to pressure her into going to the cinema to watch a film with him. Three days ago, on 2 March, Yashomati had informed her husband about Dhananjoy's behaviour. Nagardas was enraged and, after conferring with other residents of the building, complained to the head of the security agency, Shyam Karmakar. Karmakar visited the Parekh household and suggested that Nagardas prepare a written complaint. As a result, Dhananjoy was transferred to the nearby Paras Apartment, while Bijoy Thapa, who currently served at

Paras, would take his place at Anand. The transfer was set to go through on 5 March.

The Parekh family had thought the issue was handled. Naturally, Yashomati was shocked to hear that the man who had harassed her daughter had now entered their apartment while she was alone. She hurried into the lift, watching the floors pass by at a snail's pace. When she reached her front door, she rang the bell frantically but to no avail. She raised an alarm, summoning her neighbours and building staff, who helped her break into the house. Hetal's bedroom door was open; Yashomati walked right into her worst nightmare. Lying on the ground was her beloved daughter's lifeless body. Hetal's skirt and blouse had been pulled up; there was blood on her hands, her clothes and the exposed parts of her body. She had clearly been violently attacked, and the bloodstains that covered the room, including the spattering on the swing, served as further evidence. Her ripped underwear lay on the floor near the doorway.

Yashomati snapped out of the mind-numbing wave of shock to rush her daughter's limp body to the hospital. In that short time, the neighbours called a local doctor, who pronounced Hetal dead as she lay in her mother's arms. Another call was made to the family shop. Bhavesh was informed about his sister's death, and he rushed home, reaching around 7 p.m. Shaken to his core, he carried Hetal to her bed and covered her body with a sheet. A little over an hour later, Nagardas returned and called the Bhawanipur Police Station. Sub-inspector Gurupada Som and other officers rushed to Anand Apartment. As Som recorded the First Information

Report (FIR) based on Yashomati's testimony, the others began investigating the crime scene. Aside from the forensic evidence left behind, they also found a cream-coloured button and a broken chain, presumably belonging to the perpetrator. The next day, Yashomati noticed that a Richo wristwatch with a golden metal band had been stolen from the almirah in the room, and she informed the police of its disappearance.

Hetal's autopsy revealed twenty-one injuries on her body, including ones on her neck, hip and elbow. Her face and nostrils were bloodstained. The hair from the scalp matted with blood. The pattern indicated that she had been struck on the face repeatedly. There were fresh tears in her hymen and traces of blood and semen on her genitals. Though the semen sample was too disintegrated to determine its origin, it was evident that Hetal had been raped. The cause of death was concluded to be strangulation, supported by 'the fracture and dislocation of the hyoid bone'. Injuries such as these would have required a great amount of force; Hetal had experienced unimaginable violence in her final moments.

#### ARYAAN
You might be wondering, where was Dhananjoy? Sure enough, he was the prime suspect.

The police forces began their search for Dhananjoy the same night that the tragedy unfolded, but he was nowhere to be found. He had not collected his wages for the past five days, nor had he reported to Paras Apartment since he had been reassigned. Days became weeks. Dhananjoy was untraceable.

Finally, on 12 May 1990 – more than two months after Hetal's gruesome death – Dhananjoy was arrested during a raid at his ancestral village, Kuludihi. He was found hiding behind a stack of straw in his uncle's house. Once in police custody, the man who had been on the run for months was surprisingly candid. He apparently confessed to everything in one fell swoop: the crime, where he had hidden the clothes he had been wearing that day and the watch he had stolen during the attack. The police, following his instructions, were able to recover the necessary evidence. His shirt and trousers were found wrapped in a newspaper in his house. The watch was kept on a rack.

It seemed to be an open-and-shut case. The prime suspect had been arrested and confessed with a mountain of evidence against him. However, Dhananjoy's confession could not be used conclusively in the court. The Indian Evidence Act, 1872, typically deems confessions to police officers inadmissible, as they are infamous for using unethical methods such as custodial torture, as seen during the case of Sister Abhaya. Therefore, it fell on the Kolkata Police to solidify their case even further. As they questioned key witnesses and put together the timeline of events, a clearer picture began to come together, with Dhananjoy at the centre.

Despite being transferred, Dhananjoy had arrived for duty at Anand Apartment on 5 March. After Yashomati left for the temple, he had informed a fellow guard, Dasarath, that he was going to Flat 3-A to make a phone call. Around 5:45 p.m., the building's security supervisor enquired about Dhananjoy's whereabouts, demanding to know why he had disobeyed the transfer order. Dasarath, who received no response when he called Flat 3-A via the intercom system, shouted Dhananjoy's name from below. Dhananjoy had peered out from the balcony, assuring Dasarath he would come right down. He had taken the stairs, and though he had tried to hurry past the waiting men, was caught. When his supervisor asked for an explanation, Dhananjoy claimed that a personal situation had prevented him from reporting to Paras. He then left for the day. In addition to the witness testimonies of the fellow guards, a guarantee card with the seller's signature confirmed that the watch discovered among his belongings indeed belonged to Yashomati, who had bought it on 21 February 1990. A neighbour, Gauranga Chandra, also claimed that he had given the chain found at the crime scene to Dhananjoy just a month before the murder.

Here's the catch. Dhananjoy's account of the events starkly contradicted the police's version. He claimed that the entire body of evidence presented had been staged to frame him. According to him, on 5 March, he had completed his shift at Anand Apartment from 6 a.m. to 2 p.m. and then left shortly after to visit the local cinema hall to watch a film. He then collected his belongings, purchased some fruits and departed for his native village to attend his brother's sacred thread ceremony. In his telling of the story – as opposed to the testimony of the other staff members – he was not present at the complex at the time of Hetal's murder.

In fact, Dhananjoy argued that he was never given the transfer order in the first place. He pointed out that Bijoy Thapa, who was allegedly meant to take his place at Anand

Apartment, had not shown up to work there that morning either. He claimed that both the transfer order and the written complaint were fabricated, providing a plausible explanation for why the two documents had been seized on 29 June 1990 – more than three months after Hetal's death.

Dhananjoy denied harassing Hetal and refuted Dasarath's and his supervisor's testimony as being absurd. He emphasized that it was highly unlikely he would have told Dasarath he was heading to Flat 3-A if he intended to commit such a heinous crime. It made no sense for him to respond to Dasarath's call from downstairs afterwards. Additionally, why would he use the lift, knowing that the operator would see him? Interestingly, as the case proceeded, Ramdhan was declared a hostile witness – one who, despite being called by a party to testify in its favour, ends up testifying against that party. In his case, that was the prosecution. He denied having seen Dhananjoy take the elevator to the third floor and head in the direction of the Parekh's flat. In doing so, Ramdhan directly refuted Yashomati – who had stated he was the one to tell her that Dhananjoy had entered the flat – and undermined his crucial eyewitness statement. However, he did maintain that he saw Dhananjoy taking the stairs around 5:45 p.m., when he was talking to Dasarath and their supervisor before leaving the premises.

#### AISHWARYA
Let's say we believe Dhananjoy, that he was being framed by the parties involved in the case. How did he explain the presence of the watch among his belongings, as well as the chain he had been given, being found at the scene?

Dhananjoy denied that he had disclosed the location of the watch and clothes to the police, claiming it was illogical for him to keep the items that could implicate him after he had committed such a crime. The clothes found showed no evidence of blood when subjected to forensic analysis. He suggested that the guarantee card produced by Yashomati was forged by the seller, since the cash memo – which would have contained both the serial number and date of purchase of the Richo watch – was never located. Dhananjoy's legal representatives also pointed out that his house had been searched without the presence of independent witnesses, which was required by law. Another key observation was that neither Dasarath nor the security supervisor had noticed anything suspicious or dishevelled about Dhananjoy's behaviour or appearance on 5 March, despite the heinous crime he had supposedly *just* committed – and that Hetal had clearly fought back against.

> **AISHWARYA**
> I'm not convinced. It seems like he's spinning a big conspiracy where there is none.
>
> **ARYAAN**
> Though some of Dhananjoy's counterclaims were surprisingly sound, human behaviour is extremely complex. It's entirely possible that his contradictory behaviour was deliberate to confuse, or perhaps his decisions were truly illogical given what he was trying to cover up. The courts weren't convinced either.

The judge found the claim that Hetal's family, the independent witnesses and the police had all entered into some kind of secret alliance completely far-fetched. After a lengthy trial, Dhananjoy was convicted for theft and the rape and murder of Hetal Parekh by the second court of the Additional Sessions Judge at Alipore even while his lawyers argued it was circumstantial evidence. The case was appealed at the Calcutta High Court, followed by the Supreme Court of India, and both upheld the conviction. Dhananjoy's crime was categorized as a 'rarest of rare' case – one where death was the only appropriate sentence. The Supreme Court called it 'an affront to the human dignity of the society'.

Even after the decisive sentencing, more than a decade would pass before it was carried out. The execution was scheduled for 25 June 2004. Leading to the day, Dhananjoy's family petitioned the Supreme Court of India and submitted a mercy plea to the then-president, A. P. J. Abdul Kalam. Public opinion was split: several human rights activists and lawyers spoke out against the execution and organized candlelight vigils, while a bloc led by Meera Bhattacharjee, wife of the then-chief minister of Bengal, Buddhadeb Bhattacharjee, campaigned to ensure it. On 4 August, the president rejected the Chatterjee family's plea. Ten days later, Dhananjoy was hanged at Alipore Jail, Kolkata, with devotional music playing, as per his request. It was the first execution in the history of independent India. Up until his final moments, Dhananjoy had maintained his innocence. His last words, as reported by the state's hangman Nata Mullick, were, '*Ami nirdosh. Amake mere phelchhe sab*' (I am innocent. They are killing me). Students and teachers at Welland Gouldsmith School, where Hetal had studied, spent the morning of 14 August praying for Dhananjoy and Hetal, while his family remained in their home, refusing to speak with the press. They did not claim his body, and he was cremated by the state.

The case fed into the larger conversation about the death penalty, which remains a controversial topic in India even today. Some believed Dhananjoy was an innocent wronged by a system that made a scapegoat of the less privileged. This stance was supported by two statisticians at the Indian Statistical Institute, Kolkata, Probal Chaudhuri and Debasis Sengupta, who took an interest in the case. Over ten years, they closely examined the case and identified what they said were serious gaps in the evidence. Their long-awaited findings were published in a book called *Adalat, Media, Samaj Ebong Dhananjoyer Phasi* in August 2016, which was later adapted into a controversial Bengali movie in 2017.

### ARYAAN
An important aside here is that even Dhanonjoy's family denounced the movie, though they allegedly initially approved it.

The book pointed out some interesting details. Chaudhuri and Sengupta claimed the timeline drawn out by the authorities – of Dhananjoy committing the crime, interacting with Dasarath and the supervisor and then leaving the building in just half an hour – was almost impossible. They pointed out that the balcony Dhananjoy had allegedly responded from when his name was called was enclosed by a grille, which meant he couldn't have leaned out and answered. These details, along with the absence of blood on Dhananjoy's clothing and person, led them to conclude he had been falsely incriminated.

In a shocking move, the report presented the theory that Hetal's death may have been committed by her family. In particular, Sengupta and Chaudhuri suspected Yashomati's involvement. They highlighted how quickly Yashomati had assumed something was wrong and had immediately requested her neighbours and staff to force open the door instead of trying to use the intercom system. She did not call the police – they were only alerted hours later, after Nagardas had returned home. The report alleged that Hetal might have engaged in consensual intercourse, and that when she was discovered, her family had murdered her in a brutal case of honour killing. But it wasn't just the murder which raised eyebrows – it was the aftermath. They found the family's behaviour to be deeply suspicious; Yashomati had avoided appearing at court, and despite having a thriving business in Kolkata, the Parekh family relocated to Mumbai after the murder. They have since kept a low profile, her parents grieving and aging away from the public eye. One of their neighbours in Mumbai told *Telegraph* in 2004 that they had relocated to Gujarat.

> [W]e don't know where they are ... [after the verdict] The media descended on the building ... Since we closed the gates, they went into the next house and took photographs of the Parekhs' flat. It traumatised them. They did not want to talk to anyone.

## AISHWARYA

Personally, I don't find any of this strange. Everyone has their ways of dealing with grief; I think it's completely reasonable that they wanted to have a fresh start away from the painful memories of their daughter's murder. And that Yashomati would not have wanted to relive those same memories over and over in court.

## ARYAAN

I completely agree, Aishwarya. Grief's numbing effect is enough to explain Yashomati's behaviour. I think it's worth pointing out these gaps in the prosecution's case against Dhananjoy, especially since our legal system tends to be skewed in favour of those with more resources at their disposal. I wonder if things would have played out differently if Dhananjoy's legal representation had highlighted these parts of his story. Did Hetal get the justice she deserved with Dhananjoy's execution, or was there more than one victim in this case? These doubts are difficult to address, especially since death is so final.

# ACKNOWLEDGEMENTS

**FROM AISHWARYA:**

To my brother Adi, whose ability to love without demands, exceptions and qualifiers gives me an unwavering sense of belonging.

To my friends, from school, college and everything in between. Dakshita, Harsh and Raghav, for being my triple pillars of support through the most formative years of my life. Inika, for being my fiercest supporter and oldest friend. Bernie and Elizabeth, for a friendship that crosses continents, unrelenting time differences and persists despite odds.

To Shiv Nadar School, Noida and Alma College, Michigan, for giving life to my years of education. Ms Shashi Banerjee, Ms Anju Soni, Ms Nitina Dua and Col. Gopal Karunakaran, for making classrooms feel like home. Professor Gorton, Professor Dixon and Professor Hulme, for changing how I see the world and, in turn, myself.

**FROM ARYAAN:**

To my mom, for somehow raising two teenage sons alone. For that, I am sorry and grateful. To my dad, for always affording me the best education he could, despite our means. To my brother Ivan, whose innocence and honesty I see reflected in so many of the cases we cover. It is that which allows me to tap into the feeling of loving someone and wanting to protect them.

To Prashant Mausaji, Noopur Mausi, Sunny Mama, Shubhi Mama, Yuvraj, Yashasvi, Nani and Nana for cultivating a family that always felt like home. I am whoever I am – whatever I am – today because you were there for me when no one else was.

To my friends. Joe Garvey, whose confidence in himself and those around him is contagious. Lucas Gabow for showing me what true physical discipline looks like. To my Dayaa gang of friends – Arul, Aviral, Adwaith and Rudra – who saw my teenage ups and downs and tolerated most of them. Vinamre Kasanaa, for teaching me how to hack the YouTube algorithm, drink better cocktails and listen to good jazz. Kaavyya Kesarwani, for being a cheerleader behind the scenes. Aditya Shankar for preventing me from being mugged across all our travels. And the score of friends scattered around the world who always keep a warm couch ready for me.

To all my school teachers, who made me the man I am today. I still revisit my middle school years whenever I need to find the seed of curiosity which was first sowed at that time. To Ms Rupa Chakravarty, principal of Suncity School, for teaching me the value of sanskaar. To Ms Shashi Banerjee, principal of Shiv Nadar School, for teaching me the value of warmth and forgiveness. And to both of those schools for giving me unimaginable opportunities and always believing in me.

To Alma College for taking a chance on a kid from India. I

don't know if I deserved the scholarship and I feel a tad guilty for dropping out, but those were three transformative years. To Professor Hulme, Professor Dixon and Professor Gorton for seeing a spark in me that at times I failed to recognize and always giving me the benefit of the doubt, even when they shouldn't have.

To Ted and Courtney Balaker, for giving me the opportunity to see America for everything it is. Working on your film set off a domino effect that led me to NYC, for which I can't thank you enough.

And lastly, to Ms Aishwarya Singh, the better half of the podcast. She is the foundation of *Desi Crime*, the pillar that holds it up and the fighter that set this journey off in the first place. I am grateful for being legally obligated to give you 50 per cent of all my earnings.

**FROM BOTH OF US:**
To the team at Pan Macmillan India, for bringing our vision to life. Shreyoshee Bandyopadhyay, for her editorial feedback and ability to transform the written word into a story; Vidisha Ghosh, for her meticulous edits; Shreya Ahlawat and Simran Chanana, for their editorial support; Saburi, Divyanshi and Pooja, for their marketing magic and Haitenlo Semy for an amazing cover.

To the team at Desi Studios, the heart of the company. Evan, Mansi, Maria and Manav, for bringing these stories to life with skill and dedication.

To the Collective Artists Network – DC, Shoumie and Smital. While they have staked their claim to 15 per cent of what we make in perpetuity, they have helped so many of our dreams come true and will continue to. To our agents and managers, Nannditaa and Shivangi, for painstakingly working behind the scenes on everything that goes into publishing a book – the not-so-glamorous but supremely important pieces of a larger puzzle.

To the team at Audible India, for helping us transform this book into an experience of a different kind. And to Shiv Nadar School Noida, for helping facilitate the audio recording of this book.

To the men and women who protect our borders, the Indian Police and other frontline forces – firefighters, CRPF, first aid responders and more – who risk their lives in the shadows, thank you. You are the heroes of our stories, whether they get told or not.

To journalists, who get a bad rep in the modern age but are truly the fourth pillar of any democracy, especially ours. We are grateful to so many of you for your impeccable investigative work.

And to the victims and their families. You are the reason why we do this.

# REFERENCES

## 1. THE KOLKATA HOUSE OF HORRORS

Shreya Sinha, 'Kolkata House Of Horrors: The Macabre Saga Of A Man Who Lived With Skeletons For Months', *ABP News*, 21 May 2023. Available at: https://news.abplive.com/crime/kolkata-house-of-horrors-partha-de-skeletons-arabindo-de-debjani-de-robinson-street-kankal-bari-pavlov-mental-hospital-most-shocking-crimes-1603522 (accessed on 23 June 2025).

'The Tragedy Of Partha De Who Died Known As Kolkata's "Skeleton Man"', *ScoopWhoop*, 21 February 2017. Available at: https://www.scoopwhoop.com/news/why-we-need-to-remember-partha-des-story-the-man-better-known-as-kolkatas-skeleton-man/? (accessed on 23 June 2025).

Monideepa Banerjie, 'Kolkata's House of Horror: The Full Story', *NDTV*, 12 June 2015. Available at: https://www.ndtv.com/india-news/kolkatas-house-of-horror-the-full-story-770915? (accessed on 23 June 2025).

'Kolkata's house of horrors: Lonely even in death, Partha De's body finds no takers', *Hindustan Times*, 24 February 2017. Available at: https://www.hindustantimes.com/kolkata/kolkata-s-house-of-horrors-lonely-even-in-death-partha-de-s-body-finds-no-takers/story-rvaChAGXvvO4h65CxBJeTN.html? (accessed on 23 June 2025).

'In Kolkata's House of Horrors, De family's skeletons tumbled out of closet', *Hindustan Times*, 22 February 2017. Available at: https://www.hindustantimes.com/india-news/in-kolkata-s-house-of-horrors-de-family-s-skeletons-tumbled-out-of-closet/story-b7HGYSrvqKF6RCcMYTYP1N.html? (accessed on 23 June 2025).

Dwaipayan Ghosh, 'Kolkata man who "lived" with corpses found dead', *Times of India*, 22 February 2017. Available at: https://timesofindia.indiatimes.com/city/kolkata/kolkata-house-of-horror-man-found-dead/articleshow/57283078.cms? (accessed on 23 June 2025).

Anindita Acharya, 'Now, Kolkata's infamous Robinson Street horror house story on OTT', *Millennium Post*, 15 March 2024. Available at: https://www.millenniumpost.in/bengal/now-kolkatas-infamous-robinson-street-horror-house-story-on-ott-555974? (accessed on 23 June 2025).

'Man who lived with sister and dogs' corpses for months dies "mysteriously"', *Mid-Day*, 21 February 2017. Available at: https://www.mid-day.com/news/india-news/article/kolkata-corpse-case-partha-de-sister-dogs-skeletons-dies-house-of-horror-news-18014196? (accessed on 23 June 2025).

'Kolkata horror revisited: Man who lived with sister's skeleton, found dead', *Asian Age*, 21 February 2017. Available at: https://www.asianage.com/metros/kolkata/210217/kolkata-horror-revisited-man-who-lived-with-sisters-skeleton-found-dead.html? (accessed on 23 June 2025).

Pooja Mehta, 'Kolkata's House of Skeletons: De family shared a complicated relationship, say police', *DNA*, 13 June 2015. Available at: https://www.dnaindia.com/india/report-kolkata-s-house-of-skeletons-de-family-shared-a-complicated-relationship-say-police-2095306 (accessed on 23 June 2025).

Shobita Dhar and Joeanna Rebello Fernandes. 'Body shock:

Kolkata "skeleton house" case not unique', *Times of India*, 14 June 2015. Available at: https://timesofindia.indiatimes.com/india/Body-shock-Kolkata-skeleton-house-case-not-unique/articleshow/47660204.cms? (accessed on 23 June 2025).

Indrani Roy, 'A House of Horrors in the City of Joy', Rediff, 18 June 2015. Available at: https://www.rediff.com/news/report/a-house-of-horrors-in-the-city-of-joy/20150618.htm (accessed on 23 June 2025).

Upala Sen, 'The Prisoner of Robinson Street', *The Telegraph*, 27 August 2017. Available at: https://www.telegraphindia.com/7-days/the-prisoner-of-robinson-street/cid/1315832 (accessed on 23 June 2025).

'Bizarre case of Kolkata 'horror' house: Partho-Debjani's "disturbed" history revealed', *Zee News*, 20 June 2015. Available at: https://zeenews.india.com/news/west-bengal/bizarre-case-of-kolkata-horror-house%E2%80%8B-partho-debjanis-disturbed-history-revealed_1616262.html (accessed on 23 June 2025).

## 2. MURDER AT ROYAL PARK, SRI LANKA

'Attorney General begins efforts to locate Royal Park murder convict', *Hiru News*, 19 December 2024. Available at: https://www.hirunews.lk/en/391251/attorney-general-begins-efforts-to-locate-royal-park-murder-convict? (accessed on 23 June 2025).

'Locate, initiate extradition of Royal Park murder convict', *Daily News*, 20 December 2024. Available at: https://www.dailynews.lk/2024/12/20/admin-catagories/breaking-news/692193/locate-initiate-extradition-of-royal-park-murder-convict/ (accessed on 23 June 2025).

Kusal Kavinda Amarasinghe, 'The Forensic Value of DNA Profiling in Sri Lankan Criminal Law', ResearchGate,

August 2021. Available at: https://www.researchgate.net/publication/353902414_The_Forensic_Value_of_DNA_Profiling_in_Sri_Lankan_Criminal_Law (accessed on 23 June 2025).

Shenali Waduge, 'Lessons from Royal Park Murder for Sri Lankan Society', *Sri Lanka Guardian*, 13 July 2012. Available at: http://www.srilankaguardian.org/2012/07/lessons-from-royal-park-murder-for-sri.html (accessed on 23 June 2025).

Ranjith Padmasiri, 'AG instructs officials to arrest and bring back Royal Park murder convict', *Sunday Times*, 16 June 2024. Available at: https://www.sundaytimes.lk/240616/news/ag-instructs-officials-to-arrest-and-bring-back-royal-park-murder-convict-560420.html (accessed on 23 June 2025).

'Royal Park murder convict barred from leaving country', *The Island Online*, 24 September 2022. Available at: https://island.lk/royal-park-murder-convict-barred-from-leaving-country/ (accessed on 23 June 2025).

Shadows & Sin, 'A Royal Park Murder A Crime That Shook Sri Lanka' [video], YouTube, 12 April 2025. Available at: https://www.youtube.com/watch?v=E2Eo1IGXHVA&t=2s (accessed on 24 June 2025).

'Sri Lanka- Royal Park murder convict seeks second chance at life', *MENAFN*, 14 November 2019. Available at: https://menafn.com/1099272459/Sri-Lanka-Royal-Park-murder-convict-seeks-second-chance-at-life (accessed on 24 June 2025).

Storyteller, '5. Royal Park Murder: The Yvonne Jonsson Case' [video], YouTube, 3 April 2025. Available at: https://www.youtube.com/watch?v=ZZgw4bPsU9c&t=10s (accessed on 24 June 2025).

'Police hail Royal Park case judgment', *Colombo Gazette*, 11 July 2012. Available at: https://colombogazette.com/2012/07/11/shramantha-sentenced-to-death-in-royal-park-case/? (accessed on 23 June 2025).

'Sirisena Pays Rs 1 Mn Compensation in Royal Park Case', *News First*, 11 March 2025. Available at: https://newsfirst.lk/2025/03/11/sirisena-pays-rs-1-mn-compensation-in-royal-park-case (accessed on 23 June 2025).

'Top Court Rules Sirisena's Pardon of Royal Park Killer Unlawful', *News First*, 6 June 2024. Available at: https://www.newsfirst.lk/2024/06/06/top-court-rules-sirisena-s-pardon-of-royal-park-killer-unlawful (accessed on 23 June 2025).

## 3. THE 100 KILLINGS OF JAVED IQBAL

Rory McCarth, 'Killer's sentence: cut into 100 pieces', *The Guardian*, 17 March 2000. Available at: https://www.theguardian.com/world/2000/mar/17/rorymccarthy? (accessed on 23 June 2025).

'Pakistan "serial killer" arrested', *BBC News*, 31 December 1999. Available at: http://news.bbc.co.uk/2/hi/south_asia/584373.stm? (accessed on 23 June 2025).

'Death for Pakistan serial killer', *BBC News*, 16 March 2000. Available at: http://news.bbc.co.uk/2/hi/south_asia/678553.stm? (accessed on 23 June 2025).

Eniqma, '"I could have easily killed 400 more orphans" The True Story Of Javed Iqbal' [video], YouTube, 15 June 2019. Available at: https://www.youtube.com/watch?v=wIokrZsaycY (accessed on 24 June 2025).

Jason Burke, 'Confessions back suicide note claims of child killings', *The Guardian*, 17 March 2000. Available at: https://www.theguardian.com/world/1999/dec/07/jasonburke? (accessed on 23 June 2025).

Kiran Butt, Mujahid Jafri and Saad Hasan, 'Rape, dissolve in acid: How Pakistan's serial killer murdered 100 children', *TRT World*. Available at: https://www.trtworld.com/magazine/

rape-dissolve-in-acid-how-pakistans-serial-killer-murdered-100-children-12787174 (accessed on 23 June 2025).

John Philip Jenkins, 'Javed Iqbal', Britannica. Available at: https://www.britannica.com/biography/Javed-Iqbal (accessed on 23 June 2025).

Shahzada Qasim, '"Where is my child!?" - The Notorious Case of Javed Iqbal, Killer of 100 Children', Brown History, 2 April 2024. Available at: https://brownhistory.substack.com/p/where-is-my-child-the-notorious-case (accessed on 23 June 2025).

Barry Bearak, 'Manhunt's End in Pakistan: "Killer of 100 Boys" Tells All', *New York Times*, 2 January 2000. Available at: https://www.nytimes.com/2000/01/02/world/manhunt-s-end-in-pakistan-killer-of-100-boys-tells-all.html (accessed on 23 June 2025).

Mohammed Ahmed, 'Javed Iqbal: The Disturbing Case of Pakistan's Most Notorious Serial Killer', *Pakistani Index*, 16 May 2024. Available at: https://pakistaniindex.org/2024/05/javed-iqbal-the-disturbing-case-of-pakistans-most-notorious-serial-killer/ (accessed on 23 June 2025).

'Rape, dissolve in acid: How a serial killer in Pakistan murdered 100 children', *DesPardes*. Available at: https://despardes.com/how-a-serial-killer-in-pakistan-murdered-100-children/ (accessed on 23 June 2025).

Mojo, 'Javed Iqbal: The Untold Story of a Serial Killer Who Killed 100 Kids', *Times of Ireland*, 4 June 2025. Available at: https://timesofireland.com/javed-iqbal-the-untold-story-of-a-serial-killer-who-killed-100-kids/ (accessed on 23 June 2025).

'Javed Iqbal: The Monster Behind Pakistan's Worst Serial Killings', Bugged Space, 26 June 2023. Available at: https://www.buggedspace.com/javed-iqbal-the-pakistani-serial-killer/ (accessed on 23 June 2025).

Ben Kageyama, 'Why Javed Iqbal Killed a Hundred Street Children',

Medium, 4 January 2021. Available at: https://medium.com/crimebeat/why-javed-iqbal-killed-a-hundred-street-children-f593eaad536d (accessed on 23 June 2025).

Imaan Sheikh, 'The Case of Serial Killer Javed Iqbal', *The Juggernaut*, 14 July 2021. Available at: https://www.jgnt.co/pakistani-serial-killer-javed-iqbal (accessed on 23 June 2025).

## 4. GULSHAN KUMAR VS. THE UNDERWORLD

Garima Satija, 'Bombay HC Upholds Abdul Rauf's Conviction. Here's A Timeline Of Gulshan Kumar Murder Case', *India Times*, 1 July 2021. Available at: https://www.indiatimes.com/entertainment/celebs/bombay-hc-upholds-abdul-raufs-conviction-heres-a-timeline-of-gulshan-kumar-murder-case-544009.html? (accessed on 24 June 2025).

Manasi Phadke, 'A flop album, a call to the underworld, & a daylight killing — how Gulshan Kumar was murdered', *The Print*, 4 July 2021. Available at: https://theprint.in/india/a-flop-album-a-call-to-the-underworld-a-daylight-killing-how-gulshan-kumar-was-murdered/689402/? (accessed on 24 June 2025).

Mansij Asthana, '4 Disturbing Things About Gulshan Kumar Murder That Were Straight Out Of A Bollywood Movie', Mensxp, 12 August 2021. Available at: https://www.mensxp.com/special-features/features/91934-gulshan-kumar-murder-case-underworld-gangster-assassination.html (accessed on 24 June 2025).

YBP Filmy, 'Gulshan Kumar Murder case' [video], YouTube, 23 February 2024. Available at: https://www.youtube.com/watch?v=JdE_81ZFI3c&t=6s (accessed on 24 June 2025).

World Affairs by Unacademy, 'The Unsolved Murder of Gulshan Kumar | Dawood Ibrahim & The Mumbai Underworld Mystery | World Affairs' [video], YouTube, 20 April 2025. Available at:

https://www.youtube.com/watch?v=dCUWvyGCIHg&t=6s (accessed on 24 June 2025).

HarGyan, 'Gulshan Kumar Murder Case | Why Underworld Killed Gulshan Kumar? | Ayush Pal' [video], YouTube, 15 March 2024. Available at: https://www.youtube.com/watch?v=71n5k4qQfEc&t=1s (accessed on 24 June 2025).

Smruti Koppikar, 'From the India Today archives (1997) | Gulshan Kumar: A murder most foul', *India Today*, 18 January 2025. Available at: https://www.indiatoday.in/india-today-insight/story/from-the-india-today-archives-1997-gulshan-kumar-a-murder-most-foul-2666662-2025-01-18? (accessed on 24 June 2025).

Jyoti Kanyal, 'The Gulshan Kumar Murder Case: A Recap', *India Today*, 1 July 2021. Available at: https://www.indiatoday.in/movies/celebrities/story/gulshan-kumar-murder-case-a-recap-1821531-2021-07-01? (accessed on 24 June 2025).

Omkar Gokhale, 'Gulshan Kumar murder case: Bombay HC upholds conviction of Dawood aide Abdul Rauf', *The Indian Express*, 1 July 2021. Available at: https://indianexpress.com/article/cities/mumbai/gulshan-kumar-murder-case-verdict-7384018/? (accessed on 24 June 2025).

'Gulshan murder accused get life term', *Times of India*, 30 April 2002. Available at: https://timesofindia.indiatimes.com/city/mumbai/Gulshan-murder-accused-gets-life-term/articleshow/8407094.cms? (accessed on 24 June 2025).

'Mumbai police had intel on Gulshan Kumar's murder, claims Rakesh Maria', *Mumbai Mirror*, 21 February 2020. Available at: https://mumbaimirror.indiatimes.com/mumbai/other/mumbai-police-had-intel-on-gulshan-kumar-murder-claims-rakesh-maria/articleshow/74245429.html? (accessed on 24 June 2025).

Ahmed Ali, 'Mumbai: Police knew of plan to kill Gulshan

Kumar, says ex-top cop's book', *Times of India*, 20 February 2020. Available at: https://timesofindia.indiatimes.com/city/mumbai/police-knew-of-plan-to-kill-gulshan-kumar-says-ex-top-cops-book/articleshow/74216943.cms? (accessed on 24 June 2025).

'Gulshans Refusal To Pay Protection Money Led To Murder', *Business Standard*, 13 August 1997. Available at: https://www.business-standard.com/article/specials/gulshans-refusal-to-pay-protection-money-led-to-murder-197081301071_1.html? (accessed on 24 June 2025).

'Mumbai cops had detailed intel on plot to kill Gulshan Kumar: Rakesh Maria', *Business Standard*, 21 February 2020. Available at: https://www.business-standard.com/article/current-affairs/mumbai-cops-had-intel-on-killing-of-gulshan-kumar-rakesh-maria-120022100858_1.html? (accessed on 24 June 2025).

Kanchan Chaudhari, 'Gulshan Kumar murder: Bombay HC upholds life term for killer', *Hindustan Times,* 2 July 2021. Available at: https://www.hindustantimes.com/cities/mumbai-news/gulshan-kumar-murder-bombay-hc-upholds-life-term-for-killer-101625165017923.html? (accessed on 24 June 2025).

Swati Deshpande, 'Bombay HC upholds murder rap on convicted sharpshooter in Gulshan Kumar death; upholds acquittal of Ramesh Taurani', *Times of India*, 1 July 2021. Available at: https://timesofindia.indiatimes.com/india/gulshan-kumar-murder-case-hc-upholds-abdul-rauf-merchants-conviction/articleshow/84011279.cms? (accessed on 24 June 2025).

## 5. A ROYAL WEDDING AND A VANISHING: VISHAL MEHROTRA

Colin Campbell, 'Confession found in Vishal Mehrotra unsolved murder review', *BBC*, 30 July 2020. Available at: https://www.bbc.com/news/uk-england-sussex-53568304? (accessed on 24 June 2025).

Colin Campbell, 'Vishal Mehrotra: Man claims he saw murdered boy after he vanished', *BBC*, 9 May 2023. Available at: https://www.bbc.com/news/uk-england-sussex-65533405? (accessed on 24 June 2025).

Colin Campbell, 'Vishal Mehrotra: Witness believes suspicious car linked to murder', *BBC*, 10 October 2023. Available at: https://www.bbc.com/news/uk-england-sussex-67008658? (accessed on 24 June 2025).

Mabel Banfield Nwachi, 'Sussex police "committed to solving" Vishal Mehrotra murder case', *The Guardian*, 11 May 2023. Available at: https://www.theguardian.com/uk-news/2023/may/11/sussex-police-committed-to-solving-vishal-mehrotra-case? (accessed on 24 June 2025).

Colin Campbell, 'Vishal Mehrotra: Racism blamed for failure to solve 40-year-old murder', *BBC*, 11 June 2021. Available at: https://www.bbc.com/news/uk-england-sussex-57415022? (accessed on 24 June 2025).

Colin Campbell, 'Vishal Mehrotra: Police scrapped plans for schoolboy murder appeal', *BBC*, 29 July 2021. Available at: https://www.bbc.com/news/uk-england-sussex-57995512? (accessed on 24 June 2025).

'Met Police handling of boy's royal wedding day death investigated', *BBC*, 3 March 2015. Available at: https://www.bbc.com/news/uk-england-london-31717179? (accessed on 24 June 2025).

Colin Campbell, 'Vishal Mehrotra: Father pleads for fresh inquiry into son's murder', *BBC*, 13 July 2020. Available at: https://www.bbc.com/news/uk-england-sussex-53335896? (accessed on 24 June 2025).

Pooja Shrivastava, 'Vishal Mehrotra: Father condemns as police scrap public appeal', *Eastern Eye*, 29 July 2021. Available at: https://www.easterneye.biz/vishal-mehrotra-father-condemns-as-police-scrap-public-appeal/? (accessed on 24 June 2025).

Charlotte Ikonen, 'Vishal Mehrotra: Dad wants fresh inquiry into son's murder', *Wandsworth Times*, 13 July 2020. Available at: https://www.wandsworthguardian.co.uk/news/18578674.vishal-mehrotra-dad-wants-fresh-inquiry-sons-murder/? (accessed on 24 June 2025).

Mamta Mehrotra, 'Justice for Vishal Mehrotra', Change.org, 17 May 2023. Available at: https://www.change.org/p/justice-for-vishal-mehrotra-494a8b11-7ab5-45e7-9b97-f30c3dda9378? (accessed on 24 June 2025).

BBC Sounds, *Vishal*, Apple Podcasts, 10 April 2023. Available at: https://podcasts.apple.com/us/podcast/vishal/id1681787156 (accessed on 24 June 2025).

Mathew Smith, 'Vishal, PIE and 80s boarding', Indigo Jo Blogs, 22 February 2025. Available at: https://www.blogistan.co.uk/blog/mt.php/2025/02/22/vishal-pie-and-80s-boarding (accessed on 24 June 2025).

Claudia Joseph, 'Boy, eight, who disappeared from London streets after watching Royal wedding procession of Charles and Diana "may have been murdered by notorious paedophile"', *Daily Mail*, 13 January 2023. Available at: https://www.dailymail.co.uk/news/article-11633007/Boy-disappeared-watching-Chales-Dianas-wedding-murdered-paedophile.html (accessed on 24 June 2025).

Emily G. Thompson, 'The Murder of Vishal Mehrotra & The Elm Guest House', Morbidology, 5 January 2019. Available at: https://morbidology.com/the-murder-of-vishal-mehrotra-the-elm-guest-house/ (accessed on 25 June 2025).

Grace Macaskill, 'Inside chilling mystery of boy, 8, who vanished during Charles and Diana's wedding as sinister new theory revealed', *The Sun*, 19 January 2023. Available at: https://www.thesun.co.uk/news/21095070/footsteps-killers-vishal-mehrotra-charles-diana/ (accessed on 25 June 2025).

Tom Parfitt, 'What happened to Vishal Mehrotra? The unsolved case of boy who vanished after royal wedding', Yahoo News, 19 January 2025. Available at: https://uk.news.yahoo.com/what-happened-to-vishal-mehrotra-channel-4-documentary-181009339.html? (accessed on 25 June 2025).

'Vishal — cold-case podcast puts victim's family at the heart of the story', *Financial Times*. Available at: https://www.ft.com/content/4b160ee4-9bb2-4440-af8b-559ad1a136ad (accessed on 25 June 2025).

Rhiannon Du Cann, 'Heartbreaking story of boy who went missing just hours after Charles and Diana's wedding', *Express*, 25 April 2023. Available at: https://www.express.co.uk/news/uk/1762569/vishal-mehrotra-disappearance-charles-diana-wedding-spt (accessed on 25 June 2025).

## 6. A CASE STUDY IN CRIME: SAJAL BARUI

'17 years after triple murder, Sajal walks out of jail', *The Indian Express*, 11 August 2010. Available at: https://indianexpress.com/article/cities/kolkata/17-years-after-triple-murder-sajal-walks-out-of-jail/? (accessed on 25 June 2025).

Ashim Kumar Roy, 'Sajal Barui @ Papa vs State Of West Bengal on 30 August, 2011', Indian Kanoon. Available at: https://indiankanoon.org/doc/125225693/? (accessed on 25 June 2025).

Pronab Mondal, 'Sajal's saga: sex, lies and videotape', *The Telegraph*, 26 May 2003. Available at: https://www.telegraphindia.com/west-bengal/sajal-s-saga-sex-lies-and-videotape/cid/1258151 (accessed on 25 June 2025).

Kriti Shrivastava, 'The Story of Sajal Barui: Teen Who Killed Entire Family, Partied in Jail, and Is Now a Free Man', *Thar Tribune*, 29 June 2024. Available at: https://thartribune.com/the-story-of-sajal-barui-teen-who-killed-entire-family-partied-in-jail-and-is-now-a-free-man/ (accessed on 25 June 2025).

'Sajal's life term waived', *The Telegraph*, 31 August 2011. Available at: https://www.telegraphindia.com/west-bengal/sajal-s-life-term-waived/cid/1195285? (accessed on 25 June 2025).

'Two beer bottles to freedom - Sajal Barui spiked guards' drinks to walk out of hospital', *The Telegraph*, 22 May 2003. Available at: https://www.telegraphindia.com/west-bengal/two-beer-bottles-to-freedom-sajal-barui-spiked-guards-drinks-to-walk-out-of-hospital/cid/1089780? (accessed on 25 June 2025).

Jayanta Gupta, 'Justice delayed for teen killer?', *Times of India*, 1 July 2010. Available at: https://timesofindia.indiatimes.com/city/kolkata/Justice-delayed-for-teen-killer/articleshow/6112415.cms? (accessed on 25 June 2025).

'Ranjit Mondal And Sajal Barui And Etc. vs State on 31 January, 1997', Indian Kanoon. Available at: https://indiankanoon.org/doc/1735444/? (accessed on 25 June 2025).

'Sajal Barui free to choose new life', *Times of India*, 11 August 2010. Available at: https://timesofindia.indiatimes.com/city/kolkata/Sajal-Barui-free-to-choose-new-life/articleshow/6290094.cms? (accessed on 25 June 2025).

'Out of jail, painting on lips', *The Telegraph*, 11 August 2010. Available at: https://www.telegraphindia.com/west-bengal/out-of-jail-painting-on-lips/cid/1272728? (accessed on 25 June 2025).

'Underworld link found in Sajal case', *Times of India*, 19 September 2001. Available at: https://timesofindia.indiatimes.com/city/kolkata/Underworld-link-found-in-Sajal-case/articleshow/598610302.cms? (accessed on 25 June 2025).

'Murder at 16, bail at 33', *The Telegraph*, 30 June 2010. Available at: https://www.telegraphindia.com/india/murder-at-16-bail-at-33/cid/510266? (accessed on 25 June 2025).

Justice Navigator, '1993 Sajal Barui Case | Kolkata Case|TRUE CRIME STORIES|' [video], YouTube, 17 September 2024. Available at: https://www.youtube.com/watch?v=5Nzegtx9ViU (accessed on 25 June 2025).

## 7. THE GRUESOME MURDER OF SISTER ABHAYA

R. Krishnakumar, 'A CBI Special Court finds Father Thomas Kottoor and Sister Sephy guilty of murder in the sensational Sister Abhaya case of 1992', *Frontline*, 22 December 2020. Available at: https://frontline.thehindu.com/dispatches/a-cbi-special-court-finds-father-thomas-kottoor-and-sister-sephy-guilty-of-murder-in-the-sensational-sister-abhaya-case-of-1992/article33395468.ece? (accessed on 26 June 2025).

G Anand, 'Sister Abhaya murder case | Curtains down on a 28-year-old case', *The Hindu*, 23 December 2020. Available at: https://www.thehindu.com/news/national/kerala/sister-abhaya-murder-case-curtains-down-on-a-28-year-old-case/article33405445.ece? (accessed on 26 June 2025).

Rhea Mogul, 'She was murdered for catching an Indian priest and nun in a sex act. Three decades later, justice is served', *CNN World*, 24 January 2021. Available at: https://edition.cnn.com/2021/01/23/asia/sister-abhaya-murder-intl-dst-hnk/ (accessed on 26 June 2025).

Sreedevi Jayarajan, 'Explainer: What is the Sister Abhaya case and why it took 28 years for a verdict', *The NEWS Minute*, 21 December 2020. Available at: https://www.thenewsminute.com/kerala/explainer-what-sister-abhaya-case-and-why-it-took-28-years-verdict-140048 (accessed on 26 June 2025).

Dibakar Dutta, 'From "suicide" to conviction of Father Thomas and Sister Sephy: How it took 28 years for Sister Abhaya to get justice', *OpIndia*, 22 December 2020. Available at: https://www.

opindia.com/2020/12/sister-abhaya-case-father-thomas-sister-sephy-convicted-all-you-need-to-know-about-case/ (accessed on 26 June 2025).

'Sister Abhaya Murder Case: 28-Year Fight for Justice in Kerala's Most Disturbing Convent Crime', *Factual America*. Available at: https://www.factualamerica.com/crime-scene-stories/sister-abhaya-murder-case-28-year-fight-for-justice-in-keralas-most-disturbing-convent-crime (accessed on 26 June 2025).

M Nikitha, 'The Sensational Murder Case of Sister Abhaya – Timeline of Incidents', B&B Associates LLP. Available at: https://bnblegal.com/article/the-sensational-murder-case-of-sister-abhaya-timeline-of-incidents/ (accessed on 26 June 2025).

Rejimon Kuttappan, 'Explained: Sister Abhaya's Murder And The 28-Year Journey For Justice', *Boom*, 22 December 2020. Available at: https://www.boomlive.in/fact-file/sister-abhaya-case-verdict-sister-sephy-father-thomas-kottoor-judgement-explained-cbi-court-11254 (accessed on 26 June 2025).

CNN-News18, '28 Years After Murder Of Sister Abhaya, Accused Priest & Nun Sentenced To Life Imprisonment' [video], YouTube, 23 December 2020. Available at: https://www.youtube.com/watch?v=8XOF763RRag (accessed on 26 June 2025).

'The evidence that nailed Sister Abhaya's killers 28 years later', *India Today*, 24 December 2020. Available at: https://www.indiatoday.in/india/story/sister-abhaya-murder-evidence-1752581-2020-12-24 (accessed on 26 June 2025).

'A 28-Year Quest for Justice: The Mystery of Sister Abhaya's Murder', *Deccan Chronicle*, 9 May 2025. Available at: https://www.deccanchronicle.com/nation/crime/a-28-year-quest-for-justice-the-mystery-of-sister-abhayas-murder-1877880 (accessed on 26 June 2025).

'Court no to media exposure in sister Abhaya murder case', *The Hindu*, 14 September 2009. Available at: https://www.thehindu.

com/news/cities/Kochi/Court-no-to-media-exposure-in-sister-Abhaya-murder-case/article16881340.ece? (accessed on 26 June 2025).

'Sister Abhaya murder case verdict: 28 years later, both accused found guilty', *The Indian Express*, 22 December 2020. Available at: https://indianexpress.com/article/india/sister-abhaya-murder-verdict-7114553/? (accessed on 26 June 2025).

Sneha Mary Koshy, 'Sister Abhaya Murder: 28 Years On, Kerala Catholic Priest, Nun Convicted', *NDTV*, 22 December 2020. Available at: https://www.ndtv.com/india-news/sister-abhaya-murder-case-two-found-guilty-by-kerala-court-28-years-after-crime-2341922? (accessed on 26 June 2025).

'Sister Abhaya murder case | Father Thomas Kottoor, Sister Sephy sentenced to life imprisonment', *The Hindu*, 23 December 2020. Available at: https://www.thehindu.com/news/national/sister-abhaya-case-father-thomas-kottoor-sister-sephy-sentenced-to-life-imprisonment/article33400112.ece? (accessed on 26 June 2025).

Shaju Philip, 'Priest, nun get life term in Abhaya murder case', *The Indian Express*, 24 December 2020. Available at: https://indianexpress.com/article/india/kerala/abhaya-murder-case-priest-nun-sentenced-to-life-imprisonment-by-cbi-court-7116471/? (accessed on 26 June 2025).

Ramesh Babu, 'Sister Abhaya Murder: Kerala priest, nun get life imprisonment', *Hindustan Times*, 23 December 2020. Available at: https://www.hindustantimes.com/india-news/sister-abhaya-murder-kerala-priest-nun-get-life-imprisonment-story-nyiOYBzQM0ywboYzJkDSGK.html? (accessed on 27 June 2025).

'Sister Abhaya murder case: Kerala HC suspends life term, grants bail to convicted priest, nun', *The Indian Express*, 23 June 2022. Available at: https://indianexpress.com/article/india/kerala/

sister-abhaya-murder-case-kerala-high-court-grants-bail-to-convicted-priest-nun-7985974/? (accessed on 27 June 2025).

K. C Gopakumar, 'Sister Abhaya murder case | HC suspends life sentence of convicts', *The Hindu*, 23 June 2022. Available at: https://www.thehindu.com/news/national/kerala/sister-abhaya-murder-case-hc-suspends-life-sentence-of-convicts/article65556186.ece? (accessed on 27 June 2025).

Ramesh Babu, 'Nun and priest get bail in Sister Abhaya murder case', *Hindustan Times*, 24 June 2022. Available at: https://www.hindustantimes.com/india-news/sister-abhaya-murder-kerala-high-court-grants-bail-to-2-convicts-101655965738124.html? (accessed on 27 June 2025).

## 8. OCCULT SECRETS AND MASS PSYCHOSIS: THE BURARI SUICIDES

Guy Hadleigh, 'The Ritualistic Burari Deaths A Family's Mysterious End', 12 July 2024. Available at: https://www.guyhadleigh.com/blog/the-ritualistic-burari-deaths? (accessed on 27 June 2025).

'Burari deaths: Here's a look back at four cult-based mass suicides', *The Indian Express*, 3 July 2018. Available at: https://indianexpress.com/article/research/burari-deaths-delhi-cult-based-mass-suicides-5243910/? (accessed on 27 June 2025).

'Delhi Burari deaths: Cops recover handwritten notes with details of "mass murder", possible links to the occult', *Firstpost*, 2 July 2018. Available at: https://www.firstpost.com/india/delhi-burari-deaths-cops-recover-handwritten-notes-with-horrifying-details-of-mass-murder-and-possible-links-to-the-occult-4643571.html? (accessed on 27 June 2025).

Shiv Sunny and Karn Pratap Singh, 'Mass suicide, "wandering souls" rumours hit property rates in Delhi's Burari', *Hindustan Times*, 12 July 2018. Available at: https://www.hindustantimes.com/delhi-news/burari-battles-rumours-fears-of-plunging-property-rates-after-11-deaths/story-oBEpgpuTg5UKHk1UOMVWvI. html? (accessed on 27 June 2025).

'It was an accident: Report reveals how a ritual went wrong for Burari family', *India Today*, 15 September 2018. Available at: https://www.indiatoday.in/india/story/it-was-an-accident-report-reveals-how-ritual-went-wrong-for-burari-family-1340281-2018-09-15? (accessed on 27 June 2025).

Hemani Bhandari, 'Burari deaths: 11 bright people with one dark secret', *The Hindu*, 16 July 2018. Available at: https://www.thehindu.com/news/cities/Delhi/11-bright-people-with-one-dark-secret/article24428709.ece? (accessed on 27 June 2025).

Prabhash K Dutta, 'Beyond Burari deaths, occult practices are still a killer in India', *India Today*, 6 July 2018. Available at: https://www.indiatoday.in/india/story/beyond-burari-deaths-occult-practices-are-still-a-killer-in-india-1279217-2018-07-06? (accessed on 27 June 2025).

'Were occult practices behind India's "house of mass hangings"?', *BBC*, 20 July 2018. Available at: https://www.bbc.com/news/world-asia-india-44844617? (accessed on 27 June 2025).

'Burari case: Son's hallucinations of dead father behind mass suicide? Diary notings throw up morbid twist', *Financial Express*, 3 July 2018. Available at: https://www.financialexpress.com/india-news/burari-case-sons-hallucinations-of-dead-father-behind-mass-suicide-diary-notings-throw-up-morbid-twist/1229939/? (accessed on 27 June 2025).

Somreet Bhattacharya, 'Burai Mass Suicide: Locals skip "haunted" Burari house', *Times of India*, 25 October 2018. Available at: https://timesofindia.indiatimes.com/city/delhi/locals-skip-haunted-burari-house/articleshow/66354284.cms? (accessed on 27 June 2025).

'11 deaths, 11 pictures, 11 scary facts about Delhi family's mass suicide', *The Economic Times*, 3 July 2018. Available at: https://economictimes.indiatimes.com/news/politics-and-nation/11-deaths-11-pictures-11-scary-facts-about-delhi-familys-mass-suicide/house-of-horrors/slideshow/64843100.cms (accessed on 27 June 2025).

'Burari Deaths: A House, A Family, and A Mystery That Shook India', Bugged Space, 15 June 2023. Available at: https://www.buggedspace.com/burari-deaths/ (accessed on 27 June 2025).

## 9. THE SCAM CALL THAT WASN'T: THE ADITYA RANKA KIDNAPPING

Omkar Gokhale, 'Solving Crime: How a pair of forgotten red slippers helped cops nab the accused in 2013 Adit Ranka murder case', *The Indian Express*, 10 April 2023. Available at: https://indianexpress.com/article/cities/mumbai/solving-crime-forgotten-red-slippers-helped-cops-nab-accused-2013-adit-ranka-murder-case-8528968/? (accessed on 27 June 2025).

Sadaf Modak, 'Court says no motive "cogently established" against Ranka's cousin', *The Indian Express*, 13 October 2017. Available at: https://indianexpress.com/article/cities/mumbai/court-says-no-motive-cogently-established-against-rankas-cousin-4887812/? (accessed on 27 June 2025).

'Aditya Ranka murder verdict: He deserved death, says mother of victim', *Mid-Day*, 13 October 2017. Available at: https://www.mid-day.com/mumbai/mumbai-news/article/aditya-ranka-murder-verdict-he-deserved-death--says-mother-of-victim-18650192? (accessed on 27 June 2025).

'Five cases that you will never forget from Arita Sarkar's *Kidnapped*', Penguin Random House, 1 July 2019. Available at: https://www.penguin.co.in/five-cases-that-you-will-never-forget-from-arita-sarkars-kidnapped/? (accessed on 27 June 2025).

Rebecca Samervel, 'Cousin cleared of killing diamond merchant's son, friend convicted', *Times of India*, 10 October 2017. Available at: https://timesofindia.indiatimes.com/city/mumbai/cousin-cleared-of-killing-diamond-merchants-son-friend-convicted/articleshow/61013395.cms? (accessed on 27 June 2025).

'घर वालों से रुपए लेने के लिए दुकानदार ने रची थी अपहरण की कहानी, जांच में निकली फर्जी', *Hindustan*, 17 November 2024. Available at: https://www.livehindustan.com/uttar-pradesh/hardoi/story-fake-kidnapping-story-of-shopkeeper-in-hardoi-police-investigation-reveals-truth-201731866134362.html? (accessed on 27 June 2025).

Sadaf Modak, 'Ranka's killer awarded life imprisonment in 2013 Kidnapping and murder', *The Indian Express*, 13 October 2017. Available at: https://indianexpress.com/article/cities/mumbai/rankas-killer-awarded-life-imprisonment-in-2013-kidnapping-and-murder-4887773/? (accessed on 27 June 2025).

Sadaf Modak, 'Diamond broker's son murdered: Bombay HC grants bail to man sentenced to life by trial court', *The Indian Express*, 11 August 2019. Available at: https://indianexpress.com/article/cities/mumbai/diamond-brokers-son-murder-bombay-hc-grants-bail-man-sentenced-life-5895285/? (accessed on 27 June 2025).

'Case of missing slippers: How 13-year-old Aditya's kidnappers got caught', *India Today*, 15 May 2013. Available at: https://www.indiatoday.in/mail-today/story/mba-student-kidnaps-cousin-kills-him-to-pay-ipl-bet-163166-2013-05-14 (accessed on 27 June 2025).

Sadaf Modak, 'Diamond broker's son murdered: Bombay HC grants bail to man sentenced to life by trial court', *The Indian Express*, 11 August 2019. Available at: https://indianexpress.com/article/cities/mumbai/diamond-brokers-son-murder-bombay-hc-grants-bail-man-sentenced-life-5895285/ (accessed on 27 June 2025).

Crimes From The East Podcast, 'Deadly Betrayal The Adit Ranka Murder'[video], YouTube, 24 May 2021. Available at: https://www.youtube.com/watch?v=gxarw3JlDb0 (accessed on 27 June 2025).

## 10. SNUFFING OUT A RISING STAR: THE MURDER OF QANDEEL BALOCH

Sanam Maher, 'Death of a Star What Qandeel Baloch left behind', *Caravan*, 1 May 2018. Available at: https://caravanmagazine.in/reportage/what-qandeel-baloch-left-behind (accessed on 27 June 2025).

Amber Rahim Shamsi, 'Qandeel Baloch: How her murder reflects a divided country', *BBC News*, 16 July 2016. Available at: https://www.bbc.com/news/world-asia-36815808? (accessed on 27 June 2025).

'Brother of social media star Qandeel Baloch is jailed for her murder', *The Guardian*, 27 September 2019. Available at: https://www.theguardian.com/world/2019/sep/27/brother-social-media-star-qandeel-baloch-jailed-murder-pakistan? (accessed on 27 June 2025).

Hamza Ameer, 'Qandeel Baloch murder: Slain Pakistani model's brother jailed for life', *India Today*, 27 September 2019. Available at: https://www.indiatoday.in/world/story/qandeel-baloch-murder-slain-pakistani-model-s-brother-jailed-for-life-1603854-2019-09-27? (accessed on 27 June 2025).

Diaa Hadid, 'A man who strangled his celebrity sister has been acquitted in Pakistan', *NPR*, 15 February 2022. Available at: https://www.npr.org/2022/02/15/1080843294/qandeel-baloch-brother-acquittal-murder-pakistan? (accessed on 27 June 2025).

'Qandeel Baloch murder case: Brother sentenced to life imprisonment', *Business Standard*, 27 September 2019. Available at: https://www.business-standard.com/article/news-ani/qandeel-baloch-murder-case-brother-sentenced-to-life-imprisonment-119092700459_1.html (accessed on 27 June 2025).

Tara John, '"Honour Killings" and the Murder of a Social-Media Star', *Time*, 21 July 2016. Available at: https://time.com/4416688/honor-killings-and-the-murder-of-a-social-media-star/ (accessed on 27 June 2025).

Emma Stefansky, 'Pakistani Social Media Star Qandeel Baloch Murdered in Apparent Honor Killing', *Vanity Fair*, 17 July 2016. Available at: https://www.vanityfair.com/news/2016/07/qandeel-baloch-murdered-honor-killing? (accessed on 27 June 2025).

Saira Khan, 'The Outrageous "Honor Killing" of a Pakistani Social-Media Star', *The New Yorker*, 19 July 2016. Available at: https://www.newyorker.com/news/news-desk/the-outrageous-honor-killing-of-a-pakistani-social-media-star? (accessed on 27 June 2025).

Lauren Duca, 'Pakistani Model Qandeel Baloch Was Murdered by Her Brother in an Admitted "Honor Killing"', *Teen Vogue*, 17 July 2016. Available at: https://www.teenvogue.com/story/pakistani-model-honor-killing (accessed on 27 June 2025).

Arsalan Iftikhar, 'Honor Killings Are a Global Problem', *Time*, 29 July 2016. Available at: https://time.com/4415554/honor-killing-qandeel-baloch/ (accessed on 27 June 2025).

'Explained: Qandeel Baloch's brother convicted; a look at Pakistan's honour killing case', *The Indian Express*, 1 October 2019. Available at: https://indianexpress.com/article/explained/explained-qandeel-balochs-brother-convicted-for-murder-a-look-at-paks-honour-killing-case-6041199/? (accessed on 27 June 2025).

'Pakistan High Court acquits social media star Qandeel Baloch's killer after parents pardon him', *Tribune India*, 15 February 2022. Available at: https://www.tribuneindia.com/news/world/pakistan-high-court-acquits-social-media-star-qandeel-balochs-killer-after-parents-pardon-him-369882/ (accessed on 27 June 2025).

'Pakistan: Brother's acquittal in Qandeel Baloch murder challenged', *Al Jazeera*, 21 March 2022. Available at: https://www.aljazeera.com/news/2022/3/21/pakistan-appeal-over-brother-acquittal-in-qandeel-baloch-murder (accessed on 27 June 2025).

'Qandeel Baloch "honour killing": Brother sentenced to life', *The Hindu*, 27 September 2019. Available at: https://www.thehindu.com/news/international/brother-of-pakistani-social-media-star-jailed-for-life-for-her-murder/article29528917.ece? (accessed on 27 June 2025).

## 11. A HASTY CONCLUSION: THE CONFOUNDING CASE OF PRAVIN VARUGHESE

Jonah Meadows, 'Man Murdered Morton Grove SIU Student In 2014, Jury Finds', Patch, 15 June 2018. Available at: https://patch.com/illinois/niles/man-murdered-morton-grove-siu-student-2014-jury-finds? (accessed on 27 June 2025).

Kriti Mehrotra, 'Gaege Bethune: Where is the Alleged Killer Now?', The Cinemaholic, 28 April 2024. Available at: https://thecinemaholic.com/gaege-bethune/? (accessed on 27 June 2025).

Aimee Lamoureux, 'The Real Reason Pravin Varughese's Convicted Murderer Was Set Free', Grunge, 7 March 2022. Available at: https://www.grunge.com/364336/the-real-reason-pravin-varugheses-convicted-murderer-was-set-free/? (accessed on 27 June 2025).

Rob Stafford and Lisa Capitanini, '"My Client is a Victim in

This Case": New Defense Lawyer Says Downstate Man Only Offered a Ride to Suburban College Student'. *NBC Chicago*, 2 November 2018. Available at: https://www.nbcchicago.com/local/my-client-is-a-victim-in-this-case-new-defense-lawyer-says-downstate-man-only-offered-a-ride-to-suburban-college-student/141271/? (accessed on 27 June 2025).

'Jackson County judge vacates Gaege Bethune's murder conviction', *The Daily Egyptian*, 17 September 2018. Available at: https://dailyegyptian.com/86433/news/jackson-county-judge-vacates-gaege-bethunes-murder-conviction/? (accessed on 27 June 2025).

'Pravin Varughese murder: Indian-American mother's fight leads to conviction of son's killer', *Gulf News*, 5 November 2018. Available at: https://gulfnews.com/world/americas/pravin-varughese-murder-indian-american-mothers-fight-leads-to-conviction-of-sons-killer-1.2237902? (accessed on 27 June 2025).

Viswa Vanapalli, 'Pravin Varughese: How Did He Die? Who Killed Him?', The Cinemaholic, 24 March 2024. Available at: https://thecinemaholic.com/pravin-varughese-murder-where-is-gaege-bethune-now/? (accessed on 27 June 2025).

Shweta Mudaliar, 'Where is Gaege Bethune now? 'Dateline NBC' explores Illinois teen's deadly drug dispute', Meaww, 28 April 2024. Available at: https://meaww.com/where-is-gaege-bethune-now-dateline-nbc-explores-illinois-teens-deadly-drug-dispute? (accessed on 27 June 2025).

Nikita Mahato, 'Dateline NBC: Why Was Pravin Varughese's Accused Killer Gaege Bethune Released?', Coming Soon, 26 April 2022. Available at: https://www.comingsoon.net/true-crime/news/1681662-dateline-nbc-why-was-pravin-varughese-accused-killer-gaege-bethune-released? (accessed on 27 June 2025).

'Murdered: Pravin Varughese', Uncovered, 11 May 2024. Available at: https://uncovered.com/cases/pravin-varughese? (accessed on 27 June 2025).

'Jury finds Gaege Bethune guilty of first-degree murder in the 2014 death of Indian-American student Pravin Varughese', *News India Times*, 16 June 2018. Available at: https://www.newsindiatimes.com/jury-finds-gaege-bethune-guilty-of-first-degree-murder-in-the-2014-death-of-indian-american-student-pravin-varughese/? (accessed on 27 June 2025).

Jerry Brown, 'Pravin Varughese: Student's mysterious death, harrowing autopsy photos, and the mom who never gave up', Daily Crime, 19 January 2023. Available at: https://www.dailycrime.com/pravin-varughese-students-mysterious-death-harrowing-autopsy-photos-and-the-mom-who-never-gave-up/ (accessed on 27 June 2025).

## 12. THE TANDOOR MURDER

'Death for India's Tandoor killer', *Alja Zeera*, 7 November 2003. Available at: https://www.aljazeera.com/news/2003/11/7/death-for-indias-tandoor-killer? (accessed on 27 June 2025).

Vaibhav Tiwari, 'The 1995 Tandoor Murder Case That Shocked Delhi: All You Need To Know', *NDTV*, 21 December 2018. Available at: https://www.ndtv.com/india-news/naina-sahni-murder-all-you-need-to-know-about-the-tandoor-case-1966212? (accessed on 27 June 2025).

'Tandoor case: How Sushil Sharma murdered his wife Naina Sahni', *News 18*, 8 October 2013. Available at: https://www.news18.com/news/politics/tandoor-case-how-sushil-sharma-murdered-his-wife-naina-sahni-643800.html? (accessed on 27 June 2025).

Abraham Thomas, 'Tandoor murder: Supreme Court junks Delhi govt's plea', *Hindustan Times*, 5 January 2023.

Available at: https://www.hindustantimes.com/cities/delhi-news/tandoor-murder-supreme-court-junks-delhi-govt-s-plea-101672857724519.html? (accessed on 27 June 2025).

Abhinav Garg, 'Tandoor murder case: Delhi HC orders release of Sushil Sharma', *Times of India*, 21 December 2018. Available at: https://timesofindia.indiatimes.com/city/delhi/hc-does-life-term-mean-life/articleshow/67171330.cms? (accessed on 28 June 2025).

Anuj Pant, 'Sushil Sharma, Tandoor Murder Case Convict, Will Walk Free After 23 Years', *NDTV*, 21 December 2018. Available at: https://www.ndtv.com/india-news/tandoor-murder-case-sushil-sharma-tandoor-murder-case-convict-will-walk-free-after-23-years-1966271 (accessed on 28 June 2025).

'1995 Tandoor murder case: Delhi HC orders immediate release of convict Sushil Sharma', *The Indian Express*, 21 December 2018. Available at: https://indianexpress.com/article/india/1995-tandoor-murder-case-delhi-hc-orders-immediate-release-of-convict-sushil-sharma-5504051/ (accessed on 28 June 2025).

'The infamous 'Tandoor murder case: All you need to know', *Firstpost*, 8 October 2013. Available at: https://www.firstpost.com/india/the-infamous-tandoor-murder-case-all-you-need-to-know-1159475.html (accessed on 28 June 2025).

Pritam Pal Singh, '29 years after tandoor murder case, Sushil walks out of jail', *The Indian Express*, 22 December 2018. Available at: https://indianexpress.com/article/cities/delhi/29-years-after-tandoor-murder-case-sushil-walks-out-of-jail-5504666/? (accessed on 28 June 2025).

Utkarsh Anand, 'Tandoor murder case: SC commutes death sentence of Sushil Sharma to life', *The Indian Express*, 8 October 2013. Available at: https://indianexpress.com/article/india/crime/tandoor-murder-case-sc-commutes-death-sentence-of-sushil-sharma-to-life/? (accessed on 28 June 2025).

Maxwell Pereira, *The Tandoor Murder: The Crime That Shook the Nation and Brought a Government to Its Knees*, Chennai: Context, 2018.

Vivek Tanwar, 'The Shocking Tandoor Murder Case: Naina Sahni's Story', Advocate Tanwar, 13 February 2024. Available at: https://advocatetanwar.com/the-shocking-tandoor-murder-case-naina-sahnis-story/ (accessed on 28 June 2025).

Preeti, 'Tandoor Murder Case Study', Scribd. Available at: http://scribd.com/presentation/555831720/TANDOOR-MURDER-CASE-STUDY (accessed on 28 June 2025).

'1995 Tandoor murder case: A murder mystery that shook the nation', *DNA*, 21 December 2018. Available at: https://www.dnaindia.com/india/photo-gallery-1995-tandoor-murder-case-a-murder-mystery-that-shook-the-nation-2698752/india/photo-gallery-1995-tandoor-murder-case-a-murder-mystery-that-shook-the-nation-2698752/what-exactly-happened-that-night-2698753 (accessed on 28 June 2025).

Abhinav Garg, 'Tandoor murder case: Convict out on parole as state didn't respond', *Times of India*, 15 September 2015. Available at: https://timesofindia.indiatimes.com/city/delhi/Tandoor-murder-case-Convict-out-on-parole-as-state-didnt-respond/articleshow/48977345.cms? (accessed on 28 June 2025).

## 13. NOT-SO-JOLLY JOSEPH

Vivek Rajagopal, '"The Jolly Joseph Case": All you need to know about horrific Kerala cyanide murders', *India Today*, 14 December 2023. Available at: https://www.indiatoday.in/entertainment/ott/story/curry-and-cyanide-the-jolly-joseph-case-all-you-need-to-know-about-horrific-kerala-cyanide-murders-india-today-originals-documentary-netflix-2475832-2023-12-14 (accessed on 28 June 2025).

'Koodathayi case: Kerala HC not to interfere in lower court order against Jolly', *Mathrubhumi*, 6 March 2023. Available at: https://english.mathrubhumi.com/news/kerala/koodathayi-case-kerala-hc-not-to-interfere-in-lower-court-order-against-jolly-9bd1e097? (accessed on 28 June 2025).

Shalu Philip, 'The true story of the Jolly Joseph case, now subject of a Netflix documentary', *The Indian Express*, 9 January 2024. Available at: https://indianexpress.com/article/explained/jolly-joseph-murders-koodatha-netflix-9079974/? (accessed on 28 June 2025).

Evangeline Elsa, 'Jolly Joseph Kerala serial murder case: Bank raided, positive lab report and how she killed a child', *Gulf News*, 30 October 2019. Available at: https://gulfnews.com/world/asia/india/jolly-joseph-kerala-serial-murder-case-bank-raided-positive-lab-report-and-how-she-killed-a-child-1.1572433598642? (accessed on 28 June 2025).

'"Jolly forcing me to drop case": Rojo, who filed first complaint in Koodathayi murders', *The News Minute*, 16 October 2019. Available at: https://www.thenewsminute.com/kerala/jolly-forcing-me-drop-case-rojo-who-filed-first-complaint-koodathayi-murders-110608? (accessed on 28 June 2025).

Shalu Philip, 'Using cyanide, Kerala woman murdered six members of family over 14 years, say police', *The Indian Express*, 10 October 2019. Available at: https://indianexpress.com/article/india/kerala/using-cyanide-kerala-woman-murdered-six-members-of-family-over-14-years-say-police-6055693/? (accessed on 28 June 2025).

'Koodathayi case: No cyanide presence spotted in four bodies; trial to begin on March 6', *Mathrubhumi*, 5 February 2023. Available at: https://english.mathrubhumi.com/news/kerala/koodathayi-case-no-cyanide-presence-spotted-in-four-bodies-trial-to-begin-on-march-6-b254b322 (accessed on 28 June 2025).

Rashmi Kuttan, 'Koodathayi murder case: Supreme Court rejects Jolly Joseph's plea seeking acquittal', *Asianet News*, 22 March 2024. Available at: https://newsable.asianetnews.com/kerala-news/koodathayi-murder-case-supreme-court-rejects-jolly-joseph-s-plea-seeking-acquittal-rkn-saqo87? (accessed on 28 June 2025).

'Koodathayi case accused approaches court against telecast of Netflix documentary "Curry & Cyanide: The Jolly Joseph Case"', *News9*, 19 January 2024. Available at: https://www.news9live.com/state/kerala/koodathayi-case-accused-approaches-court-against-telecast-of-netflix-documentary-curry-cyanide-the-jolly-joseph-case-2411034 (accessed on 28 June 2025).

'SC rejects Jolly Joseph's plea seeking acquittal in death of her husband', *Mathrubhumi*, 23 March 2024. Available at: https://english.mathrubhumi.com/news/kerala/sc-rejects-jolly-josephs-plea-seeking-acquittal-in-death-of-her-husband-13e0803a (accessed on 28 June 2025).

## 14. MISSING SINCE 9/11: SNEHA PHILIP

Helen Elfer, 'Sneha Philip: The mystery of the woman who disappeared on 9/11', *Independent*, 11 September 2021. Available at: https://www.independent.co.uk/news/world/americas/sneha-philip-mystery-disappeared-9-11-b1917381.html? (accessed on 29 June 2025).

Michael Ruiz, 'Missing doctor who lived near Twin Towers officially died on 9/11, but sleuths suspect she was killed earlier', *FOX 13 Seattle*, 11 September 2023. Available at: https://www.fox13seattle.com/news/missing-doctor-died-9-11-possibly-killed-earlier (accessed on 29 June 2025).

Monika Joshi, 'Indian woman included in 9/11 honour roll, finally', *Rediff*, 7 August 2008. Available at: https://www.rediff.com/

news/report/roll/20080807.htm? (accessed on 29 June 2025).

'Sneha Ann Philip', The Charley Project, 12 October 2004. Available at: https://charleyproject.org/case/sneha-ann-philip? (accessed on 29 June 2025).

Dareh Gregorian, 'SOLVED: THE LAST MYSTERY OF 9/11', *New York Post*, 11 July 2008. Available at: https://nypost.com/2008/07/11/solved-the-last-mystery-of-911/ (accessed on 29 June 2025).

George Joseph, '9/11: "Sneha's room has been kept the same way for the past 15 years"', Rediff, 11 September 2016. Available at: https://www.rediff.com/news/special/snehas-room-has-been-kept-the-same-way-for-the-past-15-years/20160911.htm? (accessed on 29 June 2025).

Aishwarya Gopinath, 'Dr Sneha Anne Philip, The Malayali Who Was The 2751st Victim Of The 9/11 Attack', Pinklungi, 11 September 2022. Available at: https://www.pinklungi.com/dr-sneha-anne-philip-the-malayali-who-was-the-2751st-victim-of-the-9-11-attack/? (accessed on 29 June 2025).

Andrea Francese, '"Missing on 9/11": A New Podcast Dives Into the Mysterious Disappearance of Sneha Philip', Cheat Sheet, 26 June 2021. Available at: https://www.cheatsheet.com/news/missing-on-9-11-new-podcast-dives-into-the-mysterious-disappearance-of-sneha-philip.html/? (accessed on 29 June 2025).

## 15. THE TALE OF TWO VISHWANATHS

S. R. Krishna Kumar, 'Vishwanath Shetty vs State Of Karnataka on 5 February, 2025', India Kanoon. Available at: https://indiankanoon.org/doc/172921239/ (accessed on 10 July 2025).

Sakshi TV, 'Karnataka lokayukta Justice Vishwanath Shetty stabbed, attacker arrested' [video], YouTube, 7 March 2018. Available at: https://www.youtube.com/watch?v=MiAFaQIh2EA (accessed on 10 July 2025).

'Puttur: Accused, arrested after 13 years of murder, faces another case', DiajiWorld, 12 August 2014. Available at: https://www.daijiworld.com/news/newsDisplay.aspx?newsID=255267 (accessed on 10 July 2025).

'Puttur: Accused gets life term 20 years after murdering financier', DaijiWorld, 16 December 2021. Available at: https://www.daijiworld.com/news/newsDisplay?newsID=904890 (accessed on 10 July 2025).

'How did cricket stadium help solve 13-year-old murder mystery?', *Top Indian News*, 22 June 2024. Available at: https://www.topindiannews.com/national/how-did-cricket-stadium-help-solve-13-year-old-murder-mystery-news-19545 (accessed on 10 July 2025).

'Absconding Uppinangady murderer trapped after unlucky 13 years', *Mangalore Today*, 12 August 2014. Available at: https://www.mangaloretoday.com/main/Absconding-Uppinangady-murderer-trapped-after-unlucky-13-years.html (accessed on 10 July 2025).

'Murder accused arrested after 13 years', *Coastal Digest*, 11 August 2014. Available at: https://www.mangaloretoday.com/main/Absconding-Uppinangady-murderer-trapped-after-unlucky-13-years.html (accessed on 10 July 2025).

Press Trust of India, 'Accused in murder case arrested after 13 years', *Business Standard*, 12 August 2014. Available at: https://www.business-standard.com/article/pti-stories/accused-in-murder-case-arrested-after-13-years-114081200513_1.html (accessed on 10 July 2025).

'Here's how Karnataka cops cracked a 13-year-old murder case, all thanks to a cricket tourney', *Deccan Herald*, 23 June 2024. Available at: https://www.deccanherald.com/india/karnataka/heres-how-karnataka-cops-cracked-a-13-year-old-murder-case-all-thanks-to-a-cricket-tourney-3076816 (accessed on 10 July 2025).

Tv9 Kannada, 'How Did The Accused Sneak A Knife Into The Lokayuktha Office & Stab Vishwanath Shetty?' [video], YouTube, 7 March 2018. Available at: https://www.youtube.com/watch?v=1OL4raagl6U (accessed on 10 July 2025).

'Man accused on murder held after 16 years', *Times of India*, 6 September 2014. Available at: https://timesofindia.indiatimes.com/city/mangaluru/Man-accused-of-murder-held-after-16-years/articleshow/41847803.cms (accessed on 10 July 2025).

## 16. BURIED ALIVE: THE GRISLY MURDER OF SHAKEREH KHALEELI

'Resurrecting Shakereh Khaleeli' *The Tribune*, 29 April 2023. Available at: https://www.tribuneindia.com/news/entertainment/resurrecting-shakereh-khaleeli-503074/ (accessed on 30 June 2025).

Abhimanyu Hazarika, 'Shakereh Khaleeli murder: Swami Shraddhanand moves Supreme Court again for parole', Bar and Bench, 29 July 2024. Available at: https://www.barandbench.com/news/shakereh-khaleeli-murder-swami-shraddhanand-supreme-court-parole? (accessed on 30 June 2025).

'Here's the true story of Swami Shraddhanand, "godman" who buried his wife alive, shown in Amazon's *Dancing on the Grave*', *DNA*, 23 April 2023. Available at: https://www.dnaindia.com/entertainment/report-swami-shraddhanand-godman-shakereh-khaleeli-true-crime-show-dancing-on-the-grave-prime-video-3038092 (accessed on 30 June 2025).

Aditi Suryavanshi, 'Shakereh Khaleeli Murder: True Story Behind New Series "Dancing on the Grave"', *The Quint*, 24 April 2023. Available at: https://www.thequint.com/entertainment/hot-on-web/shakereh-khaleeli-murder-true-story-behind-dancing-on-the-grave (accessed on 30 June 2025).

Avni Arya, 'Flashback Files | Bengaluru's Most Chilling Crime: A Princess, A Swami and A Coffin Beneath Royal Palace', *Times Now*, 15 May 2025. Available at: https://www.timesnownews.com/bengaluru/bengalurus-most-chilling-crime-a-princess-a-swami-and-a-coffin-beneath-palace-what-happened-to-shakereh-khaleeli-swami-shraddhananda-article-151640131 (accessed on 30 June 2025).

'Dancing On The Grave: What is the Shakereh Khaleeli murder case the Prime Video show is based on', *The Indian Express*, 28 April 2023. Available at: https://indianexpress.com/article/explained/dancing-on-the-grave-what-is-the-shakereh-khaleeli-murder-case-8579856/? (accessed on 30 June 2025).

'HC confirms Shraddhananda's verdict', *Times of India*, 20 September 2005. Available at: https://timesofindia.indiatimes.com/india/hc-confirms-shraddhanandas-verdict/articleshow/1236575.cms? (accessed on 30 June 2025).

'Death or life term? SC divided over godman verdict', *Times of India*, 1 May 2008. Available at: https://timesofindia.indiatimes.com/india/death-or-life-term-sc-divided-over-godman-verdict/articleshow/2999764.cms (accessed on 30 June 2025).

Abhimanyu Hazarika, 'Shakereh Khaleeli murder: Supreme Court refuses to entertain Swami Shraddhanand plea for parole', Bar and Bench, 26 April 2023. Available at: https://www.barandbench.com/news/litigation/shakereh-khaleeli-murder-supreme-court-dismisses-swami-shraddhanand-plea-for-parole? (accessed on 30 June 2025).

Shweta Keshri, 'Dancing on the Grave Review: This India Today Originals will leave you hooked with its intense storytelling', *India Today*, 21 April 2023. Available at: https://www.indiatoday.in/entertainment/ott/story/dancing-on-the-grave-review-shakereh-khaleeli-chilling-murder-2362585-2023-04-21 (accessed on 30 June 2025).

'OTT series "Dancing on the Grave" to tell story of Shakereh Khaleeli murder case', *Times of India*, 15 April 2023. Available at: https://timesofindia.indiatimes.com/web-series/news/hindi/ott-series-dancing-on-the-grave-to-tell-story-of-shakereh-khaleeli-murder-case/articleshow/99518824.cms? (accessed on 30 June 2025).

Abhimanyu Hazarika, 'Shakereh Khaleeli murder: Supreme Court rejects parole plea by Swami Shraddhanand (again)', Bar and Bench, 11 September 2024. Available at: https://www.barandbench.com/news/shakereh-khaleeli-murder-supreme-court-rejects-parole-swami-shraddhanand-again? (accessed on 30 June 2025).

Arshiya Banu, 'Shakereh Khaleeli Murder: Supreme Court Upholds Life Sentence for Swami Shraddhananda', Legalit, 25 October 2024. Available at: https://legalit.ai/shakereh-khaleeli-murder-supreme-court-upholds-life-sentence-for-swami-shraddhananda/ (accessed on 30 June 2025).

Shaurya Thapa, 'The true story of Dancing On The Grave and the murder of Shakereh Khaleeli from Bengaluru', DailyO, 18 April 2024. Available at: https://www.dailyo.in/entertainment/the-true-story-of-dancing-on-the-grave-and-the-murder-of-shakereh-khaleeli-from-bengaluru-39493 (accessed on 30 June 2025).

## 17. THE SICKLY-SWEET SMELL OF MURDER: THE JOSHI–ABHYANKAR MASSACRES

Sushant Kulkarni, 'Know Your City: The Joshi-Abhyankar serial murders that struck fear in the hearts of Pune's young and old', *The Indian Express*, 1 October 2022. Available at: https://

indianexpress.com/article/cities/pune/know-your-city-joshi-abhyankar-serial-murders-fear-punes-8184128/ (accessed on 30 June 2025).

'47 years on, podcast captures Joshi-Abhyankar murders that shook Punekars', *Hindustan Times*, 14 January 2023. Available at: https://www.hindustantimes.com/cities/pune-news/47-years-on-podcast-captures-joshi-abhyankar-murders-that-shook-punekars-101673717637235.html (accessed on 30 June 2025).

SR PAY, 'Joshi Abhyankar Pune Family Murders' [video], YouTube, 29 December 2023. Available at: https://www.youtube.com/watch?v=ogP84zK9qKg (accessed on 30 June 2025).

Jake Carter, 'Pune Massacre: The Chilling Tale of the Joshi-Abhyankar Serial Murders', Anomalien, 3 August 2023. Available at: https://anomalien.com/pune-massacre-the-chilling-tale-of-the-joshi-abhyankar-serial-murders/ (accessed on 30 June 2025).

'Joshi-Abhyankar serial murders- A gang of art students from Pune who did serial killings during 1976-1977 (Crime Patrol Dial 100 Episode 46 on 16th December, 2015)', Inside Stories, 18 December 2015. Available at: https://www.insidestories.co.in/2015/12/shaitaan-joshi-abhyankar-serial-murders.html (accessed on 30 June 2025).

'4 Convicts Were Last Hanged In A Day In 1983: Report', *NDTV*, 10 January 2020. Available at: https://www.ndtv.com/india-news/joshi-abhyankar-killings-before-nirbhaya-case-4-convicts-were-last-hanged-in-a-day-in-1983-says-repo-2161621 (accessed on 30 June 2025).

Parth Kulkarni, 'Josh Abhyankar Murders', *Bloodstained – An Indian Saga*, Apple Podcasts, 30 October 2023. Available at: https://podcasts.apple.com/ca/podcast/bloodstained-an-indian-saga/id1714181571 (accessed on 30 June 2025).

Seema Khandagale, *Pune Killings: Jakkal Case*, Amazon Music, 11 January 2023. Available at: https://music.amazon.com/es-cl/

podcasts/e50c84af-3b7e-4a29-8f35-44ecb401803a/episodes/dc35570e-ebac-4b03-afe6-2ed12acf7c41/pune-killings-jakkal-case-episode-one (accessed on 30 June 2025).

Apurva Patil, '2. The Joshi Abhyankar Serial Murders', *SinsOfAsia - A True Crime Podcast*, Spotify, 30 March 2022. Available at: https://creators.spotify.com/pod/profile/apurva-patil8/episodes/Ep--02---The-Joshi-Abhyankar-Serial-Murders-India-e1gfa00 (accessed on 30 June 2025).

## 18. A DEADLY VIRAL VIDEO: THE KOHISTAN KILLINGS

'Afzal Kohistani: 'Honour killing' whistleblower shot dead', *BBC*, 7 March 2019. Available at: https://www.bbc.com/news/world-asia-47480597 (accessed on 30 June 2025).

Ashfaq Ahmed, 'How Afzal Kohistani, the brave man who challenged "honour killing" in Pakistan's tribal belt, lost his life', *Gulf News*, 7 March 2019. Available at: https://gulfnews.com/world/asia/pakistan/how-afzal-kohistani-the-brave-man-who-challenged-honour-killing-in-pakistans-tribal-belt-lost-his-life-1.62514125 (accessed on 30 June 2025).

'Kohistan video murders: Three guilty in 'honour killing' blood feud', *BBC*, 5 September 2019. Available at: https://www.bbc.com/news/world-asia-49592540 (accessed on 30 June 2025).

Frances Mao, Kelly Ng and Muhammad Zubair, 'Pakistan: Woman killed after being seen with man in viral photo', *BBC*, 28 November 2023. Available at: https://www.bbc.com/news/world-asia-67551554 (accessed on 30 June 2025).

'Honor Killings Unveiled: The Kohistan Video Scandal', Prime Video. Available at: https://www.primevideo.com/detail/Honor-Killings-Unveiled-The-Kohistan-Video-Scandal/0IQXXVAUOBACMTY3HLDGRG6XPP

ENDEVR, 'Unveiled: The Kohistan Video Scandal | Tribal Justice | ENDEVR Documentary' [video], YouTube,

9 May 2021. Available at: https://www.youtube.com/watch?v=eFVhdudc3Rk (accessed on 30 June 2025).

'HRCP strongly condemns Kohistan honour killing', HRCP. Available at: https://hrcp-web.org/hrcpweb/hrcp-strongly-condemns-kohistan-honour-killing/ (accessed on 30 June 2025).

VICE News, 'The Kohistan Story: Killing for Honor' [video], YouTube, 25 January 2016. Available at: https://www.youtube.com/watch?v=xoPXW8Qm8U8&t=22s (accessed on 30 June 2025).

Haseeb Bhatti, 'Girls in 2011 Kohistan video were killed, Supreme Court told', *Dawn*, 2 January 2019. Available at: https://www.dawn.com/news/1455038 (accessed on 30 June 2025).

'Kohistan: The reality of honour killings in Pakistan', Global Politics, 12 December 2023. Available at: https://globalpolitics.in/pakistan/pakistan-short-notes.php?recordNo=822&url=Kohistan:%20The%20reality%20of%20honour%20killings%20in%20Pakistan (accessed on 30 June 2025).

Asad Hashim, 'How a Pakistani whistle-blower was killed for 'honour'', *Al Jazeera*, 26 March 2019. Available at: https://www.aljazeera.com/features/2019/3/26/how-a-pakistani-whistle-blower-was-killed-for-honour (accessed on 30 June 2025).

'4 arrested in "honor killing" of 18-year-old Pakistani woman after doctored photo with her boyfriend goes viral', *CBS News*, 1 December 2023. Available at: https://www.cbsnews.com/news/honor-killing-pakistan-doctored-photo-woman-boyfriend-goes-viral-arrests/ (accessed on 30 June 2025).

Umar Bacha, 'Rising Honour Killings in Kohistan: A Consequence of Judicial Inefficiency?', *Lok Sujag*, 1 March 2024. Available at: https://loksujag.com/story/honor-killing-kohistan-kp-eng (accessed on 30 June 2025).

'Pakistan: Authorities must end impunity of tribal councils as so-called "honour killings" continue unabated', Amnesty International, 30 November 2023. Available at: https://www.amnesty.org/en/latest/news/2023/11/pakistan-authorities-must-intensify-pressure-to-end-impunity-of-tribal-councils-as-honour-killings-continue-unabated/ (accessed on 30 June 2025).

## 19. GONE WITHOUT A TRACE: THE SUDDEN DISAPPEARANCE OF THE CHOHAN FAMILY

Sidin Vadukut, 'The tale of the Chohan murders', *LiveMint*, 4 February 2017. Available at: https://www.livemint.com/Sundayapp/Lr81eAH30WDuSv4rN9SFtO/The-tale-of-the-Chohan-murders.html (accessed on 30 June 2025).

Real Stories, 'The Brutal Murder Of The Chohan Family | Real Stories True Crime Documentary' [video], YouTube, 28 February 2018. Available at: https://www.youtube.com/watch?v=xSkSFcOcd_U (accessed on 30 June 2025).

Tania Branigan, 'Family murdered "to take over business"', *The Guardian*, 9 November 2004. Available at: https://www.theguardian.com/uk/2004/nov/09/ukcrime.taniabranigan (accessed on 30 June 2025).

Nabanita Sircar, '5 NRIs killed in cold blood', *Hindustan Times*, 11 November 2004. Available at: https://www.hindustantimes.com/world/5-nris-killed-in-cold-blood/story-qyU4BB3ppq3mfaqrtqHNSI.html (accessed on 30 June 2025).

'Missing family inquiry after body found in UK', *New Zealand Herald*, 4 May 2003. Available at: https://www.nzherald.co.nz/nz/missing-family-inquiry-after-body-found-in-uk/CKG5I6X75WC2QDU752SIQ43GFI/#google_vignette (accessed on 30 June 2025).

BingeWorthy Documentaries, 'What Happened to Them? | The Family Who Vanished | Full Documentary' [video], YouTube, 4 June 2024. Available at: https://www.youtube.com/watch?v=rKBRyFJG5PM (accessed on 30 June 2025).

Jamie Wilson, 'New twist in saga of missing millionaire as body is found in the sea', *The Guardian*, 3 May 2003. Available at: https://www.theguardian.com/uk/2003/may/03/jamiewilson (accessed on 30 June 2025).

'The Brutal Murder Of The Chohan Family - True Crime Documentary', *True Crime Podcast 2025*, Spotify, 3 July 2024. Available at: https://open.spotify.com/episode/0ZJykwQDxJmQliMKrV1WKp (accessed on 30 June 2025).

'Chohan family killers named as Michael Schallamach murder suspects', *BBC News*, 30 June 2016. Available at: https://www.bbc.com/news/uk-england-hampshire-36666080 (accessed on 30 June 2025).

Lamat R Hasan, 'Vadukut revisits Brit-Indian family's murder in "The Corpse That Spoke"', *Catch News*, 11 February 2017. Available at: https://www.catchnews.com/culture-news/vadukut-revisits-brit-indian-family-s-murder-in-the-corpse-that-spoke-1486795832.html (accessed on 30 June 2025).

Imaan Sheikh, 'Horror in Hounslow: The Chohan Family Case', *The Juggernaut*, 27 May 2021. Available at: https://www.jgnt.co/the-chohan-family-case (accessed on 30 June 2025).

'Chohan murders: Timeline', *BBC News*, 1 July 2005. Available at: http://news.bbc.co.uk/2/hi/uk_news/4444527.stm (accessed on 30 June 2025).

## 20. TO BE HANGED UNTIL DEATH: THE CASE OF HETAL PAREKH

'Dhananjoy Chatterjee case: A noteworthy lesson for the judiciary', The Law Blog, 17 August 2020. Available at: https://thelawblog.

in/2020/08/17/dhananjoy-chatterjee-case-a-noteworthy-lesson-for-the-judiciary/ (accessed on 30 June 2025).

'As "rapist-murderer" Dhananjoy's story comes on screen, a look at the case that shook India', *The News Minute*, 4 July 2017. Available at: https://www.thenewsminute.com/news/rapist-murderer-dhananjoys-story-comes-screen-look-case-shook-india-64644 (accessed on 30 June 2025).

N Jayaram, 'How India hanged a poor watchman whose guilt was far from established', *Scroll*, 21 July 2015. Available at: https://scroll.in/article/741784/how-india-hanged-a-poor-watchman-whose-guilt-was-far-from-established (accessed on 30 June 2025).

Debasis Sengupta and Probal Chaudhuri, 'A re-analysis of the case of the murder of Hetal Parekh'. Available at: https://www.india-hanged-innocent.org/PDFs/dhananjoy-report.pdf (accessed on 30 June 2025).

Debasis Sengupta, 'Dhananjoy Chatterjee - An innocent person judicially killed by the state', *Millennium Post*, 10 September 2016. Available at: https://www.millenniumpost.in/dhananjoy-chatterjee--an-innocent-person-judicially-killed-by-the-state-161059 (accessed on 30 June 2025).

Saibal Gupta, 'In 30 years, only one death sentence for rape and murder', *Deccan Herald*, 30 December 2012. Available at: https://www.deccanherald.com/india/in-30-years-only-one-2382181 (accessed on 30 June 2025).

Amitesh Surwar, 'Hetal Parekh Murder Case: A Tragedy That Redefined Justice in India | CrimePod Castle S01E1005', *CrimePod Castle*, RSS.com, 24 November 2024. Available at: https://rss.com/podcasts/crimepod-castle/1768076/ (accessed on 30 June 2025).

'The Murderers of Dhananjoy Hazir Ho! Abolish Death Penalty', People's Union for Democratic Rights, 13 July 2015. Available at: https://www.pudr.org/press-statements/the-murderers-of-dhananjoy-hazir-ho-abolish-death-penalty/ (accessed on 30 June 2025).

'Hetal horror revisited', *The Telegraph*, 17 January 2005. Available at: https://www.telegraphindia.com/west-bengal/hetal-horror-revisited/cid/687656 (accessed on 30 June 2025).

'Case: Dhananjoy Chatterjee v. State of West Bengal (1994) 2 SCC 220', Dhyeya Law. Available at: https://www.dhyeyalaw.in/dhananjoy-chatterjee-v-state-of-west-bengal-1994-2-scc-220 (accessed on 30 June 2025).

Priyanka Dasgupta, 'Dhananjoy Chatterjee's family rejoices after Pahlaj's exit', *Times of India*, 11 August 2017. Available at: https://timesofindia.indiatimes.com/city/kolkata/dhananjoy-chatterjees-family-rejoices-after-pahlajs-exit/articleshow/60024587.cms (accessed on 30 June 2025).